A GOSPEL PRIESTHOOD

Yves Congar OP

A GOSPEL
PRIESTHOOD

Translated by P. J. Hepburne-Scott

HERDER AND HERDER

1967
HERDER AND HERDER NEW YORK
232 Madison Avenue, New York 10016

Original edition:
Sacerdoce et Laïcat, first half,
Paris, Les Editions du Cerf.

Nihil obstat: John M. T. Barton S.T.D.,
L.S.S., Censor Imprimatur: ✠ Patrick
Casey, Vic. Gen. Westminster, 28th
November 1966

Library of Congress Catalog Card Number 67-14143
© 1967 by Herder and Herder, Inc.
Printed in the United States

CONTENTS

A GOSPEL PRIESTHOOD

CHAPTER ONE

The Apostolate[1]

THE WORDS 'APOSTOLATE' AND 'APOSTLE' COME from Greek through Latin, and they have the same history in all languages. Although the word existed in classical Greek, it has become a specifically Christian, or perhaps Judeo-Christian term. *Apostellein* means 'to send', and the *apostolos* is essentially an 'envoy', someone sent. The dominant idea suggested by it is therefore not of 'propaganda', nor even of zeal—though we are apt to say of someone both zealous and disinterested that he is a regular apostle—but of being sent.

It is not an undue intrusion of philosophy into revealed truth to remark that from the moment a person is sent, he is sent *by* someone and *to* someone; the very idea of sending implies, if it is to mean anything at all, two relationships. The envoy or messenger, and so the apostle, is strictly someone who, by his obedience and fidelity, joins in a living way the person who sends him to those to whom he is sent. We shall understand the essence of the Christian apostolate when we know by whom and to whom we are sent.

By whom? By God; and I say 'God' on purpose. I admit that we may be sent directly by the hierarchy, which derives its authority from the twelve, just as the twelve had been sent directly by Jesus Christ. But Jesus himself had been sent, and in the most formal way possible he presents his 'sending' of his apostles as a continuation of that by which he has himself been sent into the world by the Father. 'As the Father has sent me, even so I send you.'[2] The early Church had a very strong sense of this kind of 'sequence' of mission. At a date when not all the writings that from the New Testament had been composed, St Clement of Rome wrote: 'The apostles have preached to us from our Lord Jesus Christ; Jesus Christ from God. Christ, therefore, was sent by God, the apostles by Christ: so both were orderly sent, according to the will of God. For having received their command, and being thoroughly assured by the resurrection of our Lord Jesus Christ, and convinced by the word of God, with the fullness of the Holy Spirit, they went abroad, publishing that the kingdom of God was at hand. And thus, preaching through countries and cities, they appointed the first fruits of their conversions to be bishops and ministers over such as should afterwards believe, having first proved them by the Spirit.'[3] More than one similar passage is to be found in Tertullian, writing at the end of the second century or the beginning of the third.[4]

This series of missionary 'sequences' from the Father to the Son made flesh, from him to the apostles and the whole chain of mission proceeding from them until it comes down to us could be considered in its *juridical* aspect; that is, from the angle of legitimacy, of authority, of the canonical conditions for the legitimate handing on of the mission. All that is very important, but it is not my intention to dwell on it. I want only to draw attention in passing to an idea that may help us to understand the meticulous care that the Church brings to all these juridical definitions and their observance. In the New Dispensation, this meticulous care plays a similar part to that represented in the Old Testament by God's vigilance over the purity and succession of the Messianic race. Writers such as W. Vischer have shown that it is this vigilance which explains episodes, sometimes disconcerting to our view, such as the deceits of the patriarchs on the subject of their wives, or the story of Thamar.[5] The messianic line could not be allowed to die out. The 'apostolic succession' is something comparable: a handing down of mission with the legitimacy and powers belonging to any mission.

But I want rather to consider the *soul* of the apostolate. 'As my Father has sent me, even so I send you' corresponds to 'As the Father has loved me, so have I loved you,' which is also in St John's Gospel.[6] The soul of the apostolate, what sets in motion this great missionary sequence that has its origins in the Father, and sets in motion all mission in the Church, starting from the Father and passing through Christ and the apostles, is *agape*.

Most of us already have a fairly clear idea of what the Bible means by *agape*, and more than one recent study (notably Nygren's) has helped us to understand it. *Agape* is love, but love of a special character. It is not the love that desires for itself: this is termed *eros*, which the New Testament uses seldom and usually in a pejorative sense. *Agape* is the love that gives, the love that loves, not for some benefit to be obtained for itself, but simply for the sake of loving. It is the love that flows from its source because one has a loving and generous heart. I think that the nearest type of it to be found on earth is the love of parents for their children. This is natural: Does not Paul say that all fatherhood (and motherhood) derives from God's fatherhood?[7] It is not for nothing, either, that *agape* is usually attributed by the New Testament *to the Father*:[8] it is because he is the source of all things, the beginning without beginning, the principle, not only of creation, but of the divine family itself, since the two other Persons, though they are perfect God, are so only by proceeding from the Father. In the same way, the soul of the whole great missionary flow or sequence is this love which is its own reason and principle—this source of love which is the property of the Father and the origin of all good, all truth and all gifts. God—the Father—loves *because* he is good, *because*, being good, he wishes to give, to communicate himself. This is the reason why there is a mission; first, Christ's own mission, and, in its flow, that of the apostles and of all that in Christian speech, merit the name of apostolate. 'God so loved (*agapan*) the world that he sent his only begotten Son. . . .' The soul of the apostolate is, then, the love that gives, *agape*.

We know *by whom* people are sent: by God, who *is agape*. But to whom are they sent? Clearly, to men. It is said of Christ: *qui propter nos homines et propter nostram salutem*. . . . These words even add a further detail of precision. Jesus did not come only for men, but for the salvation of men, who are sinners. When he himself defines in the gospels the terms of his mission, he says: 'He has sent me to proclaim release to the captives and recovering of sight to the blind';[9] 'The Son of Man came to seek and to save the lost'.[10] One of the great joys of studying Scripture is the discovery of the perfect and extraordinary agreement between passages written on different occasions by different authors and at very different dates. This is true here. On the one hand, whenever Jesus speaks of the object of his mission, he mentions the lost, the sick, sinners. On the other hand, whenever the New Testament defines the origin of this *agape* or giving-love which, as we have seen, is the soul of the mission, it does so in terms like the following: 'In this the love [*agape*] of God was made manifest among us, that God sent his only Son into the world, so that we might live through him. *In this* is love [*agape*], not that we loved God, but that *he* loved us, and sent his Son to be the expiation for our sins';[11] or, 'God shows his love for us *in that* while we were yet sinners, Christ died for us'.[12] We know, therefore, that if the body of the mission is its legitimate assignment, its soul is a special form of love, the love called *agape* in the New Testament: giving-love, love that seeks not itself but gives itself, and for this very reason is directed towards the weakest and most wretched.

All this may seem sublime, for so it is, but perhaps also a little abstract. Yet how close to the facts it is! Consider the whole life of the Church, and especially her missionary life. Remember how from the very beginning of her existence the Church began to care not only for souls, but for bodies too, to succour everywhere whatever was lost, how she founds orphanages, hospitals, schools, how, in all these things, her rule is to be as effective as possible, but she is in no sense seeking results in the human sense of the word. Humanly speaking, the missions in the Far North, for instance, or the work of a priest I know who undertakes the care of unmarried mothers; humanly speaking, I repeat, these are not repayable. They are undertakings of *agape*, treading in the path opened by the Son of Man.

Again, all this will seem extremely concrete if we consider the *implications* of the mission. Much has been written and spoken on this subject in the years between the wars (1919–39), when through many attempts, and impelled by that great pope, Pius XI, a real science of missions was brought into being. At that time people spoke in terms of 'adaptation', and the encyclical *Praecones Evangelii* of 2nd June 1951 sanctioned the idea. The creation of a *native* clergy was begun or at least intensified. But

within the framework of Catholic Action, first during its best
years between 1925 and 1940, then in the new stage developed by
the harsh experiences of the war, experiences of the prison camps,
the Resistance and so on, it began to be seen that the need for the
mission was not only abroad, overseas and in other climates, but
that wide expanses of the old Christian countries were terribly
like mission countries. You may know the title of Abbé Godin's
book, now historic in France—*La France, pays de mission?*[13]—and
how he straightaway sealed with his life the work that he had
started. Soon it became clear that the need for adaptation, the
need to be native, already recognised for foreign missions, existed
no less for the new mission field to be found in the very heart of
the old Christian countries. In the eyes of the most generous of
the priests and laymen who gave themselves to the new mission,
it became plain that the mission required something like a new
birth. Those who thought they had only to come flourishing the
truth that they possessed, and to communicate this truth from on
high, as it were, were much mistaken. A missionary could only
enter from below, very humbly, in a world foreign to his own.
The best of these apostles began to say from this time onwards
that to be a missionary is to *commune with*, to share in a *common
destiny*, it is 'to muck in with', 'to rot with'!

These are extreme terms, to be interpreted in their context.
But for my part I am struck by their depth and accuracy. If we
turn to the great classic theologian, St Thomas Aquinas, we read
that every mission has a relationship to the sender, as we have
seen, and a relationship to that to which it is sent; this is what
concerns us here. Either, he says, one may come to a place where
one did not exist before, or finding oneself there already, one
begins to exist in a new way.[14] In our countries the Church
already exists; but with regard to certain whole classes of people,
she must, if she is to be fully missionary, begin to exist in a new
way. She must be *with* these people, not just *beside* them or *in
front of* them, but *with* them. Think for a moment what it means
to be not only beside someone, but with him and for him; ask
yourself whether, in our modern societies, in which the Church
indeed erects her steeples everywhere and celebrates her age-old
ceremonies, there are not sections of humanity that the Church
is not truly *with*, although she is just by their side. I am not

thinking only of the manual workers, of the populations of industrial cities, of mines and factories. I do think of them, certainly, and they take first place in my thoughts, because these are the most deprived and at the same time the most numerous, as well as the richest in wonderful stores of generosity, and also the most 'lost' and forlorn. Also because experience shows that in present-day circumstances they represent the spearhead of this historic movement and they set the missionary problem at its most acute. But I think also of all the regions of the world of the mind where mankind strives, regions that know not the Church and perhaps are not known by her. The Church must be *with* all this, if she is to be fully missionary in the world of today.

And, most certainly, to fulfil the work of a missionary to a group of men it is not enough *to be with* them. Imagine a priest or a layman 'sent' to Arabs, for example, or to the working class district in the outskirts of our large cities, someone who would be *with* to such an extent that he really became like one of them. It is plain that he would excellently fulfil one article of the missionary programme, the one concerning adaptation or, to express it more fully, its indigenous character. But it is also plain that he would only be really missionary if, having fully become one of them, he did not cease to represent something else when among them. 'To be with' is not enough: we must *be with* on God's behalf and in God's sight, as a Church and in full view of Jesus Christ. In short, there is no mission unless that *something else* is brought to it; there is no mission unless there is tension. Without it, there will just be one more Arab, one more proletarian, one more militant worker. But there will be no mission, and no apostolate.

This is where we reach the heart of the problem of the apostolate or of the mission. It is very important to realise that the apostolate or mission—even, in a general way, the Church—admits of a kind of duality or tension between two aspects which, if the terms are explained, may be called sanctity and catholicity. Perhaps I may make my meaning clearer if I set before you separately two attitudes that can arise from a too exclusive concern for either of these two aspects.

It is possible for someone to be mainly possessed by the feeling that the Church should be a leaven in the lump, that she must go to men and be fully with them, sharing their problems and ambitions. That is good and true. But let us suppose that this person has not in the same degree, or sufficiently, the sense that the Church is something *other* than being active to the progress of history or of human happiness in their proper spheres. Then this person would run the risk of himself becoming lost in the movement of the world he wished to quicken—or with the workers' movement *with which* he had wanted to be—and then he could not bring to them this *something other* of the gospel and the Kingdom of God, the very things that form the content of our mission. He would forget, in this case, that if the Church is for the world—*not* for herself or her own glory or success or power— if she *has* a mission to the world, she is, and must first be, herself, something other than the world: an order of sanctity and salvation that does not come from the world, that the 'world' cannot understand. There is, in short, not only the *catholicity* of the Church, her extension; there is also her sanctity, which comes from elsewhere and from above.

At the opposite extreme, a person could be deeply penetrated with the feeling that the Church is something other than the world, an order apart with her own laws, her own way of life and her demands, not only for a deeper life, but for social behaviour. At the same time he might not feel, like a searing wound, the appeal of the vast world and the land of men. Such a man would observe Catholic regulations very punctiliously—if he were a priest, for instance, wearing his cassock, saying his breviary, keeping the slightest prescriptions of canon law, following the strictest and safest theological formulations: all excellent things, certainly, and you will not easily find one word against them in my life or my writings—but in short, such a man would be a very faithful minister of the Church as a body set apart, but he would have very little anxiety about bringing back men who are estranged, about their problems or about the possible values of the contributions of history. In a word, he would be a man of an order of sanctity set apart, not of an order of catholicity.

Again—and here I am saying what seems to be the lesson of both history and experience—I fear that the Church regarded in this way as apart in its sanctity, closed, very exclusive and condemnatory of anything that does not appear in perfectly regular and foreseen conditions, may take on the air of a *sect*—for this is precisely the attitude of sects, groups, set apart in sanctity, of chosen ones, caring little for catholicity or for sharing in the problems and burdens of the times. Or again, she might come to be regarded chiefly as a great clerical machine, very powerful but hardly if at all apostolic. This would produce a clergy whose first object would be to represent to the faithful the authority of 'the Church'—a Church which would be this clerical body, almost closed to the world, acting very little like the leaven in the meal.

It is obvious that I have here drawn the portrait of two attitudes which are really monstrosities, studies in teratology! Neither of these Churches is the Church of Jesus Christ and the apostles. For their Church is *at one and the same time* holy and catholic. But her holiness comes to its perfect blossoming only by grace of the apostolate which makes her fully catholic; and she is not the Catholic Church unless she is first of all holy.

I am very much struck by these words of our Lord about himself in John:[15] 'Whom the Father consecrated and sent into the world.' And again, in John (Chapter 17) there comes what is often called the priestly prayer, which I prefer to call the apostolic prayer: 'I have given them thy word, and the world has hated them because they are not of the world, even as I am not of the world. . . . Sanctify them in the truth: thy word is truth. As thou didst send me into the world, so I have sent them into the world. And for their sake I consecrate myself, that they also may be consecrated in truth.'[16] It is clear from such passages that an apostle is not the same thing as a 'militant', that is, a man having influence and recruiting partisans. It is a deplorable misuse of words to speak, as people do nowadays, in season and out of season, of 'an apostle of prophylaxis', 'an apostle of the press: of sport: of television'. I remember once at La Sainte Baume, a place of pilgrimage to Mary Magdalene near Saint-Maximin, I saw a tablet bearing these words: 'To Mr X, apostle of cycle touring'. No! It won't do! It is essential that an apostle be first sanctified, before he is sent and in order to be sent. An apostle is a man of God; his task is something quite different from propaganda, even propaganda for a good cause; he is one of the living constituents of God's plan of salvation, which passes through the Cross. He is, as it were, a living relay of the *agape* that flows from the Father to the furthest limits of the world and of history.[17] The mystery of the apostolate is of the order of sanctity. That is why Aquinas, who is anything but a sentimentalist, shows us the personalities of the apostles as completely pervaded and moulded by the Holy Spirit, who is the spirit of holiness. It is equally noticeable that the ancient liturgical texts of the rites for priestly ordinations speak little of the powers conferred on the ordained, but much more of the virtues he needs, praying God to grant them to him. Often the ordination prayers are vague about the priest's sacramental powers, for these were known and acknowledged, but the prayers implore the coming of the Holy Spirit. Because of the spread of various heresies, because of Protestantism, the Church has been forced to emphasise very strongly her authority and her powers. Let us never forget the whole aspect of charismata and of personal holiness in our conception of the priesthood and of the apostolate.

I should like to show briefly, in a somewhat more practical way, how these reflections throw light on some of our most immediate present-day problems. I do not propose to discuss in detail the question of the worker-priests, whose case has focused excessive public attention in recent years, but I hope that what follows may throw some light on a problem which is of interest to all of us.

The general trend of events is doubtless familiar. Some men, many of whom are of admirable unselfishness and faith, paid perhaps too little attention to the fulfilment of the practical requirements of their priestly condition, as a condition apart, their position of sanctity set apart; for they were literally in anguish before the gulf they had to bridge, before the need for making fresh contact and making their presence real (the 'being with'). They did not, in any case, like the word 'apart', and it is easy to understand them. The intention of Rome's intervention in the question could not be purely negative; it was to be a call to those priestly requirements, which necessarily involve positive aspects, laid down by the legitimate authority, outside whose communion there can be no apostolate in the Church.

Finally, a brief application to your life as lay people. At the end of an already solid address, I cannot undertake to give you a whole theology of the lay apostolate. I have dealt with this in a long book, which has appeared in English.[18] I merely suggest an outline for reflection.

Every Christian is called to the apostolate in the wide sense: he has not to wait for any other vocation than his vocation to a Christian life; no other mission than that of a Christian life, lived in the concrete conditions of his profession and of the circumstances and personal contacts of his life. For us, all this is not merely secular: it is an application to us of the will of God, who has given us a place in his plan of salvation. Our task, then, is, by inserting ourselves in the history of the world, to insert ourselves also, by the same act, in the sacred history which God is working out in it; to effect in it a *sequentia sancti evangelii*, a continuation of the mission of Jesus Christ, trying, after his example and by his grace, to save what without him would be lost. It is not a matter of searching for an exceptional vocation, but of living one's life under the holy will of God, in a spirit of filial obedience, fidelity and generosity, at the bidding of the circumstances into which God leads us and where he awaits us. *That*, and nothing else, is what will prove sanctifying for us. It is *there* we must bear our witness, very humbly, very simply, very faithfully. The Holy Spirit, whose hand is over all, knows what he is about. Thus, you have to act as Christians in the ordinary conditions of life, and so you will find all sorts of opportunities to serve and let your light shine.

In conclusion, I should like to make a few remarks concerning the apostolate of lay people. Though I can hardly undertake to present here a whole theology of the lay apostolate—I have already dealt with this problem extensively—I do wish to suggest an outline for reflection.

Every Christian is called to the apostolate in the wide sense: he has not to wait for any other vocation than his vocation to a Christian life; no other mission than that of a Christian life, lived in the concrete conditions of his profession and of the circumstances and personal contacts of his life. For us, all this is not merely secular: it is an application to us of the will of God, who has given us a place in his plan of salvation. Our task, then, is, by inserting ourselves in the history of the world, to insert ourselves also, by the same act, in the sacred history which God is working out in it; to effect in it a *sequentia sancti evangelii*, a continuation of the mission of Jesus Christ, trying, after his example and by his grace, to save what without him would be lost. It is not a matter of searching for an exceptional vocation, but of living one's life under the holy will of God, in a spirit of filial obedience, fidelity, and generosity, at the bidding of the circumstances into which God leads us and where he awaits us. *That*, and nothing else, is what will prove sanctifying for us. It is *there* we must bear our witness, very humbly, very simply, very faithfully. The Holy Spirit, whose hand is over all, knows what he is about. Thus, we have to act as Christians in the ordinary conditions of life, and there find all sorts of opportunities to serve and let our light shine.

That is the sphere of what we might call 'Catholics' action'. But also in the singular and with a capital A, there is 'Catholic Action'. That means taking part in an organised apostolate, under the special impulse, direction and control of the hierarchy. Granted that we are never independent of this direction and that all Christian life is subject to it, still, it is subject in a general manner, in the sense that it can only develop within the limits of dogma and by the grace of the sacraments. In Catholic Action, in the strict sense, there is much more. There is a real share in the mission belonging to the bishops, in the heart of an official movement of the Church, far more directly bound by the instructions given to the body of Christ by the episcopate, centred on the Roman See. It is not so much a personal action, *ex spiritu*, according to inward inspiration, as a corporate action of a movement under orders, in a certain way *ex officio*.

With all my heart I pray that the Spirit of Pentecost may enable you, day by day, to find how best you can serve the kingdom of God!

NOTES

1. Conference given in English to the women students of the Beaufort Society on 2nd May 1956, at Cambridge. Text published in *Bulletin d'Orientations œcuméniques* (Beirut), July–August, 1956, pp. 11–19, and, substantially the same text, in *World Mission* (New York), 1956, pp. 283–94, and in *New Life* (London), Sept–Oct, 1956, pp. 164–74.
2. Jn 17: 18; 20: 21.
3. *First to the Corinthians*, 42, Burton translation.
4. See *De Praescr.* 21:4; 37.
5. Gen 38.
6. 15:9.
7. Eph 3:15.
8. See for instance, 1 Cor 13:13, or a concordance.
9. Lk 4:18.
10. 19:10.
11. 1 Jn 4:9–10; 3:16.
12. Rom 6:8.
13. *France Pagan?*, London, 1949.
14. *Sum. Theol.*, Ia, qu. 43, art. 1.
15. 10:36.
16. 17:14, 17–19.
17. See the conclusions of Mt and Mk.
18. *Lay People* (see List of Abbrevs.).

CHAPTER TWO

Conversion

A Study in Theology and Psychology[1]

The idea of conversion

Conversion, in the most general sense of the word, is a change in the principle or principles governing the synthesis or direction of our life. In itself it does not mean conversion to God, or even to the good: one can turn to evil, one could be converted to rationalism or Marxism; there are conversions from Catholicism to Eastern Orthodoxy or Protestantism, to Judaism or to religions outside the Jewish-Christian tradition. Taken in this quite general sense, the 'converted' are those who are called the 'twice-born', as distinct from the 'once-born'. There is of course a birth which is common to all men, that by which we come to exist as men, with the qualities of human nature: and it is thus we come into the world. There are some who experience a second birth to a certain world of values, to which they have freely surrendered and given themselves. Some have discovered the great poverty of others, for example, or justice: others have had their whole life turned upside down, have been affected in such a way that they devote themselves to procuring a good or fighting an evil.

For there to be 'conversion', something else is needed besides merely intellectual knowledge or even a speculative conviction. A research worker or a statistician may know all about human poverty or hunger without being in the least converted to fighting them. There must be a personal experience by which a man has been made to question himself and induced to change something in his life. By way of comparison, think of the great difference

15

there is between a mere official report and the testimony of a witness.[2] The witness feels that he is under obligation to the truth, so that he is prepared to endure anything in order to maintain an assertion in which, for him, the *fact* is charged with a *value*. A real conversion means also that the value by which we have been captivated is of such a nature as to set the course of our life, so as to give a meaning to our destiny.

Moral Conversion and Religious Conversion

Moral conversion is a change in our ethical principles, or a transition from their neglect to their practice. Certain philosophies, such as stoicism or that of Plotinus,[3] have presented an ideal which demanded, in its own manner, a conversion of that sort.

Religious conversion in the proper sense has points of resemblance with moral conversion, but it is different. It implies not only that life has a direction which can be the object of conversion, but that this direction is determined by a personal God, and that the principle of the 'conversion' is the realisation of the true relationship which God calls us to form with him.[4]

Moral and religious conversion are often closely connected; or else the moral conversion occurs within the context of a faith which, though always professed in principle, had hardly, if at all, affected the conduct of daily life.[5] This, which some call 'mystical conversion', is the case, for example, of Francis of Assisi and Ignatius Loyola, Mère Angélique and Pascal (23rd November 1654). It is also the case of the 'second conversions' described by spiritual writers.[6] But in all these different cases there is always, it seems to me, either at the root of the moral conversion or accompanying it, a fresh discovery of the living God, of Christ and of the authentic religious relationship, and therefore a religious conversion.

The step taken by those who are called *conversi* in the ecclesiastical Latin of the patristic period can be termed moral conversion. In those days (fourth to sixth centuries) the word was used for those who embraced the religious life, sometimes without taking the habit, or of those who withdrew from the world and gave themselves to the religious life, without leaving their secular state or occupations. After the eleventh century the word acquired a precise sense in the monastic order; it was used to describe the lay brothers who had taken religious vows.

CONVERSION IN THE JEWISH AND

CHRISTIAN SCRIPTURES[7]

Vocabulary

Conversion is expressed in scripture by two Hebrew words and two Greek words. In Hebrew שׁוּב, *shubh*, to turn back, has no religious meaning in itself, but has acquired, by use, the meaning of conversion, which is expressed by the noun derived from it, *teshuvah*. To be converted is to turn back to God: there are many occasions for its use.[8] The other is נִחַם *nacham*, to regret or repent.[9]

In Greek, *shubh* is usually translated in the Septuagint by ἐπιστρέθειν, which has the same sense: to turn, to turn back, to come back, and so, in certain cases, to be converted.[10] In the New Testament it is used, for example, of turning away from darkness to light.[11] One turns away *from*, ἄπο, ἐκ,[12] and one turns *towards*, ἐπι, πρός,[13] where the verb is employed without a preposition.[14] Μετανοιεῖν, and the noun μετάνοια, were well known in classical Greek, with the meaning of changing one's mind or intention, changing the direction of one's thought. The meaning of *regret* was present and became more evident in the hellenistic age.[15] The Septuagint gives μετανοιεῖν a strong technical sense of *conversion* by making it the equivalent of ἐπιστρέφειν when the word is used in a moral or religious sense: thus the Septuagint sometimes translates *shubh* by μετανοιειν.[16] Thus μετανοιειν was ready to be used in the gospel and then in the Acts and epistles as a technical expression to signify changing one's mind, turning towards God, being converted, with all the content of *shubh* in the Prophets, but keeping the meaning of regret and repentance only secondarily.[17] In several places in the Septuagint[18] and the New Testament μετανοιειν and ἐπισρέφειν are coupled[19]—a sign of their approximation in meaning. In this quasi-equivalence μετανοιειν no doubt expresses rather the inward change of attitude, ἐπιστρέφειν the change of relationship to another (God).

In Latin the word *conversio* correctly translated the idea of returning, turning back, being converted, but μετανοιειν was translated by pœnitere, pœnitentia.[20] This had two disadvantages: it lost the expressive image of turning inherent in the Hebrew *shubh* and the Greek μετανοιειν and ἐπιστρέφειν; and although *paenitere* really came from *paene*, with the sense of 'being dissatisfied with', it came to be influenced by the word *pœna*, even to assuming its spelling. It thus received a predominant sense of onerous compensation, affliction, which did justice to only one sense, and that not the deepest, of the biblical use of μετανοιεῖν. 'Penitence' suggested, in the first place, works of penance, an aspect strongly emphasised in the Middle Ages. Still, the more spiritual knew that 'evangelical conversion' is essentially the conversion of Faith, that is, an entire submission to and confidence in the living God. 'What is the life of penitence', says Tauler, 'in its essence and truth? Simply this, to turn fully and truly away from all that is not God and to turn fully and truly to the pure and true good; and the deeper the movement of conversion, the more it does penance.'[21] This is the meaning which is supreme in the whole story of Francis of Assisi and his companions.[22]

Biblical theology of conversion

E. Würthwein distinguishes, and contrasts, the idea of penitence found in Israel before the prophets and that of conversion preached by them.[23] There were, in fact, expressions of penitence in Israel, not only occasional but legalised and ritualised in the institutions and in worship, which comprised fasting, groaning and supplications, and even such outward signs as sackcloth and ashes. Sometimes a general penance was ordered, affecting even children and animals.[24] But when the prophets came they said, in effect: all this does not amount to a return to God.[25] To the prophets the essential thing which qualifies all the rest is to establish a genuine *religious relationship*. It is the relationship by which Yahweh is in truth the *God of Israel* and Israel is the *people of God*. It is a personal relationship between a man who commits himself, his heart and conscience, and the living God, the God who has a will, and a plan which calls on man to comply with its requirements. An individual (or the people as a whole) is converted when he really lets God be God to him. This relationship takes concrete form in these three points: obeying God's will;

trusting him absolutely; turning away from the evil God hates. In fact its demands are extremely concrete in the sphere of human conduct. The Covenant requires man to observe pure justice, to treat others as his brethren, especially the poor and the weak, etc. *That* is the true fast.[26] In short, the prophets preach not so much 'penitence' as 'conversion'; for them, everything is decided on the theological, not the ethical or ascetical level.

There are certainly some passages which do not fit into the scheme: the prophets know and accept penitential rites.[27] Würthwein also places during the Exile the outstanding case of Ezekiel, who expresses a very vivid sense of personal responsibility and the possibility of man's turning towards justice or injustice.[28] Certainly the distinction drawn by Würthwein is basically correct: it has its parallels or correspondences in other domains, such as the temple and presence of God, sacrifices and feasts, etc. It is true that the prophets understood and taught that there is a way of practising religion which in reality alienates from God, or which panders to the instinct of the pagan in us to be always fleeing from God, representing God in man's image, and so making an image of him for ourselves, whereas true religion consists in letting ourselves be fashioned by God in *his* image, in unreserved faith and love. But there would be a danger in making a system of the implied opposition: the danger of failing to see that the relation of faith and *chesed*, which is the substance of the conversion desired by the prophets, *includes* and does not exclude the concrete reality of 'penitence' as sorrow for sin, contrition, amendment and satisfaction.

Protestant authors sometimes say that the opposite of sin is not holiness but faith. No; it is justice. They sometimes tend unconsciously to transpose the debate between works and faith into other domains—there is something of that in Nygren's admirable *Eros and Agape*—not seeing clearly enough the true nature of a faith which proves itself by works.[29] Würthwein's indications on the prophetical preaching of true conversion to God have therefore only to be completed by the other elements of that preaching; the statements on hating and repudiating sin, in short, on true penitence, which flows from the relationship of faith, justice, *chesed* and the knowledge of Yahweh.[30]

In the New Testament the idea of conversion is absolutely

fundamental. The gospel begins with the summons of John the Baptist, repeated by our Lord at the beginning of his preaching: 'Repent! μετανοεῖτε, for the kingdom of heaven is at hand'.[31] It is a summons to a deep and inward change of life, corresponding to the wholly new and decisive act by which God comes to free us and to pardon our sins. The conversion to which first John and then Jesus calls us demands a complete revision of the direction of life, in the light of this decisive act of God. It is man's response to the sovereign initiative of God: it implies, first, repentance or penitence, by which we forsake sin,[32] then faith, by which we commit ourselves wholly to God.[33] Finally, it implies consequences for the whole of life, which is renewed by that penitence and faith. It will have another style, one befitting the kingdom of God, summed up at its best in an attitude of non-possession, purity, readiness for any service, trust, unquestioning openness of the affections; in short, an attitude of spiritual childhood.

This gospel message is of absolute and definitive value for all men, until the end of the world. It is repeated all through space and time by the apostolate: every man is called on to repent and be converted at the proclamation of a herald of the Good News.[34]

Paul and John thought out the theological implications of the reality of the Christian life as conversion: their respective theologies are fundamentally identical. Although St John does not use the words μετάνοια, μετανοιεῖν, he presents the deepest theology (in the strict sense of the word) of conversion, as the act and process by which the believer lets himself be engendered and formed by God, in dependence on Jesus Christ. St Paul himself gradually developed, in the course of his epistles, a theological synthesis of Christian conversion, combining these three aspects: first, faith: this is not so much a consequence of penitence-conversion as its principle. Next, baptism and the new man: in which St Paul adopts some Jewish ideas on the baptism of proselytes, but Christian baptism derives all its meaning from its relation to Jesus Christ and his Pasch. Finally, a whole programme of life involved in faith and baptism. The latter, which conforms us to the death and resurrection of Christ, has a very precise and exacting *moral* content: one is converted to *serve God*;[35] one is committed by faith and baptism to a type of life which consists in putting to death the 'old man' in us and making the 'new man' real.[36] Nothing is at once more theological, more sacramental and more ethical than conversion according to Paul; nothing is more truly an act of God, engaging man in a constant effort; nothing is done more conclusively once and for all, has more constantly to be done again and again.

Components of conversion and the point of view from which the facts can be considered

We may now consider what conversion really is, as we learn it every day from what happens in our own country or in mission lands. Conversion is a personal step affecting the life of a morally adult man, one, that is, in whom the principle of moral synthesis is personally possessed and can be freely chosen or approved. It entails a whole series of moral and psychological changes and of affective and intellectual motivations. There are preparatory influences, either positive, opening the mind to certain values, or negative, helping one to transcend certain attitudes which were holding one back. Among these influences must specially be reckoned the rôle of trials, things which bring us to an impasse, disappointments, injuries.[37] There are stages, series of motivations. Augustine passed through Neoplatonism;[38] Görres returned to Catholicism through the idea of political unity, and many men of his time through that of the Church as a force for stability and order (von Haller, for example). The preparations play their part, then give way to something else, which remains. Factors dependent on environment may also play a part, usually inhibitive, as can be seen in studies of the psychology of European working classes or of conversions in mission countries, in areas subject to Islam, etc.[39] Certain cases, personally known to me, even raise the question whether a sort of atavism does not sometimes influence conversions from one religious body to another.[40] The subject is worth studying.

All this shows that conversion entails a very complex *human reality*, moral, social, historical and perhaps even genetic, which it is permissible, and of great interest, to study. If not always, at least in many cases, a purely psychological study of conversions might be made, and the most demanding theologians do not hinder us in this respect.[41]

With sufficient evidence, therefore, conversions could also be

grouped according to classes and types, if indeed their extraordinary variety can be covered by several types, and if this
classification possesses a real interest. I offer here a possible
classification, based on the psychological point of view, or on
psychologically determined motives.[42]

1. Conversions dominated by anxiety, the need to find the
truth, and intellectual motivations: a frequent case in conversions
from one communion to another; for example, Newman, Cornelia
de Vogel.

2. Conversions dominated by the desire to find a pure moral
ideal: many conversions to Christianity from paganism and Islam.

3. Conversions of an emotional type, specially frequent in
evangelistic revival meetings and the Salvation Army.

There are also gradual conversions and sudden conversions,
but in the latter the moment of abrupt decision has often been
preceded by preparation and is followed by a long and laborious
effort: this was the case, for example, with Alphonse Ratisbonne
and his vision of our Lady in Rome, 1842. It may happen that the
reasons *follow* that decisive moment when the moral or religious
'turning' occurs, which constitutes the essence of conversion: for
it often happens that the new principle of synthesis is acquired
suddenly as by an instantaneous illumination, and that the whole
complex of reasons and answers comes only afterwards. This was
the case, for example, with men like Robert Bracey,[43] but notably
in the more illustrious case, described by himself in terms of
unsurpassable sincerity, of Paul Claudel.[44] More than four years
elapsed between his illumination at Christmas, 1886, and his first
confession in 1890. *Animus*, which had to reason out the difficulties and draw the conclusions, could only follow later behind
anima.

There are conversions which are entirely personal and the
Catholic Church prefers them.[45] Certain group conversions, like
that of the Anglican monks of Caldey in 1913, fall within this
category, for they are in reality a number of personal conversions,
more or less related and simultaneous. The psychologist of religion, on the other hand, would allow a place for collective conversions. There have been examples in history[46] and doubtless
still are, in contemporary missionary records, of social groups
following their leader in a collective manner,[47] and there are also

revivals and evangelising campaigns, which lead to more or less sudden, collective 'conversions'; for instance, the work of Moody and Evan Roberts in the Welsh Revival of 1904-5, the campaigns of Billy Graham, the appeals of the Salvation Army and the like.[48] The great 'missions' of the seventeenth, eighteenth and nineteenth centuries in the Catholic Church presented features similar to those of the Protestant revivals. Basically, it depends on a kind of preaching which imitates that of the great prophets of Israel. 'Revival is the return to obedience towards God' (Finney).

It would be dangerous to insist overmuch on the spectacular and even rather romantic aspects of a sudden conversion, especially if it is the result of an emotional upheaval. Such conversions are apt to leave all the real problems to be dealt with later. In reality, the whole Christian life is conversion. Every Christian ought to strive to become, day by day, what he is, and to fulfil his spiritual being in depth.[49] We must clearly see what is implied in the practice of infant baptism, on the one hand for every Christian, on the other for the Church, in her effort to carry out a genuine pastoral work. Baptism must necessarily be followed by instruction and conversion. In the Church before Constantine, when on occasion it was dangerous to be a Christian, the Church was composed in the main of convinced men. Baptism was certainly given, almost always, to adults, previously convinced and converted. It truly represented, not only from the dogmatic but from the psychological and moral point of view, a *second birth*. Now that it is given to babies a few weeks old, there is a risk that it may appear as only an aspect of the common human birth, that by which one is sent into the world, in a certain society which, in our country, is 'Christian'.[50] But the obligation of instruction and conversion is still indissolubly bound up with it: quite simply, since it is no longer complied with *before* baptism, it must be complied with *after* it, by a personal step. The life of the Christian is strictly bound by the obligation to *become* really a Christian, after one has been made such without personal choice: that is, by the obligation of conversion.

Various psychological 'explanations' of the facts of conversion have been suggested: social pressure, the weakening of vital tone, the subconscious, sexuality, etc. These different psychological

B

explanations of the fact of conversion often emphasise some real aspect, on the phenomenal level, but they are too brief and partial to explain the whole process, especially if it is seen in its connection with the whole of life and its significance. They have often been influenced, in works of religious psychology, by the attitude adopted by E. D. Starbuck, the pioneer of such studies, towards adolescence as a favourable moment for conversion;[51] or again by the rather Protestant view of conversion as sudden and definite, with a predominant feeling of sin being overcome through a total 'surrender' to grace, to the will and service of God. William James[52] saw conversion as the end of an unconscious incubation of feelings and ideas which finally appear, or rather explode, on the level of clear consciousness, under the pressure of our desire to substitute for the decrepit or scattered elements of our mental synthesis a stronger and more unifying principle; this occurs either through an emotional shock, a new perception, or a combination of circumstances which throw light upon the wear, the disorganisation and the lack of cohesion in our previous system.

A contemporary psychologist like R. H. Thouless, while distinguishing several kinds of conversions, some of which go beyond this explanation, returns to the same thing in the long run under a different form; feelings habitually checked by a resistance which opposes their affirmation and assertion overcome this resistance and rise to the level of conscious life. This outline is particularly applicable to the conversions of young people, in which there is a desire to escape from some habit of sin which is weighing them down at the very age when they are struggling to attain and affirm their proper synthesis. But Thouless himself acknowledges that this does not take into account intellectual conversions, the larger part of which consists of conversions from one denomination to another.

Certain psychoanalysts have given a rather simple explanation of the fact of conversion; that candidates for conversion are found among persons of changeable psychic make-up, without innate unity. The need to unify themselves causes them to subordinate or repress one part of themselves for the benefit of the other part. Moreover, feeling themselves inadequate, they attach themselves to a powerful friend who completes them, calms them and enables them to compensate for their failures. But this solution of their anguish is paid for with a loss in human value.[53]

In the considerations of these psychologists there are many things which are partly true and which depend, moreover, as much upon simple description as upon explanation—if not more. It is certain that conversion occurs at the end of a crisis, accompanied by a definite disequilibrium which one is trying to overcome, as well as by a loss of inner security. That is why a young man's effort to achieve a proper balance in his personal life, or some shameful experience undergone to a point of extremity, some vice or sin, such an experience as grief, sickness, war, prison camp, or even a simple change of environment,[54] can be propitious for conversion. It is certain that this represents the attainment of a more satisfactory principle of synthesis and is an integration. But it still remains to be examined under what conditions and in what way this fulfilment and this integration come about.

As with everything which occurs in the psychic life of man, it is understandable that psychologists who explore the conscious and the subconscious endeavour to give a psychological interpretation of the facts. But two considerations seem to require that one can, and even should, go beyond these explanations.

1. *Truth as represented by the phenomenological method.* Consciousness has a content, an intentionality. It is more than a way of analysing and thus 'explaining' *the way* things happen: it is necessary to consider and try to 'comprehend' the *content and meaning* of what is happening. Now converts perceive and affirm certain things, and the convergence of their experience and affirmation cannot be without its own value. I believe that a proof may be drawn from these things, bringing with it a moral certitude of the kind based on converging testimony, in favour not only of the existence of God but of his action upon souls, as well as of the reality of certain mystical facts. Indeed, one affirmation recurs in accounts of conversions (though less in juvenile conversions, which psychologists are so ready to deal with, than in mystical conversions), namely, that a guiding and determining rôle is played by a living but transcendent and invisible person. The experience they have undergone seems to them to be not only directed towards God but conducted by him, and what they claim regarding this initiative and direction resembles in a re-

markable way what theologians call the action of grace. The final impulse, that by which the whole is illumined and decided, comes not from them but from the action of another within themselves.[55] Hence a phenomenologist of religion concludes: 'We cannot describe the structure of conversion without including the divine action as a factor for comprehension.'[56] It is perhaps awkward to speak, as does Mainage, of a 'dualism' existing in the soul of the convert; nothing, however, is more firmly attested than the certitude of moral evidence experienced by so many converts that what is happening to them does not come, fundamentally, from them but from God.

2. *From the psychological or medical point of view*, John the Baptist died simply from a hæmorrhage. But from the theological point of view his death is a martyrdom which crowns his testimony to the incarnate Word; it is related to the history of salvation and has a sacred character. This example helps us to understand that the same fact may permit of different interpretations, situated at different levels, depending on different means of knowledge and criteria. The psychologist may see in a conversion the outcome of a crisis whose development he has more or less completely and exactly analysed; he may also note a point at which an explanation based on the ordinary 'laws' of human behaviour is halted in the face of data going beyond natural measurements and order. He thus arrives—and he must make allowance for this as something possible beyond his explanation—at the point where the apologist begins to speak of a moral miracle. Nothing, on the contrary, would be more disappointing and even ridiculous than to pretend to 'explain', by some internal conflict, a fact like the conversion of St Paul. Jung is such a great psychologist that it would be no reflection on his merits to say that his ideas on this subject[57] are pitifully inadequate.

The theological interpretation of the fact of conversion is related to particular *dogmatic* criteria proceeding from the statements of Revelation and faith concerning the reality of God and his action, and *spiritual and moral criteria*, taking into account the wholeness of life, purity, the spiritual fruits of the motivation, the fruitfulness and the higher well-being which will flow from it. For a conversion coming from God is not merely a psychological fact, it is a spiritual fact; it is not only an end, a refuge after storm; it opens, rather, a source for others, entering into the inexhaustible history of charity, and the return of creation to God by means of light, freedom, the cross, and love.

Theology of conversion

1. Classical theology has hardly been concerned with conversion, apart from its study of the decisive act of justification.[58] Justification, which is the borderline case, demonstrates in all their force the affirmations of theology about conversion, as supposing a gracious and sovereign act of God. This is done in the baptism of infants without any conscious human activity on their part. We are then in the presence of conversion as an act of God (of grace) in the pure state. It is rather curious to note that Protestantism, which originally insisted upon pure grace and the passivity of man, has come round, on the one hand, to emphasising the rôle of experience in conversion, and on the other hand to questioning and even rejecting infant baptism, for theological reasons. But Protestants faithful to a traditional position on the sacramental value of baptism, even of small children, distinguish between regeneration, produced at baptism by an act of God[59] and conversion, implying a free act of man.[60]

In fact, what is ordinarily called conversion takes place in the conscious life of an adult and generally entails a whole process of preparation and gradual approach. It is rare for it to be absolutely instantaneous and identified with justification. In this gradual advance, theology (at least that which follows the Augustinian-Thomist tradition) affirms the necessity of actual grace from God, that is, action upon the intelligence and the will; a theological point which has recently received fresh attention during the controversy provoked by the work of H. Bouillard;[61] see the bibliography below.

2. But if Catholic theology clearly affirms the primacy and the decisive rôle of grace—which precedes any merit on man's part in such a way that the very beginning of conversion is in fact the fruit of grace[62]—it also affirms no less clearly the reality and the rôle of human freedom.[63] Since Augustine's time theology has even tried to analyse as closely as possible the alternate play of grace and freedom: attempts at explanation abound. Fénelon's, for example, may be read in his *VIme Lettre sur la Religion*. 'The

alternate play of grace and freedom' is perhaps an unfortunate expression, suggesting that the one operates against the other, whereas grace makes freedom effective. Without entering into the details of an analysis involving more detailed study, we shall stick to biblical texts and the experience of converts, showing how the God of grace and the freedom of man approach each other in a kind of dialogue or reciprocal conditioning, rather like a game of dominoes, in which I may play my six if my opponent has played his. Biblical religion, the religion of the Covenant, is built up on dialogue. When one reflects, particularly in St John's Gospel, on those who c me to faith, it is plain that souls placed in the presence of what will possibly become for them the truth of Jesus Christ (which approaches them at first under the form of some sign or occasion), will begin to declare themselves for or against, according to a fundamental disposition, in which the decisive fact is ultimately a psychological opening or closing of the self.[64] The question is to know whither our love is leading us. If it is open to the call and demands of another, it will go as far as charity. In the light of faith, the love of God will become, above all things, this principle for a new synthesis, capable of modelling and unifying our entire personality. For conversion will go as far as that. One may say of it what Kierkegaard says of faith: 'Belief is not an undertaking like another, one more qualification applied to the same individual (we would add: an idea or a system of ideas); no, risking belief, man himself becomes another.' In a letter of 21st July 1849, to Albéric de Blanche, Marquis of Raffin, Donoso Cortès put it in this way: 'The mystery of my conversion (for every conversion is a mystery) is a mystery of love. I did not love God, and God wanted me to love him: and because I love him, I am now converted.'[65]

Theology analyses the typical acts of conversion-justification. According to Aquinas and the Council of Trent, they are faith, joined with fear and hope, the beginning of love, repentance and a firm purpose. It is clear that all depends on faith. But theologians know that life does not always respect classifications and that it is, above all, synthetic and concrete, not analytical.[66]

Denominational conversions

By this we mean conversions which take place between one

Christian communion and another. It is clear that the conversion of a Catholic to another communion represents, from the Catholic point of view, an apostasy.[67] The Catholic Church tries, on the contrary, to attract members even of other Christian communions and bring them into her fold. Here I should like, very briefly, to emphasise the *meaning* of denominational conversions and the conditions under which they may legitimately be sought.

Who could deny that to seek them is legitimate in principle? That becomes evident as soon as the existence of a given religious truth is acknowledged, together with the fact that only one Church is true, having existed among us since Christ and the apostles. No one can blame a man for trying to make others share in a truth which he holds: no one can blame a Catholic for trying to attract to his Church and her communion the greatest possible number of men, believers or not, already Christians or not. But this can never mean that adherence to an organisation may be brought about by any means whatever, in the same way that any undertaking recruits members or clients. While the end itself is legitimate and praiseworthy, there might be ways of pursuing it which would not only be dishonest but would betray and distort the truth itself. The apostolate is not a form of propaganda like any other; it is a spiritual, even supernatural, process which derives from supernatural faith and charity. That being so, it is vital that freedom and honesty of means be safeguarded at every step of the road towards truth. One would fail in this if one were to use psychological, moral or social pressure, such as mass propaganda—the notorious 'Rape of Souls' which gave its name to Chalotin's famous book. The difference and the distance between 'proselytism' and 'evangelisation' or, as certain Protestant authors put it, between mission and propaganda,[68] must be respected. There is an increasing tendency among Catholics to seek in the essential condition for an act of faith, which is that it should be free, the foundation for a healthy tolerance.[69] In the case of a man who is a possible candidate for conversion, one must respect the gravity of the problem, of the search, and the profundity of the questions he asks himself and which he finds a stumbling-block. Nothing is more saddening than to see the simplicity with which some Catholics think to answer and dispose of all questions with some ready-made formula. Often spiritual profundity is on the side of the one who is undergoing the difficulties; even one who has the faith and, in one sense, 'has' the truth, can only keep himself on the level of both at the cost of perpetually seeking and of a spirit of interrogation and open-mindedness. Neither certitude nor the absolute value of truth is here excluded, but rather apologetical haste and over-simplified dogmatism without spiritual truth.

The very purpose of the apostolate and of evangelisation is not to recruit adherents to a group, to gain in human influence, but to help men to fulfil themselves in God and with God, that is, according to the positive plan of salvation which God has realised 'in Christ and in the Church'. 'I came that they may have life and have it more abundantly'.[70] The application of such methods in conversions from atheism to God, or from a non-Christian religion to the Christ of the gospel and the Church, can easily be seen. But the method is the same, *mutatis mutandis*, for all conversions to the Catholic Church. In changing from another Christian communion to Catholicism one goes from a state wherein the heritage of Jesus Christ, the treasury of the means to salvation and communion, is found more or less seriously impoverished or deformed, to the true ark of salvation, wherein the truth of revelation is fully safeguarded and the fullness of the means of grace, instituted by God, is perfectly preserved, offered and put into operation. The Catholic Church is that *communio sanctorum* wherein the plenitude of the *sancta* can procure, intrinsically, the full realisation of the *sancti*.

This does not mean that all was false and valueless in the communion to which one had belonged. In it there already existed *sancta* and very real values, but imperfect, more or less distorted and mixed with error. Consequently, in being converted from a non-Catholic Christian communion to the Catholic Church, nothing which was already held of the true, the good, the Christian, has to be renounced, but it is to be restored to its true place, corrected, affirmed, completed and fulfilled, through communion with a unity which is the fullness of grace and truth. Conversion, in itself, is a fulfilment. Far from being pure theory, this is a fact attested by the blessed experience of many converts.[71]

It must be admitted, however, that this fact, though experienced and acknowledged in the depths of the soul, does not prevent certain converts feeling, if not regret, at least some mixed sentiments of distress and disillusionment. On the human level—considered not on the surface, from the utilitarian angle, but in depth, we might say, on the level of a certain religious anthropology—not all that was left behind may have been recovered, or at least there may be no conscious feeling of it. Newman's case is typical. Neither grace nor truth makes everything easy, at the level of feelings of difficulty or distress. But, 'a thousand difficulties do not make a doubt'. Newman, in the darkest of the sunless years he had to go through, never ceased to say that he regretted nothing: 'I have never for a moment wavered in my trust in the Catholic Church, since I was received into her bosom.'[72]

This nature of denominational conversions entails certain aspects of practical importance. Theologically, the term 'abjuration' is not false, for there really are errors to renounce, at least objectively, but the term 'profession of faith' is more correct, more comprehensive, and at the same time less objectionable psychologically. The Holy Office has preferred it in recently approved formulas, which place more stress on the positive adherence to Catholic truth than on the rejection of error.[73] In this light, with greater insistence on the positive side, denominational conversions, which have always existed in the Church, begin to lose, if they ever had it, their polemical sharpness and any aspect of rivalry. They take their place in the great context of efforts inspired by the Holy Ghost with a view to uniting all Christians in one single visible Church of Christ and his apostles. These efforts look far beyond the necessarily individual cases of personal conversion. They follow a collective approach of disunited Christians to one another, and of all who are at present divided in separate communions towards a point of unity which is at the same time a point of fulfilment. But the conversions themselves, which represent a personal entry into unity and a sort of personal anticipation of it, may be considered no longer in the spirit of rivalry or denominational victory, but in that of spiritual emulation, so well expressed by Bishop Charrière of Fribourg, Geneva and Lausanne, in his letter to Mgr Brilioth in February 1946: 'Nor can union be realised in the manner of a triumph of one over another, like that which is seen on the temporal plane. . . .'[74]

NOTES

1. First version appeared in English in *Thought* (Fordham University), vol. 33 (1958), no. 128, pp. 5–20. Second version, revised, in *Parole et Mission*, no. 11, Oct. 1960, pp. 493–523. For bibliography on conversion, see pp. 237 ff.
2. On this analysis of 'witness', see Gabriel Marcel, 'Le témoignage comme localisation de l'existentiel' in *NRT*, 1946, pp. 182–91; J. Guitton, *La pensée moderne et le catholicisme, VI. Le problème de Jésus et les fondements du témoignage chrétien*, Aix-en-Provence, 1948, pp. 174f.
3. On Stoicism, see J. Behm in *TWB z. NT*, vol. IV, p. 976. Plotinus traced an itinerary of conversion, consisting in raising oneself above sensible images and the varied objects of the world, detaching oneself from the affections and from action, withdrawing into oneself, abolishing all memory of the past, all parcelling out of consciousness, all distinction of subject and object, in order finally to coincide, in ecstasy, with the supreme intelligible. On the idea of conversion in platonism, with the use of the words *epistrophe* and *metanoia*, see A. D. Nock, *Conversion*, Oxford, p. 179f.
4. See J. Guitton, *Le temps et l'éternité chez Plotin et saint Augustin*, Paris, 1933, pp. 230f.
5. Paul Bourget was wrong when, professing himself henceforth a Catholic (and a monarchist), in the preface to *Le Disciple* in 1899, he objected to the term *conversion* in his case: 'One is converted', he wrote, 'from a negative, not from an attitude of pure expectation. . . .' On the contrary!
6. On these conversions, see H. P. de la Boullaye, in *Dict. Sp.*, II, col. 2259f.
7. On the whole subject, see P. Galtier, art. 'Conversi' in *Dict. Sp.*, II, col. 2218–24; on the first sense, G. B. Ladner, *The Idea of Reform. Its Impact on Christian Thought* . . ., Cambridge, Mass., 1959, pp. 345, 417; for the second sense, *ibid.*, pp. 366f; for the medieval monastic sense, T. A. Brockhaus, *Religious who are known as Conversi*, Washington, 1945; K. Hallinger, 'Woher kommen die Laienbrüder?' in *Anal. Ord. Cisterc.*, 12 (1956), pp. 1–104. On 'conversion' read also Étienne Gilson, *Héloïse and Abélard*, London and New York, 1952, chap. I.
8. E.g., Am 4:6f; Is 9:12; 19:22; Jer 3; Ezk 33; Deut 4:30; Dan 9:13; 2 Chron 26:13.
9. E.g., 1 Sam 15:29; Ps 110:4; Jer 8:6. It is used with and after *shubh*, for example in Jer 38:18–19.
10. See Hos 14:2f; Am 4:8; Jn 2:13; Is 55:7; 6:10 (quoted Mt 13:15; Mk 4:12; Ac 28:27); Jer 31:14; Deut 30:10.
11. Ac 26:18.
12. Ac 8:22; Rev 2:21f; 9:20f; 16:11; Heb 6:1.
13. See 1 Pet 2:25.
14. Lk 22:32; Ac 3:19.
15. See A. H. Dirksen, *The New Testament Concept of Metanoia*, Washington, 1932, pp. 165–96; J. Behm in *TWB z. NT*, vol. IV, pp. 973–5.
16. E.g., in Wis 48:16; Is 46:8.
17. J. Behm, pp. 994f.

18. Jer 38:18–19.
19. Ac 3:19; 26:20.
20. See Dirksen, pp. 66–7.
21. Tauler, *Sermon* 12, 3; ed. Hugueny-Théry-Corbin, vol. I, p. 276.
22. See Excursus 3. 'Busse' in K. Esser and L. Hardick, *Die Schriften d. hl. Franziskus v. Ass*, Werl i. W., 2nd ed., 1956, pp. 199f.
23. E. Würthwein, 'Busse u. Umkehr' in *TWB z. NT*, vol. IV, pp. 976–85.
24. See Jn 3:7; Jud 4:10f.
25. See Am 4:6–11.
26. See Is 58:4b and 5–7; Zach 7:5f.
27. Is 22:12f; Joel 2:12.
28. See Ezek 3:19; 18:21–3, 27–8; 33:9, 11, 12, 14, 19.
29. Is not Würthwein also guilty of a certain error of method? On the one hand he analyses 'the cultural-ritual form of penitence', on the other, the prophetic idea of conversion. In the one he finds 'things', rites, in the other, something very spiritual. But he could have looked for the religious sentiments meant to be expressed in these rites, at the different concrete moments of the process of penitence, contained in the verbs *shubh* and *nacham*. The analysis of those words, which he does not attempt, would have enabled him to see what is common ground, after all, to penitence and conversion, and how the latter contains the truth of the former, even in the Prophets.
30. This aspect, on the contrary, is what Dirksen has seen and illustrated, at the risk of not sufficiently bringing out the originality of the gospel *metanoia*, the professed subject of his very erudite monograph.
31. Mt 3:2; see Mk 1:4, then Mt 4:17; Mk 1:15.
32. Mt 3:8; 'works worthy of penance'.
33. 'Repent and believe the gospel'; Mk 1:15; Ac 20:21; 26:18; Heb 6:1.
34. Mk 6:12; Mt 12:41; Lk 5:32 and parallels; 24:47 and Ac, *passim*; *TWB z. NT*, p. 999.
35. See 1 Thess 1:9–10; Gal; Rom 1:25; 12:1–2.
36. 2 Cor 4:16; 1 Thess 1:9–10; 4:4–5; 9–12; Rom 1:25–31 and 12:13; Col 3:5–9, 12–14; 4:17–20, etc. See M. E. Boismard, 'Conversion et vie nouvelle dans saint Paul', in *Lumière et Vie*, no. 47, (1960), pp. 71–94.
37. Providence makes use of them; see Hos 2:8f; Is 19:22. It was the case, for example, with Racine, for which see F. Maurice, *La vie de Jean Racine*, Paris, 1928, pp. 237f.
38. The latest and certainly the best study of the well-known problem in this form is that by John O'Meara, *The Young Augustine*, London, 1954.
39. See for example, S. Ligier, *L'adulte des milieux ouvriers*, 2 vols, Paris, 1951; *Les Conversions. Compte rendu de la 8e Semaine de Missiologie de Louvain* (1930), Louvain, 1930.
40. See A. von Ruville, *La marque du véritable anneau*, p. 193.
41. See M. Penido, 'Conversion, subconscient et surnaturel', in *Divus Thomas*, (Frib.), 1930, pp. 305–16.
42. It is that of M. T. L. Penido, *La conscience religieuse*, Paris, 1935, pp. 41–131.
43. See *Roads to Rome*, pp. 10f.
44. His account (written in 1909) first appeared in *Revue des Jeunes*, 10th Oct. 1913: reproduced by T. Mainage, *Témoins du renouveau catholique*, pp. 65f, in *Pages de Prose*, collected and presented by A. Blanchet (Gallimard), pp. 275f; etc.
45. Cardinal Vaughan wrote in 1896: 'The conversion of souls one by one, precisely as they enter the world and depart from it to their particular judgement

one by one, is the result that I look for. . . .' Introductory letter to Fr Ragey (*La crise religieuse en Angleterre*, Paris, 1896, p. vii).

46. E.g., the Saxons.

47. E.g., the Basutos, after the conversion of their chief Griffith: see *Grands Lacs* (Namur), July 1949, pp. 1–13, 17–19.

48. There is abundant literature on revivals. On the Salvation Army, see G. Swarts, *Salut par la foi et conversion brusque*, Paris, 1931.

49. A point often emphasised in our time; for example, J. Guitton, 'La conversion du pécheur, gloire de Dieu' in *Monde moderne et sens du péché. Semaine des intellectuels catholiques*, 1956, pp. 234–44; E. Roche, 'Pénitence et conversion dans l'Évangile et dans la vie chrétienne', in *NRT*, 79 (1957), pp. 113–34; P. A. Liégé, *Reviens au Seigneur ton Dieu*, Paris, 1959; P. Bruch, *Die Bekehrung aus Grundvoraussetzung christlicher existenz*, Graz, 1959.

50. See, from Pascal, the comparison of the early Christians with those of today, in *L'oeuvre de Pascal*, op. 6, NRF, p. 339, or in the small edition of L. Brunschwigg, pp. 201f.

51. *Psychology of Religion*, London, 1889.

52. *Varieties of Religious Experience*, 1902.

53. See Santo de Sanctis, 'La conversione religiosa' Bologna, 1924 (critique of A. Gemelli in *Vita e Pensiero*, Sept. 1924); E. Harms, *Psychologie und Psychiatrie der Konversion*, Leiden, 1939.

54. See V. Monod, 'Le voyage, le déracinement hors du milieu natal constituent-ils un des éléments déterminants de la conversion religieuse?' in *RHPR*, 1936, pp. 385–99.

55. Lacordaire wrote, in a letter of 11th May 1824, about his own conversion: 'It is a sublime moment, when the last ray of light penetrates the soul and attaches to a common centre the truths which are scattered there. There is always such a distance between the moment which follows and that which precedes it, between what one was before and what one is afterwards, that the word "grace" has been invented to explain this light from above.' (Foisset, *Vie de Lacordaire*, vol. I, p. 61). Aquinas, who insists strongly on the rôle of free will (Ia IIae, qu. 113, art. 1. 3; *Com. in Joan.*, c. 4, lect. 2), insists no less on the decisive character of grace: *Ipsa praeparatio mentis humanae est ex virtute divina. Nam licet facilitas qua mentes praeparantur sit causa conversionis, tamen ipsius facilitatis et praeparationis causa est Deus; Converte nos Domine ad te, et convertemur . . .* (Lam 5:21). (*Com. in 2 Cor* c. 2, lect. 3), *Per quondam interiorem instinctum quo Deus per gratiam tangit cor ut convertatur ad ipsum . . .* (*Com. in Galat.*, c. 1, lect. 4); etc.

56. G. van der Leeuw, *La religion dans son essence et ses manifestations*, Paris, 1948, p. 522.

57. Quoted by Thouless, 1950 edition, pp. 189f.

58. The two principal references are *Sum. Theol.*, Ia IIae, qu. 113 (and parallel passages), and the Council of Trent, session VI, especially cc. 5 and 6. See R. Aubert, *Le problème de l'acte de Foi*, Louvain, 1945, pp. 76f.

59. See Jn 3:7.

60. See Ac 3:19. For example, J. Strachan in *Hastings' Encyclopaedia*, vol. IV, pp. 107 and 108.

61. *Conversion et grâce chez saint Thomas d'Aquin*, (Paris, 1944).

62. See the canons of the second Council of Orange, Denz. Bann., nn. 174f; R. Aubert, *op. cit.*, pp. 36f; Council of Trent, Denz. Bann., nn. 797f, 813, and *Index Systematicus*, X and g.

63. See Denz. Bann., *Index Systematicus*, VI d; VII g; X g.

64. See a fine passage of E. Le Roy: 'Now comes into play a more concrete and intimate psychology than that of the schools: a psychology of inward opening. When a truth approaches us, and already makes itself known, although one has not yet succeeded in embodying it in an explicit idea, there is a moment of decisive darkness, when the future of the light depends on the attitude, welcoming or hostile, we adopt towards it; the conclusion begins to be formed for birth, consent or refusal, self-surrender or retreat, and that is the hour of freedom' (*Compte rendu de l'Académie des Sciences morales et politiques*, 1936, p. 912). That hour of freedom is equally the hour of grace.

65. Quoted by J. Chaix Ruy, *Donoso Cortès, théologien de l'histoire et prophète*, Paris, 1956, p. 121.

66. See E. Hugon, 'La notion théologique de la psychologie de la conversion, in *Revue thomiste*, July–Sept, 1919, pp. 226–41.

67. See Denz. Bann., n. 1815 and n. 1794; CIC, c. 2314. See the theological commentaries of R. Aubert, *op. cit.*, pp. 200f; K. Rahner, 'Ueber Konversionen', in *Hochland*, Dec. 1953, pp. 119–26 (repeated in *Theological Investigations*, vol. III).

68. C. Keysse, J. P. Lange.

69. See CIC, c. 1351, and a declaration of Pius XII on freedom of conversions in his speech of 6th Oct. 1946, to the Rota (*Osservatore Romano*, 7th–8th Oct.). In the *Ecumenical Review*, July 1959, pp. 405–21, and Oct. 1959, pp. 23–43 (reprinted separately, 96 pp.), may be found a very well documented review of recent Catholic publications on the question of religious freedom: A. F. Carrillo de Albornoz, 'Roman Catholicism and Religious Liberty.'

70. Jn 10:10.

71. See Newman, *Loss and Gain; Difficulties felt by Anglicans*, vol. I, p. 350; *Essay on the Development of Christian Doctrine*, pp. 199–203; Wenceslas Ivanov, 'Lettre à Charles du Bos,' in *Correspondance d'un coin à l'autre*, Paris, 1931, pp. 175–6.

72. See in L. Bouyer, *Newman, His Life and Spirituality*, a letter of 1862 to *The Globe*, and a passage in his *Journal*, 8th Nov. 1860.

73. See my note on 'Abjuration' in *Catholicisme*, vol. I (1948), col. 39–40.

74. See the pastoral letter of Mgr Stohr, bishop of Mainz, 22nd May 1952.

On the meaning and conditions of denominational conversions, see Newman, *Grammar of Assent*, pp. 194–203; Letter of 24th Feb. 1887 to G. T. Edwards, secretary of the Evangelical Society (in Ward, *Life*, vol. II, p. 527); Yves de Montcheuil, 'Pour un apostolat spirituel', in *Construire*, IX, 1942, pp. 132f; P. Mulla, 'Perspectives d'après-guerre en pays de mission et conditions d'une évangélisation libre et efficace', in *Studia Missionalia*, Rome, vol. I, 1943, pp. 137–65; Y. M. J. Congar, *Divided Christendom*, London, 1937; 'Proselytism and Evangelization', next chapter in this book; H. Duméry, *Les trois tentations de l'apostolat moderne*, Paris, 1948; 'La tentation de faire du bien', in *Esprit*, Jan. 1955, pp. 1–34 (reprinted under the same title with other studies, Paris, 1956); K. Rahner, quoted above, n. 67.

CHAPTER THREE

Proselytism
and Evangelisation

IN SPITE OF SOME AMBIGUITIES WHICH THE author has doubtless not been careful enough to eliminate, A. J. Cronin's novel, *The Keys of the Kingdom*, is a striking presentation of a problem on which everyone engaged in apostolic work ought to have reflected.[1] It is the problem of the apostolate in relation to complete respect for conscience and its freedom. The question is (seeing that the truth is in the Church, or rather, that the Church *is* the truth); should one make it the purpose of one's activity to lead men to hold the Church's doctrines and practise her precepts, or should one rather remain open to a notion of the Kingdom of God and of salvation which goes beyond this narrowly denominational point of view and results in an attitude towards souls more respectful of the privacy of their freedom and the mystery of grace? In other words, it is the question whether our apostolate aims at serving the Church or at serving souls. I propose to give the name of 'proselytism' to that activity which seeks the victory of our own denomination: what seeks men's spiritual good, their life and progress in Christ, I shall call 'evangelisation'. The debate is therefore between these two.

I am well aware that at the level of theoretical principle, this is an unreal problem. The distinction is not one of law; it cannot form the foundation of an ecclesiology. The essential problem here is one of attitude, on the level of the 'hypothesis', of psychological facts and tendencies. The ensuing reflections, if followed to their conclusion, will make it clear what I mean by this.

A Jocist 'militant' at a difficult juncture, and showing signs of discouragement and disaffection, was asked by one of his friends: 'What's wrong? You are well liked in your section, the chaplain likes you. . . .' The militant replied: 'Oh yes, the chaplain likes me all right, but it isn't me he likes, it's the JOC he likes in me."

This incident is a fair illustration of the danger against which Cronin's book is warning us, the danger of aiming not at the inner, personal good of men, but at the victory of our own group, the success of our organisations. If we examine ourselves in all honesty we shall have to admit that what we are really working for, in many cases, is not so much that goodness should come into a soul, that God should be better known and served, as that people should join our group, that there should be many in our organisations, that we should have influence over men, and especially over those who are themselves influential, that we may be able to use So-and-so, to make him act in our interests, etc. Every priest, even the most disinterested, who has long been careful about the purity of his apostolate, will be led by such an examination of conscience to recognise in his activity some element of proselytism. I invite those of them who may read this to question themselves candidly.

In a remarkable missiological study, published during the war and little known amongst us, Paul Mulla[2] gave a warning against hasty and merely external conversions, made to swell the 'bag'. He saw in them 'the result of a hasty zeal which takes the individual, detached from his social background and personal history, as an abstract being, a *homo missiologicus*, destined to swell the registers of the Church, an apostolic "game-book", if he is not reserved for a spectacular exhibition or an advertisement.'[3] The author applied these remarks even to the apostolate in European countries, and still more precisely to the conversion of known intellectuals. Certain Catholics seem not so much to expect from these men an adherence freely formed by a long interior process of maturing as to try to persuade them that really they 'already belong to us'.[4] To such an extent in their minds is the haste for victory added to the zeal of the gospel!

We priests must purge ourselves of political clericalism. We must purge ourselves of all possible traces of moral and psychological clericalism. By political clericalism I mean making use of the influence we derive from the priesthood and our mission for the benefit of political forces. By moral and psychological clericalism I mean seeking and enjoying the influence possessed by the clergy over the conduct of the laity, and even over their spiritual conduct in so far as our actions are the expression of our desire and quest for influence.

This is an extremely important point. In a country like France, for instance, where the critical spirit is so developed and has long been dominant, immense possibilities are closed to our apostolate, simply because we are distrusted. Trust and distrust are feelings which are simple and sometimes confused, but extremely powerful, affecting positively or negatively the relations between one person and another. Distrust represents a complex—that is, 'a permanent association of images, coloured by a determinate emotive state and consequently tending to a determinate purpose of direction'—an extremely powerful complex, taking years or it may be decades of patient and completely unselfish action to dispel. The most convincing reasons, the most generous enterprises, the greatest goodwill, prove ineffective and fall into a mysterious impotence, simply because those to whom all this is directed do not trust us. Distrust creates an impenetrable barrier: it shuts eyes, ears and hearts. A whole mass of sometimes admirable efforts in the sphere of social and international concord, and especially in the sphere of the apostolate, are made, through distrust, of no effect.

More precisely, people distrust us because they fear that we are trying to get a hold on them: they are afraid of being 'used'—'for the glory of God', of course, but used and influenced all the same —of being made to accept a mass of things far beyond their real convictions or likings, of having their hands forced. Women are less afraid of this than men, which is one reason why they come more willingly to church. But where women submit, men jib; they don't like to be told what they must do, what they must think, what place to take, what attitude to adopt. Many lapses from all religious practice among the former students of our religious colleges spring from these feelings. It is certainly no accident that in many places Catholicism has become a religion of women, or rather, that it has ceased to be a religion for men.

The complex and the reflexes which we have described have certainly much to do with it.

In this connection I am inclined to see a danger in certain ways of developing or maintaining a mystique of conquest. We use this word with such a good conscience that we don't notice it, but there is something aggressive and unpleasant about it. 'I am not here to be conquered', is the reaction of many who feel they are the object of our enterprises. 'I refuse to let anyone try to *get* me.' And feeling their freedom menaced, they protect it by keeping at a distance. Here, too, the best-intentioned apostle is in danger of considering the people to be evangelised, not as persons whom we can help, help to perfect what belongs in them to God and the Church, but as material in which the missionary can obtain his best returns, and whom he has to transfer from the hostile or indifferent world to one which is friendly; to the *clientèle*, shall we say?

Some remarks in this sense were suggested to me by Henri Perrin's fine book, *Priest-Workman in Germany*,[6] which in many respects is so moving. After describing his concrete outline of what might be called a pastoral or apostolic anthropology, I pointed out that in the very zeal to which he bears witness there is danger of a certain lack of discretion. 'In his book there appears a desire to "hook", to tackle everyone he comes across. Apostolic zeal is clear enough, but it is a zeal always in danger of turning into a desire for influence, into tactlessness, a sort of professionalism of conquest. These are the dangers besetting us. But on the other shore of the narrow strait, through which our apostolic voyage lies, we are beset by a no less grave danger, that of apostolic timidity and cowardice, to which even more of our colleagues succumb.'[7] The problem of proselytism *versus* evangelisation is thus complicated by the fatal tension between zeal and tactlessness.

The problems are immense, urgent and, alas, insoluble, in the sense that it is impossible to solve them with a dialectic formula, and it is useless to look for one. By that I mean a form of words which would provide an objective solution of general validity, independent of our interior attitude, needing only to be applied as required. These problems are far rather of a sort which are not susceptible of a solution external to ourselves, such as might exist

apart from our conscious fidelity to all the facts, honestly acknowledged. Faced with such situations, we have only one possibility
which is not a betrayal: to be prepared to experience in ourselves
the sort of laceration involved in being true to all the facts, and
to try to purify the springs of action in ourselves.

This will mean, in practice, deepening and purifying our love,
a love which is really love; not, that is, asserting ourselves, even
in the masked and apparently disinterested form of serving our
Church, but seeking the good of the other person and, to that
end, accepting the other, with a total respect for that profoundest
movement in which he is truly *himself*. And we must do so as if
it concerned ourselves and our own good, and that deepest movement which expresses ourselves, and which we accept with so
profound an agreement.

The deepening and purifying of the love to which we are thus
called will apply more precisely to pastoral or apostolic charity.
This must not be a remote, ethereal sentiment, so 'supernatural-
ised' that it is emptied of all human content and reduced to an
abstraction. It is a sharing in the *agape* of God, manifested in
Jesus Christ, who characterised his mission as total self-consecra-
tion, 'to seek and to save that which was lost'. In this perspective
our apostolic charity will be devoted heart and soul to the evangelisation, that is, the service of men, desiring only to help them
to fulfil themselves in goodness, according to God and Jesus
Christ.

Thus the avowed intention to be apostolic fishers of men, the
desire to convert, must never stray from the path laid down, from
us to the other man, by a real love, a love which is humble and
serving, respectful and disinterested. One thing is certain, that
proselytism is very apt to begin at the precise point where the
undertaking, instead of going forward in love alone and under the
inspiration of a genuine love, begins to go astray from or beyond
it. And this, it must be admitted, is the fatal danger of every
organisation. For every organisation, though originally provoked
by the spirit and wholly inspired by it, soon exists by itself,
independently of its inspiration. It is then that it tends to become
an end instead of a means, and to make use of the spirit of
proselytism, instead of existing only by the spirit of evangelisation.

Obviously we have still to examine the reason by which the proselytising attitude seems to justify itself and almost to be inevitable. That reason is the conviction, worthy of all respect, that we possess the truth, that the Church is the truth. Therefore, since her dogmas are the truth, since salvation is to be found in her sacraments, what else have we to do but to lead men to submit to their discipline? Hence, for example, that concern and that question so commonly encountered when someone is dying: 'Has he received the sacraments?' In *The Keys of the Kingdom*, Francis does not even think of trying to induce his atheist friend Dr Tulloch, dying of the plague, to confess and be anointed. This earns the old Scotsman's profound gratitude: 'Man, I've never loved ye so much as I do now, for not trying to bully me to heaven. . . .' But it moves Mother Mary Veronica to a shocked rebuke, to which the poor priest humbly replies: 'God judges us not only by what we believe, but by what we do.'

Francis' reply may be a little extreme, but who dare say that it is wrong? As I shall shortly point out, these are things that cannot be made into a theory just like that, for they would only become mere indifferentism, but at the level of the practical attitude, in a concrete situation, they are authentically true. It is doubtless in this gulf between law and fact, between thesis and hypothesis, that a place must be found for an attitude full of tolerance and very delicate respect for the mystery of grace and freedom.

Perfect agreement between law and fact, between the objectively true forms of religion and the interior good of souls, is a reality which belongs to the age to come. For it is a part of that visibility, that triumphant victory of the truth, which is an aspect of glory, reserved for the advent of justice. Then God will render to every man according to his works, the secrets of all hearts will be revealed, error, evil and death will be done away, the good and the true will triumph in glory. But in the present dispensation, which is the era of the Church, we are under the rule of the advent of mercy, in which Christ saves rather than reigns. We are not in the time of the harvest, but in that of the sowing and the growth of the seed; when the tares are growing up with the wheat, and the time has not yet come to separate them; when the growth of God's seed is a mystery and God's work is done even with things which to us seem bad. Under these conditions we have no right to deny that some man's way is good, though it may not be our way. We cannot claim to see him arriving at once just where we want him to go. We must sow generously, honestly and in trust, and leave the result to God.[8]

That is why we must avoid the rather sectarian form of certitude and zeal which leads us to classify men, and also things or events or decisions, into good and bad, sheep and goats, as if this were not unwarrantably to anticipate the judgement of God; as if there were here, on earth, a kingdom of the good, defined with certitude and accuracy by the canonical frontiers of the Church, inside which everything is good—and a kingdom of evil, consisting of everything we think to be outside those frontiers, in which everything is bad. Whence we might draw the conclusion that everything not officially Catholic is condemned and lost.

This point of view—which as a doctrine would scarcely be supported by modern theologians—if translated into a concrete attitude, would lead to the worst forms of intolerance and proselytism. And it would show, not only a lack of respect for the mystery of freedom and the growth of God's seeds, but in the end a lack of faith and trust in the truth.[9]

It would take too long, and be too ambitious, to develop here all the consequences of these considerations from the point of view of the idea that the priest should have of his ministry. A tendency towards proselytism will obviously produce an emphasis on a sort of automatism of the function: a tendency towards evangelisation will produce an emphasis on the influence of the spiritual man. With these two tendencies correspond, respectively, an emphasis on the aspect of the system or the mechanism, and an emphasis on the aspect of life, in the idea formed of the Church. Thus we return to one of the fundamental themes of *The Keys of the Kingdom*, where we follow a kind of encounter and dialogue between the 'organised Church' and the 'life-Church'.

In those memorable pages in which Cardinal Manning, two years before his death, recorded his reflections on the obstacles to the growth of the Catholic Church in England, he gave as his fifth point, 'sacramentalism' and as his sixth, 'functionarism', the lack of attention paid to the religious man.[10] By 'sacramentalism' he meant 'the danger which besets all priests, of becoming sayers of Masses or purveyors of sacraments'. By 'functionarism' he meant the tendency 'to rely, in our actions, not on our personal fitness, but on the official function'. Manning notes that St Paul, 'inwardly conformed to his divine Master, won souls without recourse to the sacrament, because it was within.'

This point is of great importance. St Paul tells us himself that he prefers to use his spiritual gifts rather than his titles to authority.[11] With how many priests, on the contrary, the *function* and the authority attached to it conceal the person or the *spiritual man*! How often a personal question put to them is answered with a ready-made formula, copied, just as it is, from the system! It is the price paid for an objectivity and a dogmatism which are indeed great treasures, but do not escape the danger of failing to appreciate the resources of the life of the Spirit in our souls. During an interview between the hero of *The Keys of the Kingdom* and the former rector of his seminary, now his bishop, the latter says: 'You're not one of our ecclesiastical milliners who must have everything stitched up in neat little packets—convenient for handing out. And quite the nicest thing about you, dear boy, is this—you haven't got that bumptious security which springs from dogma rather than from faith.' Here again we find a hint of that fallacious distinction between dogma and faith, but here it is employed without any spirit of system, in a sense which is perfectly acceptable and in any case quite clear, to contrast a functionarism of the ready-made with the living communication of the convinced soul.

An attitude of authority adopted in the name of the function; system; ready-made religion—these things are logically connected. They go easily with a certain spirit of domination or superiority, of 'bumptious security'. On the other hand, the more our priestly action is nourished on the source of our life and our personal spiritual gifts, the more easily we shall preserve that humility in the presence of souls which inspires respect for their inner freedom. A tendency towards a service of the system and the group, by setting in motion their objective means, over which we have power, ministers to that terrible priestly pride which is one of our great temptations. A tendency towards the service of men, starting from what we possess of ever-renewed life, demands much more humility from us, more feeling of our own insufficiency, and an effort to purge ourselves of the spirit of triumph or possession.

The system calls for submission and is content with external conformity. Life calls only for conviction, the free adherence of the person. Hence, according to whether we adopt the viewpoint of proselytism or of evangelisation, there is a certain difference in our appreciation and esteem for freedom of conscience. In the former, attention is directed to the conquest of adherents for the group. We naturally desire that the conquered should become good Christians and have a personal interior life. But to bring them to this we trust mainly to the collective and objective means employed by the Church, and the priest's ministry is devoted mainly to putting these into action; the sacraments, dogmatic instruction, societies for piety and edification, Church activities, religious press and propaganda, etc. But from the viewpoint of evangelisation, attention is devoted primarily to a man's growth in goodness. I know the great resources represented by these objective means entrusted by God to the ministry of his Church, and I want men to come to them. But I would not have anything done, in their approach to the genuine form of the true life, which is not the fruit of an inner movement, whose freedom has been respected at every point.

When, in connection with papal infallibility, Gladstone expressed the fear that an Englishman might have to choose between obedience and the voice of conscience, Newman replied, quoting numerous theologians, that the Church has always upheld the primacy of conscience.[12] Conscience, he said, is 'the first Vicar of Christ'. For the positive authority of the pope would be nothing if he had not the natural authority of conscience, on which, in the last resort, is founded all real obedience and adherence itself, in so far as it is honest and true. Newman concluded with a touch of humour: 'I think it is better not to talk religion at a banquet, but if I were in fact obliged, some day, to propose a religious toast, I should certainly drink to the pope, if you like, but, you understand, to conscience first and the pope second.'

This idea, that outward adherence is worthless without the inward, personal adherence which is the soul of it; that the Church does not seek to act through external means of organisation or compulsion, but through free conviction and uncon-strained love, seems to be a point especially dear to the ecclesi-astical thought of Pius XII. He returned to it several times and, to quote only the first and last in date of his solemn declarations, in the encyclical *Summi Pontificatus*, 20th October 1939, and the speech to the Sacred College on 20th February 1946.[13]

But respect for spiritual freedom is something so delicate, so exacting, that a man can hardly be sure he has never failed in it. He may be convinced of its importance and determined to prac-tise it, and then one day it appears that in some circumstance or other he has displayed the reflexes of proselytism. So readily does our zeal accept certain habits of *esprit de corps* or competition! Or perhaps some indiscretion, venial in itself, provokes reactions which have regrettable and sometimes disastrous results. We can never be too respectful of the freedom of those to whom we are sent. A soul, especially a modern soul, must never feel itself besieged, only loved and respected—or if it feels itself besieged, let it be by God, who stands at the door and knocks. For my own part I can never meditate too often on the lesson of the Grand Inquisitor.[14] And there is also the fact that the most serious complaints made against us, and the distrust of us felt by so many, spring from the fact that, rightly or wrongly, they suspect us of the Grand Inquisitor's spirit.

In conclusion I should like to emphasise one final point which, important as it is for summing up the implications of the pre-ceding reflections, goes beyond the problem before us.

We cannot proceed, without careful adjustments, from an ab-stract general truth to a concrete attitude, nor transpose a con-crete attitude, true in itself, into an abstract general doctrine.

If, starting from the attitude of evangelisation, I were to trans-pose it as such into an ecclesiology, that is, into a theory of the nature of the Church, I should be in danger of ignoring the very fact of the Church, the usefulness of groups and the importance of the means of grace, such as doctrine and the sacraments. If, starting from abstract ecclesiology, I were to translate it as such into practice, I should run the risk of crushing the frail and holy freedom of persons under the rights of the truth in itself. Because the Church *is* the truth, I should see only error and damnation outside explicit adherence and submission to her objective forms.

The attitude I have defined as evangelisation is a spirit. A system must not be made out of it: to give it expression as an ecclesiology it is not enough to generalise it by making it abstract. So no one must find in my reflections an argument against the activities and works of the apostolate: that would be foreign and indeed contrary to my intention. It is necessary to seek out and attract those who are not Christians, to group and incorporate those who are. I am not in the least opposed to mission or parish, for both are necessary. But both must be run in the spirit of evangelisation, not in the spirit of proselytism. It is a spirit that is here in question, not a theory, which in any case would be false. In the language of scholasticism, it is a matter of a *quo*, not of a *quod*. It is something that must be experienced, that can only be experienced, and about which I have written only from the need to express myself, in order to share in this ideal with other minds. Also, as I said before, there is no dialectic solution to this question of the kind that can be objectively formulated. The problem must be solved inwardly. We cannot measure out the spirit and suggest, for example, seventy per cent, for the spirit of evangelisation and thirty per cent, for organisation, or *vice versa*. It can all be organisation, and it must all be 'spiritual apostolate', in Montcheuil's sense. The Church must use herself and all her resources, but spiritually, not carnally, using them as if not using them. Thus, 'we put no obstacle in any man's way, so that no fault may be found in our ministry, but as servants of God we commend ourselves in every way; as poor, yet making many rich, as having nothing, and yet possessing everything'.[15]

NOTES

1. Article published in *Rythmes du Monde*, no. 2 (1946), pp. 58–68.
2. Cronin's novel is open to more than one criticism on the score of ecclesiology. It seems to admit a certain opposition between what might be called the 'hierarchy-Church' or the 'organised Church' and the 'love-Church' or the 'Church as life'. It at once recalls the 'Spirit Church' and the 'body-of-bishops Church' of Tertullian in his Montanist days. But the genius and balance of a Catholic ecclesiology consist in justifying and realising the unity of the two elements, admittedly unequal in value, but both necessary to the People of God as the Church.

    Here and there, too, Cronin suggests a certain distinction, and even disconnection, between *belief* and *faith*. It seems that for Francis, the attractive hero of the novel, there is an interior attitude, consisting of tolerance, humility, kindness and, secondarily, of trust in God, which constitutes true religion or faith, by which one is saved; and next, somewhat externally to this fundamental attitude, beliefs. What counts is not what is believed but the manner of life. The fundamentally Christian way depends on each man's heart, not on his head, and can be found among Methodists as among Catholics, among non-Christian Chinese as among the baptised.

    Supposing that the tolerance preached by Cronin in the person of his hero is only the practical consequence of this sort of theoretical position, it must meet with serious criticism from Catholics. For it would be bound up with a sort of indifferentism, now outmoded even among those Christian communities most affected by nineteenth-century liberalism: it would certainly incur the condemnation levelled by Pius IX against a 'liberalism' which is quite different from tolerance, and which, as a thesis and even the principle of thought, was at bottom only a humanitarian rationalism, derived from the sources which outside the Church nourished the mysticism of Freemasonry.
3. P. Mulla, 'Perspectives d'après-guerre en pays de mission et conditions d'une evangélisation libre et efficace', in *Studia Missionalia*, Rome, I, 1943, pp. 137–65. See p. 158.
4. P. 159.
5. P. 161. These lines should be compared with the accurate pages of Fr de Montcheuil, 'Pour un apostolat spirituel', in *Construire*, IX, 1942, pp. 132f. More than one passage might be quoted here.
6. London, 1949. (See also *Priest and Worker*, London and New York, 1964.)
7. *Vie Spirituelle*, March 1946, p. 441.
8. When Theodore Ratisbonne, still a Jew, was pursuing his philosophy course and finding Judaism in it, Abbé Bautain said to him: 'Be a good Jew; God will do the rest.'
9. From a somewhat different point of view, the same thing is noted by Abbé Pardoen in a review of *The Keys of the Kingdom* (*Cahiers des Auxiliaires laïques des Missions*, July 1945, p. 24): 'The problem of tolerance is much wider than Mr Cronin thinks. It is not only respect for convictions, it is also respect for the truth itself, wherever it is found.'

10. Published by S. Purcell in his *Life of Cardinal Manning*, vol. II, pp. 782f (London, 1895).

11. 1 Cor 1:17; 2 Cor 10:7–8; 1 Thess 1:1–7; Philem 8; 2 Tim 1:14.

12. In his letter to the Duke of Norfolk, *Certain Difficulties felt by Anglicans in Catholic Teaching considered*, vol. II (1875), pp. 261f.

13. *Summi Pontificatus:* 'Her (the Church's) aim is supernatural unity in universal love, felt and practised, not a merely external uniformity, superficial and therefore weakening.' 'It must not be forgotten that every rule of social life which . . . relies on the sanction of a merely external authority is essentially insufficient and fragile.'

Speech of 20th February 1946: 'The Church is not an empire, least of all in the imperialist sense now commonly given to the word. In her progress and expansion she follows a path opposite to that of modern imperialism. She progresses principally in depth, only then in size and extent. She seeks first man himself; she tries to form man. Her work is done in the depths of each man's heart. . . . The Church acts in the innermost centre of man, of man in his personal dignity as a free creature, in his infinitely higher dignity as a child of God. . . . With this doctrine and this practice compare the imperialist tendencies as they are found in actual fact. You will not find in them any principle of inner equilibrium . . . their equilibrium, their very cohesion, are maintained only by the force of outward constraint, not in virtue of men's inward adherence, men's aptitude and promptness to take the initiative and assume responsibility.'

14. In Dostoyevski, *The Brothers Karamazov*, Book V, ch. 5. I shall refer to this again.

15. 2 Cor 6:3, 4, 10.

CHAPTER FOUR

St Paul's Casuistry[1]

THAT CASUISTRY OF SOME KIND IS NECESSARY no one, surely, will deny. Both the defenders and the historians of casuistry have noted, moreover, that our Lord in the gospels, the apostles in the Acts, and Paul in his epistles, sometimes employed it. To confine myself to Paul, I give below, in their probable chronological order, an intentionally very wide list of the passages which may concern the subject:

1 and 2 Thess (end of AD 51 or in 52): 1 Thess 4:11–12 and 2 Thess 3:6–15, on the general obligation of all the faithful to work; 1 Thess 2:7–9 and 2 Thess 3:6–9, on Paul's resolve to support himself by his work.

1 Cor (spring of 55) 4:12; 9:4 and 6:23 on the same subject; 5:3–5, 9, 13; the case of the incestuous man, conduct towards him, his excommunication; 6:1–8, disputes between Christians not to be brought before pagan judges; 7:2–16, marriage between Christians and unbelievers; 7:17–24, remaining in the state in which one was called, application to slaves; 7:1–16, 25–40, marriage and virginity; 8:1–10, 33, food offered in sacrifice to idols; 11:2–16 and 14:33b–35, women's head-dress; 11:17–34, especially 33–4, conduct of eucharistic synaxes; 14, especially 26–40, charismatic gifts; 16:1–4, rules for the collection.

2 Cor (56–7) 6:14–18, no association with unbelievers; 11:9, on the Apostle's work.

Gal (57) 2:11–14; Paul disagrees on this occasion with the casuistry of Cephas at Antioch.

Rom (57) 14:1–15, 6; on certain observances concerning foods and days.

Phil (56–7): nothing.

Philem (61–2): slavery.

Coloss (61–2) 2:16–23; allusion to observances; 3:22 to 4:1, on slaves.

Eph (61–2) 6:5–9, some words on slaves and masters.

1 Tim (67) 1:20, excommunication of Hymenæus and Alexander; 2:9–15, dress and deportment of women; 4:3–6, against false teachers who forbade marriage and certain foods; 5:3–16, widows; 6:1–2, slaves.

2 Tim: nothing.

Tit: 1:5–9, qualities required in presbyters; Paul reviews the different states of life; 2:9–10, slaves.

It is not always easy to distinguish between decisions of casuistry in the strict sense and statements of practical rules of conduct in a given state of life, which abound particularly in the Pastoral Epistles and Ephesians (5:21 to 6:9).[2] Casuistry, 'the method or department of moral theology which studies cases of conscience',[3] begins at the point where one is not satisfied with rather general moral rules, but tries to clarify a concrete problem of conscience, arising from the obscurity or complexity of the circumstances of the act, or of the rules which may govern it, or even from a certain conflict between different aspects of duty.

From among the points in the above lists which involve casuistry I shall here deal with the apostle's manual work, the meats used in idol-worship and the observances concerning foods and days. My chief aim will be to discover the criteria on which the apostle relies; these may well represent something of permanent validity for Christian pastoral work.

THE APOSTLE'S MANUAL WORK[4]

Paul's attitude to the subject of his means of livelihood was not uniform. He gratefully accepts[5] the successive gifts sent him by the Philippians to Thessalonica,[6] to Corinth[7] by Epaphroditus, and finally during his captivity, from Ephesus.[8] On the other hand, at Thessalonica and Corinth he insists above everything on supporting himself by the work of his hands;[9] at Corinth, by working at skins and tents in Aquila's workshop,[10] and the same at Ephesus during the two or three years of his stay.[11] In his extraordinary farewell speech to the elders of Ephesus, so genuinely Pauline in its themes and even its language, he not only recalls that he has himself worked with his hands but exhorts the elders to follow his example. There were therefore some cases where he made a rule of living on the faithful, and some cases where he wanted to provide for his own and his fellow-workers' support.[12] It is this difference of attitude that makes it possible to speak of casuistry in this matter.

Paul is perfectly aware that from the point of view of rights the minister of the gospel is authorised to demand his support from the community of the faithful. First of all, as he says himself, it is a natural right, in the sense that it is implicit in the nature of things.[13] Further, it is a right sanctioned by divine law, first by the law of Moses, for when God commands: 'You shall not muzzle the ox when it treads out the grain',[14] he really means work in the spiritual field; 2 Cor 9:8–11: then by our Lord's own command, bidding that those who preach the gospel should live by the gospel.[15] The apostle's rights are therefore certain. But, he says to the faithful of Thessalonica, Corinth and Ephesus, 'we have not made use of this right'.[16] What are the higher motives which impelled him, in these cases, to a decision so burdensome to his poor body? Reading all the many explicit texts in which he explains his motives, we find four which are the principal ones.

The first was a practical motive, and was no doubt the immediate cause of his choice of the different lines I have pointed out. As an apostle, Paul did not want to give any grounds for reproach,[17] which might cause any hindrance to the gospel.[18] It seems clear that he abstained from claiming his upkeep from the faithful in places where he was challenged. In order to be unchallengeable he wished to be seen to be totally disinterested.[19] We must remember, too, on this subject, the general concern, so marked in the apostolic age, for the good name of the faithful among all their fellow citizens.[20] They had to live, in the world, as a 'fragrance' of Jesus Christ. All the more reason, then, for the ministers of the gospel to commend themselves even to the pagans by a blameless life.[21]

If Paul wishes to give no grounds for reproach, it is in order that the preaching of the gospel may not be hindered in any way. He wants still more to be a living model, both to the faithful[22] and to the rest of the Lord's ministers.[23] The shepherd must be a pattern to his flock.[24] Both in Asia Minor and at Ephesus Paul was surrounded by converts who were used to living at other people's expense.[25] At Thessalonica he was faced with Christians who argued that as the last days were near, therefore they need not work, and so they led idle lives, encouraging a meddlesome spirit, inclined to mind other people's business, and little calculated to recommend Christians to the good opinions of pagans. At Corinth he was faced with the pretensions of laxist, libertarian 'spirituals', whom we shall meet again. To all these he preached an ethic, in fact an anthropology, of work.[26] For him it was a question of good order—a motive which seems to have been specially dear to him[27]—of justice,[28] of good repute among the heathen,[29] and finally a condition for carrying out the programme of Christian *agape*; see below. Paul makes this article of work such a decisive point of Christian life that he bids the faithful of Thessalonica avoid the company of those who disobey it: 2 Thess 3:6 and 11. It was natural that as Paul was constantly repeating: 'Be imitators of me, as I am of Jesus Christ',[30] he should have held fast, on such a decisive point, to setting the example himself, so that no one could upbraid him for imposing on others duties which he had not performed himself.[31]

But when Paul commends his industrious example to the ministers of the gospel in particular, he is certainly thinking still more of motives for work which may be called mystical. He insists on the fact that the preaching of the gospel is not, to his mind, a right, deriving from an authority, but a duty, a charge, an obligation.[32] The right he certainly possesses, along with the quality and ἐξουσία of an apostle. But in general Paul does not like to argue from his authority: he prefers to speak as a religious man, in the name of his love, of his greater sufferings and the spiritual gifts he employs in abundance.[33] The apostolate is not his own possession, it is a service, bringing into action resources of which he is only the steward.[34] That being so, the only reward for the work contributed by the apostle is the fruit of the work itself—the increase of the faith and charity of the baptised, in extent and depth.[35] In short, the apostle seeks a gain only for his Lord, the real Lord of the field in which he labours, and in the faithful: not for himself. Paul knows well that it would be normal for the apostle to receive, in exchange for spiritual blessings, what is necessary for his support, but he wants to follow out the logic of an attitude of duty and service and to radiate an example of it, to the point of accepting none of the rights normally inherent in his service, which he regards only as a duty and a charge. He is the δοῦλος, the man-of-all-work, of Jesus Christ,[36] on the pattern of him who, being in the nature of God, for love of us took on himself the nature of a slave.[37]

Paul's final motive for working with his hands is a consideration drawn from Christian *agape*: gratuitous and creative love, justified by its source, not by its object, reflected on earth most closely by the love of parents. He wants only to give, not to receive. For the Lord has said: 'It is more blessed to give than to receive'.[38] Again, he says: 'God loves a cheerful giver'.[39] So he has firmly decided that if he returns to Corinth a third time he will no longer live at the community's expense: 'for children ought not to lay up for their parents, but parents for their children': 2 Cor 12:13-15. This joy in giving, in the spirit of *agape*, is moreover one of the motives which impels the Christian to work. Paul says so expressly to the Ephesians.[40]

This is a motive which has been a living force in traditional theology on the temporal possessions of the Church, as is testified by scores of texts from the popes, the councils, the Fathers and the statutes of monastic and ecclesiastical institutions. It is necessary, they say, to work so as to be able to practise charity.[41] That is something we must never forget.

These motives, so powerful in Paul's missionary heart, also throw light on the strictly apostolic character of poverty. It was while thanking the Philippians for the gifts he had gladly accepted from them that he said: 'Not that I complain of want: for I have learned, in whatever state I am, to be content. I know how to be abased, and I know how to abound: in any and all circumstances I have learned the secret of facing plenty and hunger, abundance and want. I can do all things in him who strengthens me. Yet it was kind of you to share my trouble'.[42] These words well express the rule of *apostolic* poverty, as Jesus himself practised it during his public life: not the modest sufficiency of Nazareth, not the total destitution of the cross, but a sovereign liberty for the service of the gospel and the kingdom, indifferent to the alternations of comfort and want. During his public ministry, Jesus was sometimes served by devoted women who assisted him out of their property[43] or was entertained by friends, rich or of modest means: at Bethany he would have lacked for nothing.[44] At other times, worn out and exhausted, with no time to eat, he had not even anywhere to lay his head.[45] He had himself taught his apostles the law of apostolic readiness for service, at every opportunity, indifferent to comfort or want; see Lk 10:5f. The prophets too had known these alternations of warmly comfortable hospitality[46] and severest want.[47] So it was with Paul: it was his lot to be well treated by devoted friends, even too well, as at Malta, for example,[48] but also to live in hunger, cold and nakedness.[49] But 'who shall separate us from the love of Christ? Shall tribulation, or distress, or persecution, or famine, or nakedness, . . .?'[50] Apostolic poverty is the correlative of the freedom of apostolic service: the ideal of both is simply freedom and disinterestedness for the gift of self and the service of the gospel, independently of abundance or penury, favour or opposition. In any case, if the minister of the gospel has the necessaries of life, he must not seek anything more.[51]

FOOD SACRIFICED TO IDOLS[52]

This question was put to Paul by the Corinthian community at the beginning of 55.[53] It had been raised more than six years earlier, at Antioch and in the young Christian communities planted by the missions in a pagan society, and the apostles at Jerusalem had had to refer to it in connection with the question of circumcision.[54] It was still a burning question some forty years after Paul's first letter to the Corinthians, as we see from the letters to the Churches of Revelation, 2:14 and 20. In these conditions it seems justifiable to regard the question of these foods as a problem facing the Christian conscience, not only because of the facts, the concrete situation in which Christians and pagans shared a common life in the setting of cities where the cult of the pagan deities was still active and entered into daily life, but as a problem made more acute by certain positions of principle, by a certain interpretation of Christianity common among certain classes of Christians converted from paganism. Considered as a party, this current of opinion appears to be complex: it is seen in its peculiar components and particular features at Antioch and Corinth, at Pergamus and Thyatira; in some places and at some times, as at Corinth in 55 and 56, it is complicated by certain Jewish-Christian features. Considered as a tendency, it appears to be a mixture of half-repudiated paganism with an antinomian and libertarian mysticism, under the aegis of a gnostic attitude.[55] Perhaps this tendency dates from the origins of the Antioch Church. Proud of possessing the Spirit, certain Christians of Corinth had formed their own consciences in matters which they thought indifferent but were actually very grave: consorting with pagans; eating foods sacrificed to the gods (in the language of Jews and Christians, *idolothuta*), not only in their own homes, having bought them in the market, but occasionally at banquets in company with pagans, no doubt even in places devoted to pagan rites; a sexual life regarded in a naturalistic manner; lax complacency over grave public sins (the incestuous man); a way of celebrating the eucharist which was pagan rather than Christian in spirit, and slighted the demands of Christian *agape*; disorder in meetings, where charismatic manifestations prevailed over edification and charity; etc. All this was connected together, and sprang from a vindication of freedom. Here I confine myself to the consumption of foods used in the pagan sacrifices.

Paul settles the case by distinguishing different aspects:

1. The idols are non-existent, for there is only one God.[56] It is the ancient monotheistic principle, the basis of Israel's whole religion and even morality, and in no way rejected by the Christians: they have simply extended it to Jesus Christ, the Son of God, whence we have the sublime formula of 1 Cor 8:6, for which we gladly accept Sagnard's translation: 'For us [there is only] one God, the Father, from whom [come] all these things and to whom we [go]—and one only Lord Jesus Christ, by whom [come] all things and through whom we go.'[57] It was in virtue of the monotheistic principle that the rabbis called foods used in idol-worship 'offerings made to the dead', or 'offerings in honour of the non-

C

beings'.[58] From the non-existence of the idols it follows that in regard to what concerns them, and in particular to food which may be offered to them, we have absolute freedom of judgement: 'We all have knowledge'.[59]

2. For this reason everything sold in the market may be freely eaten.[60] In the first place, the food sold from the pagan temples is not, in fact, anything sacred, for the idols are nothing at all. In the second place, all that God has made is good: that is the conclusion of a logical monotheism, a conclusion repeatedly drawn and expressed in the bible.[61] With Paul this conclusion takes the form of a quotation from Psalm 24:1: 'The earth is the Lord's and the fullness thereof'.[62] The conclusions of monotheism are therefore directed, as in 8:6,[63] to the twofold assertion that all things are *for* God and *from* God: a *theo*-logical idea in the strict sense of the word, which is also the soul of all Aquinas' *theo*-logy.[64] Clearly this recognition of the fact that everything is *for* God and *from* God issues immediately in thanksgiving: 'If I partake with thankfulness, why am I denounced because of that for which I give thanks?'[65]

3. On the other hand, eating *as an act of religion* is absolutely forbidden to Christians, 1 Cor 10:14–22—that would be idolatry. For though the idols are not divine, they are, or they represent, so many demons,[66] an idea adopted by St Augustine. St Paul takes this occasion to develop a wonderful theology of communion by participation in the sacrificial meal or the cultural sacrifice, in paganism, in Judaism and in Christianity. 'I do not want you to be partners with demons. You cannot drink the cup of the Lord and the cup of demons. You cannot partake of the table of the Lord and the table of demons.'[67]

4. 'We know that "all of us possess knowledge". "Knowledge" puffs up, but love builds up.'[68] The mystical libertarians of Corinth believed, like good Greeks, that wisdom and science were supreme values.[69] They took for granted that knowledge, 'lights', judgement, were autonomous and supreme, and made this idea the basis of complete freedom of behaviour. But, as Buchsel acutely remarks,[70] the highest gift of the Spirit is not freedom, nor yet knowledge, but love. Freedom and love are not, of course, opposed: to act out of love is to act freely, but the terms of the proposition are not interchangeable; to act freely is not necessarily

to act out of love. To Paul, my knowledge that the idols are nothing is the firm ground of my freedom in the matter of food offered to idols, but charity, 'the bond of perfection',[71] may impose limits on the exercise of my freedom. Only on this condition will my freedom be spiritual, not carnal, truly flowing from the Spirit, who pours his love out into us.[72] 'For you were called to freedom, brethren, only do not use your freedom as an opportunity for the flesh, but through love be servants of one another.'[73]

Thus *agape* may lead me to *renounce* a genuine right in order to fulfil the law of Christian life, which is not vindication of rights, but *service*.[74] We have already seen, on the subject of manual work, how keenly aware Paul was of this law. While the Corinthians made their freedom an absolute, even using it in things intrinsically bad, Paul refrained out of charity from using an acknowledged right. It is not for nothing that the hymn to charity, which 'does not insist on her own way',[75] occurs in the first letter to the Corinthians. In the grave faults affecting the Corinthian Church Paul diagnosed a lack of charity.

In the case of things sacrificed to idols, this limitation on the exercise of freedom, caused by the demands of *agape*, had to apply on certain occasions. If a Christian were invited by a pagan he could eat without scruple the meat which had been offered to idols but bought on the market. But if another guest remarked that it was offered meat, he must, says Paul, abstain from eating it, out of respect for the conscience of his informant: if the guest were a pagan, so as not to let him be tempted to think one was eating offered meat precisely as such; or if (as seems to me more likely) the guest were another Christian, whose conscience was not so well informed and who had scruples, so as not to give him scandal. This consideration of scandal to the faithful, so strongly emphasised by our Lord himself in the gospel,[76] is extremely active in Paul's conscience. He develops it in detail in connection with the sacrifice-foods,[77] and his motive is the same as that of the gospel: 'Sinning against your brethren, you sin against Christ.'[78]

Paul's anxiety not to give scandal was also apostolic. It is amazing to see how far this champion of the pure gospel could carry his case for adaptation, for the sake of the same gospel. In this, too, he appealed to the Corinthians to become imitators of himself. 'Give no offence to Jews or to Greeks or to the church of

God, just as I try to please all men in everything, not seeking my own advantage, but that of many, that they may be saved.'[79]

We know to what lengths Paul went in his 'all things to all men' and 'to the Jews as a Jew'. This man, who waged such a struggle against the Judaizers, made astounding concessions. After writing 'circumcision counts for nothing', he caused Timothy, son of a Jewish mother, to be circumcised, 'because of the Jews',[80] and no doubt he would have agreed to the circumcision of Titus, but that it might have seemed a concession of *principle* to the Judaizers.[81] After speaking against the observances of the Law, he took a vow[82] and later made the concession, to James and his party, of joining with four men who had taken a Nazirite vow and paying the expenses of their purification and sacrifices.[83]

But between Paul and James the difference of outlook was still real. To demonstrate this properly one would have to study a whole set of problems raised in the apostolic Church by the Jewish-Christian tendency, of which James was the commanding figure, on the one hand, and the bold decisions of Paul on the other. I confine myself here to noting a sign of that difference in this very case of food offered to idols.

The meeting at Jerusalem, during which the question was expressly discussed and the apostles' 'decree' was issued, was very probably later than the writing, not only of the first letter to the Corinthians, but of the letter to the Galatians, neither of which make any allusion to it.[84] There the question is dealt with in a narrower way than by Paul: it chiefly concerns the difficulties which the consumption of certain foods may present to mutual intercourse and good understanding between Jewish and Gentile converts. James begins his speech by observing that, if God calls from the Gentiles a people preserved for his Name, there is nothing in that which does not agree with the words of the prophets, and therefore nothing which violates the setting in which Jewry awaited the Messiah.[85] He then proposes his own private casuistry: 'that we write to them to abstain from the pollutions of idols,[86] and from unchastity and from what is strangled and from blood'.[87] His motive is that these are the elementary and indispensable conditions of the Mosaic books, of which the Gentile converts cannot be ignorant, because there are synagogues of the Jewish communities everywhere.[88] James formulates his solution by way of prohibitions imposed in the form of law: certain things are forbidden. 'They have a strictly ritual character and answer the question . . ., what must be required of the Hellenist Christians in order that the Jewish Christians may not have to fear legal contamination by meeting them? James is not presenting them with a code of moral life, as many of the ancients understood the text, viewing it as a prohibition of idolatry, fornication (or adultery) and murder. James wished to retain only those laws of purity whose religious significance appeared universal . . ., impurity, or concubinage, figured in this context, not for its moral aspect, but as a source of legal contamination.'[89] It was, in fact, a question of fundamental legal principles: of the command against eating the blood and strangled meat.[90] Thus James finds the principle of his casuistry in the minimum of 'necessary' prescriptions, admitting of no dispensation.

But Paul—and the so-called western text of the Acts certainly seems to have intended to make some correction of the primitive version of Acts 15:29 in his favour[91]—finds the solution of the problem of the sacrifice-foods and, more generally, of the relations between the Jewish and Gentile Christians, not in a legal and ritual minimum, but in the maximum of the demands of charity. If complete freedom flows from faith, charity binds the faithful to the obligation, (i) to offend no one, and (ii) to give themselves to others by the service and sacrifice which is expressed in offerings.[92] It has been clearly shown what a tremendous part, of a truly ecclesiological and mystical character, was played in Paul's apostolic ministry by the collection for the 'saints'.[93] It was an essential part of the solution which the apostle wanted to bring to this acute problem, imperilling the unity of the Church herself: the problem of the relation or communion between Gentile and Jewish converts, in particular those of the Mother Church of Jerusalem. But Paul found this solution first and last in charity, which he made the animating principle of his casuistry. In this matter, 'St Paul's originality lies not so much in the notion of conscience as in the primacy he gives to charity as the rule of conduct'.[94]

In the Church at Rome, sprung largely from Judaism, there were certain Christians, 'weak in faith', who thought themselves obliged to observe certain days and to abstain from flesh.[95] Paul, in informing us about the facts, deals with the case, which (whatever Augustine may have thought) is different from that of the sacrifice foods,[96] as elsewhere.[97] But though the cases are different, the principles of solution employed by Paul are the same. They may be summed up in these four points:

1. Judgement must be formed from the viewpoint of faith. Now faith is the ground of a complete freedom in the use of all that God has created, which is good: nothing is impure in itself.[98] Freedom, therefore indifference. Foods do not commend us to God, any more than abstention from them.[99] The essential thing is therefore that whatever one does should be done *for the Lord*.[100]

2. Therefore, 'nothing is unclean in itself, but it is unclean for anyone who thinks it unclean'.[101] The erroneous conscience is binding, and so is the doubtful. 'Happy is he who has no reason to judge himself for what he approves. But he who has doubts is condemned if he eats, because he does not act from faith: for whatever does not proceed from faith is sin.'[102] With this firm pronouncement of Paul we may compare the *logion* recorded by Codex Bezae, after Luke 6:4: 'The same day, seeing a man working on the sabbath, Jesus said to him, Friend, if you know what you are doing, you are happy, but if you do not know, you are accursed and a transgressor of the law.' These words are added after the important passage in which Jesus justifies the breaking of the sabbath by the example of David, to which he gives a prophetic sense, foretelling that in the messianic order the distinction between things profane and things sacred, withheld from the use of the faithful, will be abolished. But the breaking of the ancient ban was permissible only for one who knew that he had come into the kingdom of grace and freedom. The man who believed himself to be still under the law was bound to obey it: though his conscience might be erroneous or doubtful, it made

him personally guilty if he broke its commands. There can be no doubt that this was the casuistry governing the concessions made by Paul, which we have mentioned above (his 'to the Jews as a Jew').

3. While the objective judgement must be formed from faith, the practical conduct is entirely subject to the demands of charity. This strengthens the obligation already laid on us by justice, not to judge another.[103] Here Paul speaks in the first place to the 'weak in faith', tempted to accuse of laxity those who know themselves to be free in the matter of foods and days. They are not to judge the 'strong', who do what they do 'in the Lord' and for him,[104] and the Lord accepts them among his own.[105] In any case, we must not judge: God alone is the judge of all, for to him every man will give account of his deeds.[106]

4. Charity obliges the 'strong', for his part, not to give scandal to the weaker brother.[107] Once again, Paul would have us renounce a privilege, rather than use it at the cost of charity.[108]

But we must not only avoid giving offence to the weaker brethren: it is still more important to guard the unity of the faithful. I believe that in Rom 14:20 ('Do not, for the sake of food, destroy the work of God') Paul is thinking rather of the concord of the community than of the personal conscience of a particular brother.[109] The work of God is, in fact, *par excellence* the edification of the community of the faithful, the body of Christ: its method is 'mutual upbuilding' and its aim is 'peace'.[110] Now it is *agape* alone which builds up;[111] it alone unites the faithful 'so that they may form the perfect divine totality, the body of Christ.'[112]

In concrete fact, *agape* requires that in order to 'maintain unity in the bond of peace'[113] we should refrain from obstinately following our personal point of view, even when it is lawful. Once more, Paul confronts the Christian in the end with the example of Christ, who did not seek his own advantage but the glory of the Father;[114] Christ, who died and who lives, not for himself but for us and for God.[115] And here we should recall the whole astounding exhortation of Phil 2:1-11.

Thus a solution drawn from *agape*, unlike a purely legal or moral solution, goes beyond the limits of a merely personal problem and stands on the level of a life of communion with others, united in edification, that is, in health and progress in Christ. In short, the apostle derives his principles of casuistry from the demands of the Christian life.

The three examples we have analysed suffice to give us an idea of Paul's casuistry and the principles underlying it. At no point does it develop in a juridical or legalistic outlook, as rabbinical casuistry did and still does. [116] Both the gospel and Paul, however, have retained something of this casuistry, even something juridical. I mean the rules of procedure on the treatment of members of the community who violated its internal discipline.[117] In this field the juridical point of view was wholly in place, although, as it concerned the law *of the Church*, it could not be developed as *law*, absolutely autonomously, without reference to the aim of love and the essentially moral, even mystical nature of the life of the Christian, as member of the Church. Thus canon law—this is one of its original features—has always given and still gives great weight to the consideration of the moral ends and the good of the private conscience of the individual.[118] The juridicalism of the Church, necessary, beneficial and holy as it is, could not, without abuse or decadence, turn to pure juridicalism.

Juridicalism is found in two circumstances. First, when the obligatory value of the duty imposed is developed *for its own sake*, without factual consideration of the purpose of justice and love, by which alone it is justified and must be measured. According to the remark of Cardinal Cushing, Archbishop of Boston,[119] St Paul's saying: 'Love is the fulfilment of the law'[120] comes to be replaced by 'the law itself is the fulfilment of the law'. Secondly, it is found when the outward matter of actions and obligations is considered without reference to their meaning, and the outward matter of the law, in consequence, without reference to its spirit. Several examples could certainly be quoted in illustration of both these defects.

A juridical spirit of this sort leads men almost inevitably to seek means of getting round the law or whittling away its obligations. Having abandoned the point of view of an ethic of Good and the Call to perfection, for a point of view of mere legal obligation, a wholly juridical casuistry of the permitted and the forbidden is then developed, in order to find, not the maximum of good, but the maximum of freedom from legal restrictions, with a merely formal respect for the letter of them. 'There is a natural tendency which drives one, in the moral as in the legal order, to find out all about the interpretation of the laws, not so as to observe them more strictly but, on the contrary, to retain only what one cannot avoid without mortal sin, or even so as to be able, cynically, to get round them more easily.'[121] It was against a casuistry understood in this sense that Pascal protested: it seemed to him that it would end by nullifying the idea of sin.[122] Pascal's reaction sprang from an exacting and profound religious conscience, but even so it did not derive from the true Christianity of Paul. For in the apostle's eyes the perverted casuistry against which Pascal protested would have been an undertaking calculated to favour the liberty of the flesh,[123] but above all it would have seemed, by its legalism, to be still doing the work of the law, and therefore tending to multiply occasions of sin, transforming them into transgressions;[124] the law is 'the power of sin';[125] 'the letter kills'.[126]

Casuistry of the gospel kind does not, for all that, despise the letter: the juridical laws form part of the given facts of the action, but they do not exhaust them. In any case, in their practical application they must be seen in the light of the aim and in view of it; that is, in the last resort, of charity. In theological tradition this is the principle which must regulate, for example, the use of dispensation,[127] and the reason why neither the divine law nor the primary natural law can be made matter for dispensation, for they express the intention of him who is the very beginning and end of all creatures. But again, charity is not taken by St Paul simply as a purely 'moral' principle, inspiring the law and compensating for its occasional rigours, but as the spiritual principle of Christian life, which consists in imitating God, as he has manifested himself, as unconditioned Gift, in Jesus Christ.

Here again, the Pauline ethics and casuistry are profoundly distinct and remote from the morality and casuistry of Stoicism, taken as these are from the perfection of man, who must aim at remaining his own master.[128] The whole conduct of the Christian must be determined from the point of view of *God*. Without prejudice to the transference of monotheistic themes to Christ, it is dominated by an actualisation of the very mystery of God, who is *agape*, in his creature. For the Gospel as for St Paul, the essential principle of ethics is *agape*: it sums up the whole conduct of the Christian and all the relations of which his life is woven on the horizontal plane of existence, under the vertical relation towards the Father and Jesus Christ, created in him by the gift of *agape*. 'Therefore be imitators of God, as beloved children; and walk in love, even as Christ loved us, and gave himself up for us, a fragrant offering and a sacrifice to God.'[129] That is why Paul's casuistry is scarcely a casuistry at all: it does not seek its determining considerations on the level of the horizontal date of action, but in the vertical line. It is 'divinising', not moralising. Always borne forward towards the accomplishment of the mystery of God in the world, it has a creative value as a proclamation of salvation, it is kerygmatic and missionary.

In this perspective, it is not only Stoicism which is superseded: the law of the Mosaic dispensation, too, is both superseded and fulfilled in the new conditions.[130] The Christian is emancipated from the law as external precept: not only from the ritual prescriptions of the Mosaic law, but from all law *qua lex*, in this sense that all law is carnal and Jewish, whenever it is taken as law, and not as the response of *agape* to the demands in us of the *agape* of God. From such a law the Christian is free.[131] But also, the whole ethical content of the law is found to be a demand, an appeal, of *agape*. There is no debt but loving, and therefore whoever loves, thereby fulfils the law,[132] the whole fullness of which consists in loving one's neighbour as oneself, after God.[133] The Christian is called and dedicated to fulfil the demands of this *agape*. In this sense he is subject to them: so Paul can call them a law, a precept,[134] the law of Jesus Christ. He must ever be striving, in the successive circumstances of life, to behave according to those demands, that is, to look for the will of God *in casu*, on the basis of the renewal of our minds by his Spirit.[135] Thus we shall fulfil God's design, his mystery,[136] which culminates in making us all the one body of his Son.[137]

These are aspects or facts which Catholic moral theology has vigorously revaluated during the last decades. It has tried, in fact, to restore to morality all its spiritual dimension of Christian life, under the action and call of God. There has been a restoration of the Thomist concept of prudence, 'that effort to unite with the divine intentions in our whole life';[138] there has been revaluation of the idea of the living imitation of Christ;[139] a resumption of the idea of Christian freedom, in the framework of a moral life dominated by the good and by charity;[140] a return to the school of *agape*;[141] a readiness to base moral theology firmly on the ontological foundations of the Christian life;[142] finally, an assimilation of that part of truth vindicated, sometimes ambiguously, by the movement upholding the *Situationsethik*.[143]

A Catholic theology faithful to biblical thought and the tradition of the Church cannot, we know, adopt the viewpoint of the *Situationsethik* purely and simply, without reservations. A pure ethic of situation, as Karl Rahner noted in 1950,[144] would result in dissolving all obligation and could become a modern form of laxism. Pius XII, in two solemn discourses in the spring of 1952,[145] and the Holy Office in an instruction of 2nd February 1956,[146] have condemned a pure *Situationsethik* for setting up an individualistic autonomy of conscience, for forgetting the universal validity of the divinely given rules of action (and particularly of the negative precepts which no situation can excuse us for infringing), and for coming near to robbing the objective rules of their content. The pope recalled (and this was indeed the meaning of the theological movement we have been describing) that prudence, understood in St Thomas' sense, satisfies all the valid requirements of an 'ethic of situation'.

In the *theo*-logy of Aquinas[147] the fulfilment of man is wholly relative to God, humanism is wholly theological. This humanism has two poles: charity, the virtue of the divine purpose, and prudence, the virtue of the means, wholly 'informed' by charity. Casuistry has no place in the setting of a prudent life, seeking to respond to the demands of charity. Not a casuistry which claims to give, ready-made, the solution to 'cases' by pure deduction from general principles, or so-called principles: that would be to ignore the specificality of the practical order, as Aquinas sees it, and to betray the lessons of Paul. Nor yet a casuistry limited to the legal or juridical aspect of things.[148] But rather, in the line of Paul and even, we hope, in his school, an attempt, pursued in the communion of the Church,[149] to respond to the intentions of God, who is *agape*, in the situation in which we are placed.[150]

NOTES

1. Paper published in German in *Verkündigung und Glaube. Festgabe für Franz X. Arnold*, Freiburg, 1958, pp. 16–41. I have made some additions.
2. Included in these statements are the rules on the position of women (1 Cor 11:2–16 and 33b–35; 1 Tim 2:9–15) and on widows (1 Tim 5:3–16) or slaves.
3. R. Brouillard, art. 'Casuistique' in *Catholicisme*, vol. 2 (1950), col. 630.
4. 1 Thess 2:7–9; 2 Thess 3:6–9; 1 Cor 4:12; 9:4 and 6–23; 2 Cor 11:9; Ac 18:3; 20:33–5.
5. Phil 4:10–20.
6. Phil 4:16.
7. 2 Cor 11:9.
8. Phil 4:18.
9. 1 Thess 2:5–9; 2 Thess 3:7–9; 1 Cor 9:4–18; 2 Cor 11:7–10; 12:13–18.
10. Ac 18:3.
11. Ac 20:31–5.
12. Ac 20:34.
13. 1 Cor 9:7; see v. 11 and Rom 15:27.
14. Deut 25:4.
15. 1 Cor 9:14, referring to Mt 10:10 and Lk 10:7. See 1 Tim 5:17–18 and see K. Schuler, *Vom Evangelium leben. Der Lebensunterhalt der Diener des Evangeliums untersucht nach dem N.T.*, Rome, 1947. Here note, 1 Cor 9:13–14, the application to the gospel worker of the command operative in the sphere of worship and sacrifice, that 'those who serve at the altar share in the sacrificial offerings', see Rom 15:16; Phil 2:17.
16. 1 Cor 9:12.
17. 1 Thess 2:10; see 2 Cor 11: 8–12.
18. 1 Cor 9:12.
19. See Neh 5:10, 14f.
20. See 1 Thess 4:12; Rom 12:17–18; 15:2; 1 Cor 10:32; 2 Cor 4:2; 6:3f; Phil 2:15; 4:5; Col 4:5–6; 1 Tim 3:7; Tit 3:2; 1 Pet 2:12, 15; 3:15–16. Also in the gospel, Mt 5:16.
21. 1 Tim 3:2 and 7; 6:14; Tit 6:7.
22. 2 Thess 3:6–9.
23. Ac 20:35.
24. 1 Tim 4:12; Tit 2:7–8; see 1 Pet 5:3.
25. Eph 4:28.
26. See B. E. Allo, *Le travail d'après St Paul*, Paris, 1914; F. J. Leenhardt and A. Pittet, *Le chrétien devant le travail*, Geneva, 1941; E. Mauris, *Le travail de l'homme et son oeuvre*, Neuchâtel-Paris, 1950; see E. Hauck, *Die Stellung des Urchristentums zu Arbeit und Geld (Beitr. z. Fördg. christl. Theol.*, 2. Reihe, Bd. 3), Gütersloh, 1921. Manual work was already held in honour by the Rabbis: see B. Rigaux, *Les Epîtres aux Thessaloniciens*, Paris, 1956, p. 709.
27. See 1 Thess 4:11; 5:14; 2 Thess 3:6 and 11; the ἄτακτοι 1 Cor 11:10; 14:23, 33 and the whole chapter; Col 2:5; 3:15.
28. If any one will not work, let him not eat', 2 Thess 3:10.

29. 1 Thess 4:12 and see above, n. 19.
30. 2 Thess 3:7–10; 1 Cor 4:16; 7:7–8; 11:1; Phil 3:17; Ac 20:33; see 1 Tim 1:16; 2 Tim 1:13.
31. See Mt 23:3; Lk 11:46; Gal 2:14; Ac 15:10.
32. See 1 Cor 9:16–17; see Ac 9:15–16; 22:14–15; 26:16–18.
33. For example, see 1 Thess 2:7–12; 1 Cor 7:25 and 40; 2 Cor 10:7–8; 11:23f; 12:1f, 11f.
34. 1 Cor 4:1; see Tit 1:7.
35. See 1 Cor 9:16–18, 23; Phil 4:17.
36. Rom 1:1; Phil 1:1; Tit 1:1.
37. Phil 2:7.
38. Ac 20:35.
39. 2 Cor 9:7; see 8:10.
40. Ac 20:35; Eph 4:28.
41. For example, see Tertullian, *Apol.*, 39; Cyprian, *Epist.*, 5, 7, 12:14; Ambrose, *De off.*, II, 28 (*Aurum habet ecclesia, non ut congreget, sed ut eroget*); Conc. Chalcedon., can. 3 (and see W. Bright, *The Canons of the First Four General Councils*, 2nd ed, Oxford, 1892, pp. 153f); M. R. Mayeux, 'Les biens d'Église considérés comme patrimoine des pauvres à travers les conciles occidentaux du VIme siècle', in *Inspiration religieuse et Structures temporelles*, Paris, 1948, pp. 138–209; J. Leclercq, 'La vie économique des monastères au moyen âge'; same vol, pp. 211f; Gratian, *Decr.*, C. 8, xii, qu. 1; C. 30, xii, qu. 2 (Friedberg, I, 679, 697; A. L. Gabriel, 'The Practice of Charity at the University of Paris, during the Middle Ages: Ave Maria College', in *Traditio*, 5 (1947), pp. 335–9, etc.
42. Phil 4:11–14.
43. Lk 8:2–3.
44. See Lk 10:38f; Jn 11:3. See Mk 1:30; Lk 4:39 (Peter's mother-in-law); Mk 14:14; Lk 22:11f (the owner of the Cenacle); etc.
45. Mt 8:20.
46. Elisha with the Shunamite woman, 2 Kings 4:8f.
47. Elijah fleeing from the wrath of Jezebel, 1 Kings 19:3f.
48. Ac 28:7f.
49. 2 Cor 11:27.
50. Rom 8:35.
51. See 1 Tim 4:7, 10, 17, 19.
52. On this question, see M. Rauer, *Die 'Schwachen' in Korinth und in Rom nach den Paulusbriefen*, 1923, pp. 40–52; H. von Soden, *Sakrament und Ethik bei Paulus Marburger. Theol. St.*, 1 (1931), pp. 1f.
53. See 1 Cor 8:9–13 and 10:14–33.
54. Ac 15:5f.
55. On the pseudo-spirituals confronting Paul, I should like to combine the conclusions of the three following authors: W. Lutgert, *Freiheitspredigt und Schwarngeister in Korinth* (*Beitrage z. Fördg. christl. Theol.*), Gütersloh, 1908 (on the antinomian, libertarian and Gnostic spirituals, converts from paganism): Büchsel, *Der Geist Gottes im NT*, Gütersloh, 1926, pp. 367f (pneumatic-gnostic tendency, turned into a party claiming to be 'of Christ'): E. B. Allo, *La Première Épître aux Corinthiens*, Paris, 1934, pp. 80–7 (the 'party of Christ' of 1 Cor is made up of ill-converted ex-pagans, seeing the gospel only as a philosophy or mysticism, of the same kind as that of Hellenism; eventually they allied with the more or less gnosticising Jewish-Christians who had come from other churches to form a party against Paul: 2 Cor).

J. Dupont (*Gnosis* . . ., Paris, 1949, pp. 180–6, 259–61, 265f), holds that Paul's opponents at Corinth are the Jews: their libertarianism was based on their consciousness of possessing the charismata of *gnosis*. To H. Schleier (paper translated in *Le Temps de l'Église*, Paris-Tournai 1961, pp. 298f), the error of the Corinthians lay in believing that the last days had arrived, that the gifts of baptism were the same as those of the kingdom, especially if they were enriched by charismata, and that they no longer needed rules. The *gnosis* of the Corinthians was not, then, the Gnostic system in the strict sense of the word, a system which does not seem to have then existed. On the other hand, the idea of such a system and of a Gnostic sect in the proper sense has recently been supported by W. Schmithals, *Die Gnosis in Korinth. Eine Untersuchung zu den Korintherbriefen*, Göttingen, 1956. The debate continues.

56. 1 Cor 8:1–6; 10:19.

57. F. M. M. Sagnard, 'A propos de 1 Cor 8:6', in *Ephemer. Theol. Lovanienses*, 26 (1950), pp. 54–8.

58. See Büchsel, art. εἰδωλόθυτον in *TWB z. NT*, vol. 2, p. 376. The pagans, on the other hand, called them ἱερόθυτον (offered in sacrifice), see 1 Cor 10:28, according to the text followed by the majority of critics.

59. 1 Cor 8:1.

60. 1 Cor 10:25–30.

61. Gen 1:31; Wis 3:11; 7:29; Ecclus 39:21–35; etc.

62. 1 Cor 10:26.

63. Quoted above.

64. On this point, see the illuminating pages of M. D. Chenu, 'Le plan de la Somme Théologique de S. Thomas d'Aquin' in *Rev. Thomiste*, 1939, pp. 93–107; *Introd. à l'étude de S. Thomas d'Aquin*, Montreal and Paris, 1950, pp. 258f.

65. V. 30, see 1 Tim 4:4–6.

66. V. 20.

67. Vv. 20b and 21. Apart from von Soden, quoted above, n. 52, there are few works to quote on the connection between *communion* as an ecclesiastical value and participation in the ritual sacrifice or meal. The article κοινωνία by F. Hauch, in *TWB z. NT*, vol. 3, pp. 805–6, is rather short.

68. 8:1.

69. 1 Cor 1:22.

70. *Der Geist Gottes im NT*, pp. 373–4.

71. Col 3:14.

72. Rom 5:5.

73. Gal 5:13–14. On the carnal use of freedom, see G. Dehn, *Gesetz oder Evangelium . . .*, Berlin, 1938, pp. 177f, and the Catholic studies quoted below, nn. 138 and 140.

74. This is one of the points on which, in spite of some apparent resemblances, the Christian ethic differs profoundly from the Stoic. The Christian man is no more the Stoic man than the world to which the Christian man is sent is the Stoic world. The Stoic sage sought freedom in the ways of conformity with the order of the world; his cosmos was that of the physical laws, expressive of the divine reason. The Christian's cosmos is that of a free design of God, who is *agape*. Therefore the holy Christian seeks freedom in the way of conformity with the will of God, by love and therefore by service. See G. Tellenbach, *Libertas, Kirche und Weltordnung im Zeitalter des Investiturstreites (Forschg. z. Kirchen-u. Geistesgesch.*, 7), Stuttgart, 1936, pp. 1–9; H. Greeven, *Das Hauptproblem der Sozialethik in der neueren Stoa und im Urchristentum (Ntl. Fchg.* 3, Reihe, 4 H.), Gütersloh, 1935, especially ch. 5, pp. 141–59.

75. 1 Cor 13:5; 10:33.
76. Mt 7:27; 18:5–6; Mk 9:41–2; Lk 17:2.
77. 1 Cor 8:7–13; see Rom 14:13–21.
78. 1 Cor 8:12.
79. 1 Cor 10:32–3, and see 9:19–22, 'To the Jews I became as a Jew'.
80. Ac 16:3.
81. See Gal 2:3–5.
82. Ac 18:18.
83. Ac 21:23–7.
84. The dating of the 'apostles' decree' depends on how the problem of the relations between Gal 2 and Ac 15 is solved. Personally I accept the view of those who hold that this probably calls for a critical examination of the text of Acts. Several Catholic exegetes hold that Luke, compiling a genuine history in a *theological* setting, has conflated two episodes which the other documents, especially Gal 2, oblige us to distinguish: viz., a first debate, attended by the whole apostolic college and presided over by Peter, on the obligation of the Mosaic law, in particular of circumcision (Ac 15:1–12; Gal 2:1–10): and a second debate, in the framework of the Jerusalem community only, presided over by James, and dealing with the dietary obligations to be observed in order to enable Jewish and Gentile converts to eat together (Ac 15:13–29; 21:18f). This line is followed by J. Dupont (notes on the Jerusalem Bible in fascicules, and article in *Rech.S.R.*); S. Giet ('L'assemblée apostolique et le décret de Jérusalem' in *Rech.S.R.*, 39 (1951 = Mél. J. Lebreton, I), pp. 203–20; P. Benoit, 'La primauté de S. Pierre selon le N.T.' in *Istina*, 2 (1955), pp. 305–34; see p. 308. A. S. Geyser ('Paul, the Apostles' Decree and the Liberals in Corinth', in *Studia Paulina*, 1953, pp. 124–38), clearly distinguishes the two situations, but does not clearly separate the two episodes in time: he has difficulty in explaining why Paul does not allude to the 'decree' in the passage in 1 Cor on the sacrifice foods.

On the other hand, still more recently, M. K. Thieme ('Diaconie primordiale, remède au schisme primordial', in *Dieu Vivant*, no. 26 (1954), pp. 101–23, and 'Le plan des Actes des Apôtres et la chronologie de son contenu', (*ibid.*, pp. 127–33), and then H. M. Féret, much more precisely (*Pierre et Paul à Antioche et à Jérusalem. Le 'conflit' des deux apôtres*, Paris, 1954), have maintained that the meeting at Jerusalem, which Acts 15 describes as a single episode, is of earlier date than the writing of 1 Cor and Gal. Féret's explanation is criticised by J. Dupont, 'Pierre et Paul à Antioche et â Jérusalem', in *Rech.S.R.*, 4 (1957), pp. 42–60 and 225–59 (this second article appeared after mine was written).
85. Ac 15:13f.
86. This refers to the meats offered to them; see Ac 15:29 and 21:25.
87. 15:20.
88. V. 21.
89. J. Dupont, note on Ac 15:20 in the Jerusalem Bible.
90. See Gen 9:4 (to Noah and his descendants): Lev 17:10–14; the ban on taking part in meals where the flesh of sacrificial victims was eaten, see Ex 34:15 (renewal of the Covenant after the incident of the golden calf).
91. By introducing into the text the 'golden rule' of charity and the mention of the Holy Spirit, adding, after 'unchastity': 'and whatever you would not have done to you, do not to others', and '. . . if you keep yourselves from these, *helped by the Holy Spirit*, you will do well.' (Codex Bezae.)
92. On the offerings as sacrifices, see Phil 4:18; Heb 13:16.
93. Texts: 1 Cor 16:1–4; 2 Cor 8:1–15; 9:1–14; Rom 15:25–32; texts of the

year 57. Add Ac 24:17. See E. B. Allo, 'La portée de la collecte pour Jérusalem dans les plans de S. Paul' in *R. Bibl.*, 45 (1936), pp. 529–37; L. Cerfaux, 'Les "saints" de Jérusalem', in *Ephem. Theol. Lovanienses*, 2 (1925), pp. 510–29; 'S. Paul et l'unité de l'Église', in *NRT*, 53 (1926), pp. 657–73; *The Church in the Theology of St Paul*, London and New York, 1959.

94. J. Dupont, 'Syneidesis, Aux origines de la notion chrétienne de conscience morale', in *Studia hellenistica*, 5, Louvain, 1948, pp. 119–53, p. 153. On the notion of conscience, see C. Spicq, 'La conscience morale dans le N.T.' in *R. Bibl.*, 1938, pp. 50–80; J. Selzenberger, *Syneidesis im N.T.*, 1961.

95. See M. J. Lagrange, *Épître aux Romains*, Paris, 1922, comm. and app., pp. 335–40; M. Rauer, *op. cit.*, n. 23, above. The vegetarian idea may have originated from Orphism and Pythagorism (Lagrange, p. 358), but also from the Essenes, (then from the Ebionites and the Therapeutae) and from the Judaizing tendency headed by James. It may have envisaged a return to the conditions of Paradise (Gen 1:19–30; men began to eat meat after the flood, Gen 9:1–7), which the prophets foretold would be restored in the last days; Is 11:5–9; 65:25.

96. Rom 14:1–15, 6.

97. Col 2:16–23 and 1 Tim 4:3–6.

98. Rom 14:14 and 17; see 1 Tim 4:3–6.

99. 1 Cor 8:8, but only the attitude of the heart, see Mk 7:1–23; Mt 15:11.

100. Rom 14:6–8; the Kingdom of God is not a matter of food and drink: Rom 14:17.

101. Rom 14:14.

102. Rom 14:22–3.

103. Rom 14:1, 4, 10; Col 2:16.

104. Rom 14:6f.

105. 14:3.

106. 14:10f, see Mt 7:1; Lk 6:37; Rom 2:1, 16; 1 Cor 4:3–5; 10:29; Jas 4:11.

107. Rom 14:13–15.

108. Rom 14:16 and 21; see 1 Cor 8:13; 10:23.

109. See G. Bertram, art. ἔργον in *TWB z. NT*, vol. 2, p. 640.

110. Rom 14:19; 15:2.

111. 1 Cor 8:1.

112. Col 3:14–15, interpreted by A. Fridrichsen, 'Charité et perfection. Observations sur Col 3:14', in *Symbolae Osloenses*, fasc. 19, Oslo. 1939, pp. 41–5. On the Pauline 'edification', see L. Cerfaux, *op. cit.*, pp. 195–6; P. Vielhauser, *Oikodome, Das Bild vom Bau im christl. Literatur vom N.T. bis Clemens Alexandrinus*, Heidelberg, 1939; O. Michel, art. οἶκος, οἰκοδομέω in *TWB z. NT*, vol. 5, pp. 122f; P. Bonnard, *Jésus-Christ édifiant son Eglise, Le concept d'édification dans le N.T.*, Neuchâtel-Paris, 1948.

113. Eph 4:3.

114. Rom 15:1–6.

115. Rom 14:9; 6:10–11.

116. For the NT period, besides Strack-Billerbeck, see Staffer, *La Palestine au temps de Jésus-Christ*, 5th ed., Paris, 1892, pp. 334f, (the sabbath); J. Bonsirven, *Le judaisme palestinien au temps de Jésus-Christ*, Paris, 1935, vol. 2, p. 178. Contemporary examples in A. Koestler, *Analyse d'un miracle*, Paris, 1949, pp. 351–9.

117. See e.g., the discipline expressed in Mt 18:15f with the rabbinical texts quoted by Strack-Billerbeck, vol. 1, pp. 787–92 and vol. 4, pp. 291–335, and still more with the Qumrân Manual of Discipline. V. 24–VI. 1, or the Damascus

Document, (in G. Vermès, *Les manuscrits du désert de Juda*, Paris, 1954, p. 174). On the excommunications carried out by Paul, see 2 Thess 3:6, 14–15; 1 Cor 5:3–5, 13; Rom 16:17; 1 Tim 1:20; 5:20; Tit 3:10–11. Many parallels have also been pointed out between Jewish law and the procedure followed over the choice of Matthias: E. Stauffer, 'Jüdisches Erbe im urchristlichen Recht', in *Theol. Literaturzeit.*, 1952, col. 201–6.

118. A fact pointed out by Pius XII in his address to the professors of the Gregorian University, *AAS*, 1953, pp. 687–8. To give only a few examples: J. Trummer, 'Mystiches im alten Kirchenrecht', in *Oesterr. Archiv f. Kirchenrecht*, 2 (1951), pp. 62–75; Ch. Lefevre, 'La doctrine de l'Hostiensis sur la préférence à assurer en droit aux intérêts spirituels', in *Ephemer. Juris can.*, 8 (1952), pp. 24–44.

119. Speech to the Congress of Canon Law at Boston, 12th–13th Oct. 1954.

120. Rom 13:10.

121. A. Valensin, 'Fondements et limites du devoir de franchise', in *Vérité et Vie*, series xviii, Strasburg, 1952–3, no. 165, p. 11.

122. On Pascal and casuistry, see E. Baudin in *Rev. S.R.*, 18 (1929), pp. 205–23.

123. Gal 5:13.

124. See Gal 3:19; Rom 5:20.

125. 1 Cor 15:56.

126. 2 Cor 3:6.

127. See e.g., Bernard, *De praec. et dispens.*, c. 2, n. 5 (*PL*, vol. 182, col. 863–4); *Sum. Theol.*, Ia IIae, qu. 96, art. 6; qu. 97, art. 4; qu. 100, art. 8 and parallels.

128. To the references quoted above, n. 32, add R. Thamin, *Un problème moral dans l'Antiquité, Étude sur la casuistique stoicienne*, Paris, 1884. Note especially, on pp. 287–8, how in the preface to his famous *Dictionnaire des cas de conscience*, 1715, Jean Pontas frankly admits that he takes many of his solutions from Roman Law and from Seneca.

129. Eph 5:2.

130. See Mt 5:17. For what follows, see S. Lyonnet, 'Introduction à Gal. et a Rom.' in the *Bible de Jérusalem* in fascicules (1953), and 'Liberté chrétienne et loi de l'Esprit selon S. Paul', in *Christus. Cahiers spirituels*, no. 4 (1954), pp. 6–27. He clearly shows how Aquinas and traditional theology have adopted this Pauline doctrine.

131. Gal 5:13; Rom 6:14.

132. Rom 13:8.

133. Gal 5:14; Rom 13:9–10.

134. Gal 5:14; Rom 13:9.

135. Rom 12:2; see Col 1:9; Eph 1:9; Rom 16:25.

136. 1 Tim 1:4–5.

137. Col 3:14–15.

138. Phrase of T. Deman, in *Prudence chrétienne. Cahier de la vie spirituelle*, Paris, 1948, p. 30. See especially, in France, the works of A. Gardeil (*La vraie vie chrétienne*), H. D. Noble, T. Deman (treatise on Prudence, in the French translation of the *Summa*, Paris, 1949), J. Leclercq (*La conscience du chrétien. Essai de Theologie morale*, Paris, 1947), and P. Delhaye, 'La theologie morale d'hier et d'aujourd'hui', in *Rev. S.R.*, 27 (1953), pp. 112–30. In Belgium, the works of Dom O. Lottin and Canon J. Leclercq (e.g., *L'enseignement de la morale chrétienne* (*Les livres du prêtre*, 3), Paris, 1949). In Germany, J. Pieper, *Traktat über die Klugheit*, Leipzig, 1938; M. Pribilla, 'Klugheit und Kasuistik' in *Stimmen der Zeit*, 133–4 (1938), pp. 210f (the 'case' should not be a formula of ready-made recipes, but should aim at forming the conscience); etc.

139. F. Tillmann.
140. R. Egenter, *Von der Freiheit der Kinder Gottes*, Freiburg-i-B., 1941; O. Karrer, *Die Freiheit des Christenmenschen in der kathol. Kirche*, Einsiedeln-Cologne, 1941.
141. P. Lippert, *Vom Gesetz u. von der Liebe*, Munich, 1932; G. Gillman, *The Primacy of Charity in Moral Theology*, London, 1960; V. Warnach, *Agape. Die Liebe als Grundmotiv der neutestl. Theologie*, Düsseldorf, 1951 (English trans. in hand). To these should be added the three volumes of Fr B. Häring, translated into English under the title *The Law of Christ*, New York, 1964; R. Carpentier, 'Le primat de l'amour dans la vie morale'; 'Le primat de la charité en morale surnaturelle'; 'Le primat de l'Amour-Charité comme méthode de théologie morale', in *NRT*, 83 (1961), pp. 3–24, 255–70, 492–509.
142. E.g., G. Ermecke, 'Das christliche Gewissen und die christl. Gewissensbildung in Moraltheologie u. Moralverkündigung', in *Theol. Quartalsch.*, 131 (1951), pp. 385–413.
143. Exaggerated in T. Steinbüchel (*Christliche Lebenshaltungen in der Krisis der Zeit u. des Menschen*, Frankfurt a. M., 1949). See the criticism in *Herder Korrespondenz*, July 1950, pp. 456–9. This assimilation is better presented in R. Egenter, 'Kasuistik als christliche Situationsethik' in *Münchener Theol. Zeitsch.*, 1 (1950–4), pp. 54–65, and W. Dirks, 'Wie erkenne ich was Gott von mir will?' in *Frankfurter Hefte*, April 1950.
144. 'Situationsethik u. Sündenmystik', in *Stimmen der Zeit*, 145/5 (1950), pp. 330–42; *Gefahren im heutigen Katholizismus*, Einsiedeln-Cologne, pp. 31f. See *Lay People*, pp. 417–20.
145. Speech of 25th March to the Family Day (*AAS*, 1952, pp. 270–8), and to the World Federation of the 'Jeunesses féminines catholiques', 18th April 1952 (pp. 413–19).
146. In *AAS*, 1956, pp. 144–5. There is a good commentary by P. J. Fuchs in *NRT*, 78 (1956), pp. 798–818.
147. See above, n. 128.
148. As J. Klein would have it, 'Ursprung und Grenzen der Kasuistik', in *Aus Theol. u. Philos. Festschrift Fr. Tillmann*, ed. T. Steinbüchel and T. Müncker, Dusseldorf, 1950, pp. 229–45. Klein's historical investigation, interesting as far as it goes, is partial and incomplete. Moreover he assumes, here as elsewhere, an irritating opposition, inherited from R. Sohn, between law and morality or spirituality.
149. In this ecclesial status of prudence, which finds a place in what Aquinas says (*Sum. Theol.*, IIa IIae, qu. 49, art. 3 and parall.) on the docility of the prudent man, is contained all the light a Christian needs to seek, not only in the advice of those more enlightened than himself, but in the knowledge of the tradition of the fathers, the saints and the theologians.
150. *Addenda:* It was only after the writing and publication of this paper that I came to know of the work of H. von Campenhausen, *Die Bergründung kirchlicher Entscheidungen beim Apostel Paulus* (*Sitzungsber. d. Heidelb. Akad. d. Wiss.*, Philos.-hist. Kl.), Heidelberg, 1957; the author shows that Paul derives every concrete decision from the centre of the faith and the Church.

Paul sometimes makes *peace* play a similar rôle to that of *agape*, as a principle of 'casuistry'; see J. Comblin, *Théologie de la Paix, Principes*, Paris, 1960, p. 248.

The inspiration and principles of this 'casuistry' of St Paul, drawn from *agape*, correspond with: 1) the apostolic *exhortation*: this does not enunciate a command of the legal type, but is an urgent appeal, in the name of God's mercy: see H. Schleier, *Le temps de l'Église*, Tournai-Paris, 1961, pp. 85f: 2) the very nature and rule of the exercise of authority in Christianity: see my study 'La hiérarchie comme service', in the collection *L'Épiscopat et L'Église universelle*, Paris, 1962, pp. 67–99.

CHAPTER FIVE

The different Priesthoods
Christian, Jewish and Pagan[1]

MODERN CATHOLICISM IS GIVEN TO SEARCHING for what may be called the 'specifically Christian'. In this it is guided by the Holy Spirit who, in the words of Irenaeus, 'continually rejuvenates the apostolic tradition preserved in the vessel of the Church and communicates its youth to the vessel which contains it'.[2] It is even forced to it, in a way, because it is confronted, inevitably and sometimes violently, with all sorts of ideologies, neo-pagan, totalitarian and others, from whose propaganda there is no escape, as well as by the dialogue with men of other religious positions. It is a difficult situation, but thousands can testify that on the whole it has benefited us and has prompted us to renew our understanding of the gospel.

The priesthood is one of the facts or notions in which the 'specifically Christian' appears most vividly when we study the words of the New Testament attentively. It stands out clearly at the outset in the vocabulary. But it may be suspected also that over and beyond the vocabulary it is the whole *meaning* of the priesthood which is in question.

Here are the facts. The word *hiereus* (priest, sacrificer) appears more than thirty times in the New Testament, and the word *archiereus* more than one hundred and thirty times. The use of these words is so constant that it clearly shows a deliberate and highly significant intention, especially as the writers of the first Christian generations very carefully follow the same line. With them, as with the New Testament, *hiereus* (or *archiereus*) is used

74

to denote either the priests of the levitical order or the pagan priests.[3] Applied to the Christian religion, the word *hiereus* is used only in speaking of Christ[4] or of the faithful.[5] It is never applied to the ministers of the Church's hierarchy. There is only one exception, in the Epistle of Clement of Rome to the Corinthians (about AD 95), in a passage which is, however, important and would suffice, without other indications, to let us know that in the lifetime of John the Apostle—who at that time was drawing up the final text of his Revelation and had not yet published his gospel as a whole—the Christian community was familiar with a hierarchic title of priesthood, distinguishing the ministers, in respect of the priestly character, from the whole body.[6]

The apostles and the early Christians were dominated by the sense that they possessed all things in Jesus Christ. To them, the whole relation of man to God—rule of life, temple, priesthood, sacrifice—was established in Jesus Christ, whose life and very self become ours by faith. The Epistle to the Hebrews, the supremely priestly document of the New Testament, is filled with this affirmation; its message is summed up in these words: 'Now the point in what we are saying is this: we have such a high priest, one who is situated at the right hand of the throne of the Majesty in heaven, a minister (*leitourgos*) in the sanctuary and the true tent which is set up not by man but by the Lord.'[7]

But although there is only one, sole priest of the Christians, he is not alone. If there is one truth everywhere proclaimed in the gospel and Paul, it is that Christ is the firstborn among a great multitude of brethren, and that he communicates to many what he has accomplished for all. He is the temple, but the faithful are temples with him. The sole temple of the Messianic age is his body: his personal body, which is risen, and his 'community-body', the community of Christians. He is priest and sacrifice, but the faithful are priests and sacrifices with him—this is attested in more than fifteen passages of the New Testament.[8] They define very precisely the priestly character and the sacrifices of the body which is the Church; not the offering of material objects, but the building up, by the faith of the believers, of a spiritual temple, *in which the living man offers himself as a spiritual sacrifice.*

Here as everywhere, Christianity appears as the fulfilment of what the prophets had preached. Truly, the more one studies the bible, the more one sees that the prophets, as the Fathers said, were the first Christians. The prophets had foretold and welcomed, not the suppression of the temple and the worship, but their *spiritual* fulfilment. God would always dwell with his people, but not in a local manner: he would dwell where he reigned, by obedience and faith. There would always be sacrifices, but not of *things* external to man himself. The true sacrifice would be that of life itself, wholly rendered to God by faith and love, in affectionate and filial devotion to his will. In its very essence and intimate reality the *Ecclesia* would be temple, sacrifice and priest. It is by fulfilling its own nature that Christianity has, of itself, a priestly character.

All this being so, what can be the priesthood which is peculiar to the ordained ministers? The New Testament, as we have seen, does not explicitly call them 'priests'. It indicates them by the names of functions, services. Our Lord, making a very clear and formal contrast on this point with the pagan order of life, declared that in the Messianic community there would be no degree of power other than positions of service.[9] The ministers of the Christian hierarchy are described in the New Testament and in Christian writings up to the end of the second century by the names of functions: *episkopos* (overseer), *presbyter* (elder, counsellor), *deacon* (minister, servant), *hegoumenos* (chief), president. To these we should have to add the lists of 'charismata' or spiritual gifts, granted 'for the building up of the body of Christ': apostles, prophets, teachers, evangelists, pastors.[10]

These were different functions, of unequal value in the hierarchy, but under different aspects they all aimed at one and the same end: the building up of the body of Christ, which is both temple and sacrifice, by the service of the gospel. It is very remarkable and noteworthy that the New Testament transposes into terms of gospel and faith what the Old Testament had chiefly conceived in terms of worship and ritual. To take only two examples; Paul writes: 'Do you not know that those who are employed in the temple service get their food from the temple, and those who serve at the altar share in the sacrificial offerings?' (Thus far the law of the Old Testament, but now the rule of the Messianic age): 'In the same way, the Lord commanded that those who proclaim the gospel should get their living by the gospel.'[11] It appears that in place of a priesthood of a ceremonial worship there is henceforth to be a ministry of the gospel. And in fact, when Paul lists the ministries for which spiritual gifts are granted, he names apostles, prophets, teachers, evangelists: all ministers of the gospel.[12] Is this not because sacrifice is now to be that of living faith, animating all life in filial obedience to God? Again: 'Offer your (living) persons as a living sacrifice, holy and acceptable to God: that is the spiritual worship (or, reasonable service) you owe him.'[13] The meaning and content of this are made clear in the following verses, 2 to 13, which should be studied. There it will be seen that there is a real identity between the programme of construction of the body of Christ by a surrender of self and everything that builds up the community of men in Christ, because this community is also the temple built of living stones.[14]

We find, in fact, that Paul attributes a priestly value to this ministry of the gospel. It consists in arousing, fostering and educating in the faithful a faith which, permeating the whole of life, constitutes the spiritual sacrifice of Christians. The two crucial texts (we italicise the words which are cultural and sacrificial and therefore priestly) are the following:

1. Rom 15:16: 'That I should be a minister (*leitourgos*) of Christ Jesus unto the Gentiles, in the *priestly service* of the Gospel of God, so that the *offering up* of the Gentiles may be acceptable, sanctified by the Holy Spirit.'

2. Phil 2:17:[15] 'If I am to be *poured as a libation* upon the *sacrificial offering* of your faith . . .'

We might also quote 2 Cor 5:18-20, connected with Eph 5:2 and other themes, such as the collection.[16]

Where, in all this, is the eucharist? Where is the obviously priestly function of celebrating the Lord's Pasch till he come again? They are at the heart of all we have said. But the reality of the link between all this and the eucharistic offering is deeper than any written statements of it which we can quote. It must be perceived in a living contemplation of the Christian mystery.

If in the Christian régime there is no other sacrifice than that of man himself, neither is any sacrifice acceptable (*euprosdektos*) to God but that perfectly pure and filial sacrifice of Jesus Christ himself.[17] It is clear that this 'once for all' does not exclude the 'repetition' (in Péguy's sense) of that offering which is accomplished by the liturgical ministers in obedience to 'Do this in commemoration of me'. Truly, 'no one has ascended into heaven but he who descended from heaven':[18] that access to the Holy of Holies, constantly promised to us in the Epistle to the Hebrews, is ours only if we are found in him, in his ascent or 'passing', if we form with him one body of Pasch, of sacrifice, of death and resurrection. And how do we do this, if not by the sacramental appropriation of the body of Christ, which is effected, first in baptism, then in the communion of his body, delivered up for us?

On the other hand, the priestly programme of the spiritual sacrifice of Christians, whether we consider it from the side of the apostolic ministry (building up the body of Christ) or from the side of the faithful,[19] consists in forming one single body, which is the body of Christ, offered to God the Father. Augustine, with his brilliantly profound perception of the Christian mystery, wrote, at the end of one of the most magnificent passages ever penned by a Christian: 'This is the Christians' sacrifice: we are one body with Christ, as the Church celebrates in the sacrament of the altar, so well known to the faithful, wherein is shown that in that oblation the Church is offered.'[20] The point of view of 'forming one body' is intimately connected with the offering of the sacrificed body of Jesus Christ. Study of the use of the word *soma* in the New Testament reveals this connection: *soma* is the 'community-body' of Christ, the Church, which is also the temple of God; but it is so only in union, through the Eucharist, with the *soma*, the body of Jesus Christ, which is the body offered up and sacrificed, on the cross, then in his eucharistic memorial.[21]

To sum up, while the ministerial or hierarchical priesthood of the body of Christ is essentially a ministry of living faith, that is, a spiritual sacrifice of the faithful, it is also, essentially and decisively, a ministry of the eucharistic celebration. It is only by my communion in the eucharist that I can offer that spiritual sacrifice, in spirit and in truth, which God seeks from his people, now become the body of Christ. That celebration is sacramental and liturgical.[22]

It is right to insist on this collective, visible, liturgical and sacramental character of the sacrifice of Christ, which the Christian apostolate has received power and command to celebrate. I am fully aware that the way in which I have presented the facts, though it is accurately and fairly based on the texts and is, indeed, necessary for a full grasp of the profound demands of the Christian sacrifice, might guide the mind to a purely personal and ultimately individualistic inwardness, which is not that of Christianity. The personal and inward quality of the prophetic religion could lead, if it alone were regarded, to the merely moral interpretation of Philo. But Jesus Christ—in whom and by whom alone is fulfilled God's will to accept only the sacrifice of man's filial and loving obedience—has 'handed over' his sacrifice to us, so that we can unite ourselves to it and achieve our own in it, in a celebration which is communal, visible, liturgical, public: in a word, ecclesial. It is in this celebration that Christian worship is really accomplished. It is in our union with his celebration by the ordained priests that, in the words of *Mediator Dei*, 'the true believers are distinguished from false Christians and the unorthodox'.[23] Here I should develop at length[24] the whole doctrine of the encyclical, were my plan not less ambitious; it is to define what is specific in the sacrifice and priesthood of the gospel, by comparison with the Aaronic sacrifice and priesthood on the one hand and with the pagan on the other.

If, then, this liturgical celebration is to be the Christian worship, the act of the priesthood of the New Testament, it must never become a legal, ritual performance, made up of something external to man himself. It is because of their profound realisation of this necessity that the Fathers—especially Augustine, but also Origen and others—so often employ phrases in which the content of the eucharist seems to be not so much the 'real presence' as the living faith or the unity of the Christians themselves. The fact is that from the point of view of the gospel, and in the Messianic régime, the two are inseparable. The eucharist of the New Testament is not a rite which could exist apart from our giving ourselves to God and to one another, in order to form one body of sacrifice in Jesus Christ, delivered for us. It is the special message of the New Testament that the inner meaning of things is henceforth given with the things themselves, and cannot be separated from them. The Law was a sheer obligation which did not contain the corresponding grace; but the law of the New Testament, Aquinas says, is principally the grace of the Holy Ghost.[25] However beautiful, ritually, the celebration may be, if it does not include the accomplishing of the spiritual sacrifice of men, if it is not fitted, in itself, to make their sacrifice real, it is not really and truly the sacrifice of the *New Testament*.

All this really needs to be expounded, perhaps even documented, at greater length, but I am not attempting more than a mere outline. I should also have liked to sketch out at least a few pastoral applications. But the essentials, I think, have been stated about the priesthood in the New Testament. From this we can surmise what it means to be a priest of the gospel.

We can also obtain a slightly clearer idea why the New Testament, systematically and certainly intentionally, has avoided using the term *hiereus*, sacrificer, for the Church's ministers, while still using it for the Jewish and even the pagan priests. Did it not mean to make a clear distinction between the Christian priesthood and the Jewish or pagan priests? We can adopt this hypothesis and try to see exactly where lay the originality of the Christian priesthood, compared with the Aaronic priesthood and that of the pagan religions.

1. From our present point of view, Judaism may be characterised by the duality of the priestly and prophetic functions. We are speaking of developed Judaism after the eighth century BC, for in earlier ages the different functions were often combined and often seem to have been incompletely dissociated from certain 'religious' ideas or practices similar to those of the surrounding pagan peoples. But at least from the eighth century and in the circumstances of the Exile, man's relations with God were realised in two ways. The contrast between them must not be exaggerated, as it often was by nineteenth-century Protestant critics, but it is very important to realise clearly their duality and their difference. On the one hand, the way of worship, the sphere of the levites and priests; on the other, the way of prophecy.

Worship was governed by the law given to Israel since the time of Moses, to make it a people apart, wholly dedicated to the acknowledgement of the true God in the midst of idolatrous nations. The law, entrusted to the loyalty of the priests, organised the life of the people as a consecrated people, set apart, and therefore wholly priestly,[26] according to the extremely meticulous prescriptions in which God's rights were asserted. The closer the

approach to Yahweh's dwelling-place, the stricter these prescriptions became, and likewise the separation, the consecration and
the holiness. Leviticus meticulously regulated the sacrifices, the
different kinds and their ritual, the investiture of the priests, the
distinction between pure and impure, the festivals, etc. Throughout the sacred land of Israel a system of purifications and prohibitions was in force: abstention from sexual relations in certain
conditions: purification after even accidental approach to a corpse,
distinction between pure and impure foods, ablutions, etc. But
the levites were subject to stricter regulations than others, and the
priests' ministry in the temple to regulations stricter still. The
temple itself comprised a succession of enclosures, from the court
of the Gentiles to the sanctuary itself, access to the holy places
becoming ever more limited and difficult. To the actual sanctuary
only the ministering priests could penetrate, bound to stricter
rules of legal holiness: into the Holy of Holies, only the high
priest, once a year, after offering a sacrifice for his own sins and
another for those of the people.

The sacrifices consisted of the offering of animals or the firstfruits of the crops, and of course they were often accompanied by
a very profound religious sentiment. Israel's prayer is still a
school of the Lord's service for the Church. Nonetheless, the fact
remains that the legal sacrifices consisted of *things*: the spirit of
worship was, as it were, separated from its body, until the prophets proclaimed, as a foreshadowing of the Gospel, the idea of
sacrifices consisting of the dispositions of the heart and of thanksgiving.

The prophets, in fact, preached the soul of religion, and a
religion in life and in history. *A religion in life*, consisting of the
dispositions of the heart: justice and right (Amos), mercy and
right (Hosea, Micah), mercy and 'knowledge of the Lord'(Hosea),
a religion summarised in those wonderful verses: 'I will betroth
you to me for ever; I will betroth you to me in righteousness and
in justice, in steadfast love and in mercy. I will betroth you to me
in faithfulness, and you shall know the Lord.'[27] The cultural
sacrifices as such were rather the object of severe criticism from
the prophets. Not that they were opposed to the cult in principle:
several of them were priests. But they held that the *things offered
in worship*, and the temple itself considered as a thing, rather kept

men away from Yahweh than brought them into communion with him, unless men approached them in the dispositions of the heart we have named. What God wanted was that the soul of worship should be present with its body, that he should be offered a religion, a cult and sacrifices, which expressed a life of loving obedience to his will.

Also, *a religion in history*. We know that the function of prophecy was not only to predict the future—though the prophets did in fact predict it more than once—but, still more, to illuminate the events of their time in the light of the will, the demands, of God's justice.[28] We think of Isaiah, at the time of the Syro-Ephraimite coalition, at the invasion of Sennacherib, then his prophecy of the captivity. We think of the theme of the 'remnant', and how the prophets, in a natural disaster which might have been viewed as a total destruction, revealed a merciful design of God, looking to the future, full of hope, foreshadowing the mystery of the Church. All the time, the prophetic teaching is instigating and educating faith in the living God who acts in history, and demands from his believers a response of faith, not only among the timeless repetitions of a sacred liturgy, but from the midst of the events of time.

Furthermore, when Israel, conquered and enslaved, saw its temple razed to the ground, its leading men taken captive or forced to live without sacrifices, without the Holy of Holies, in the midst of an idolatrous nation, the priestly type of religion seemed clearly inadequate. It is perhaps from this time and situation that we should date the remote origins—impossible to discover precisely—of the institution of a type of worship different from the temple worship; the worship, that is, of instruction and praise, of faith and prayer: the synagogue. However that may be, in our Lord's time we see, alongside the sacrificial worship of the temple, a synagogal worship everywhere in use. And we may be allowed to note here that while our Lord respected the temple, we never see him offering sacrifice there. He prays there, he teaches; in short, he performs acts of synagogal worship. But we frequently see him taking part in the worship of the synagogue, a liturgy of the word and prayer.

Aquinas, who had a keen sense of the development, the stages and the originality of the Christian economy,[29] has a passage of wide import and great depth. 'As to those matters that regarded the spiritual worship of God, consisting in the teaching of the Law and the prophets, there were, even under the Old Law, various places, called synagogues, appointed for the people to gather together for the praise of God, just as now there are places called churches, in which the Christian people gather together for the divine worship. Thus our church takes the place of both temple and synagogue: since the very sacrifice of the Church is spiritual, wherefore with us the place of sacrifice is not distinct from the place of teaching.'[30] The idea here propounded in passing by Aquinas touches, so far as our subject is concerned, on a decisive point. To know what it means to be a priest, not of Moses but of the Gospel, we have only to apply to the priesthood what is here said of worship. The special characteristic of the gospel age, and therefore the 'specifically Christian' thing by comparison with the Mosaic system, consists in this, that worship is spiritual, 'in spirit and in truth'.[31] That does not mean that we have simply allegorised or moralised the demands of the Law, as the Hellenised Jews did, especially Philo. But everything has become reality in man himself, by the action of the Holy Spirit. Truly there is no worship, no sacrifice, but that of man himself, in his life, consecrated and offered. The notion of priesthood must follow precisely from that.

The priesthood of the New Testament is no longer the priesthood of Aaron, but a priesthood from above, 'after the order of Melchizedek', which carries out a worship according to the programme of the prophets. It is a prophetic priesthood. Origen understood this well when, about the middle of the third century, he wrote the wonderful passage we shall now quote. He holds that Joshua (Jesus), son of Nun, successor to Moses, is the type of Jesus, *qui post mortem Moysi suscepit imperium*: for Moses is the Law, and Jesus (Joshua) is the freedom of Christ. And he comments thus on the verse: 'Moses, my servant, is dead':[32]

We must mention the death of Moses, for unless we understand in what sense Moses dies, we shall not see how Jesus reigns. If then you see Jerusalem destroyed, the altar laid waste, the sacrifices, offerings and libations offered no more, no priests, no high priests, no levites, when you see that all this has vanished, you can say that Moses, the servant of God, is dead. If you never see a man coming three times a year to offer me gifts in the Temple, if you see no paschal lamb slain, no unleavened bread eaten, no firstfruits offered, no consecration of any of these things: then you can say that Moses, the servant of God, is dead. On the other hand, when you see the Gentiles coming to the faith, churches being built, altars, not sprinkled with the blood of beasts, but consecrated with the precious blood of Christ; when you see that the service of the priests and levites is not the blood of bulls and of goats, but the word of God by the grace of the Holy Spirit: then you can say that Jesus has received and obtained the headship after Moses;—not that Jesus who was son of Nun, but Jesus the Son of God. When you see that Christ is sacrificed as our Pasch and that we eat the unleavened bread of sincerity and truth, when you see in the Church—like fruits of the good soil, bringing forth thirty, sixty, a hundred fold,—widows, virgins and martyrs; when you see the seed of Israel multiplied in those who are born, not of blood, nor of the will of the flesh, nor of the will of man, but of God, and when you see the children of God who are scattered abroad coming together into one; when you see the people of God keeping the sabbaths, not by withdrawing slothfully from the common affairs of men, but by abstaining from the deeds of sin; when you see all that, you can say: 'Moses, the servant of God, is dead, and Jesus the Son of God has received the headship.'[33]

This is not the place, nor have we the space, to develop the immense spiritual, pastoral and even eschatological consequences of this teaching. It would mean outlining the whole programme of the Catholic priesthood, the spiritual attitudes it demands and the work it has to carry out. The subject is immense and in many respects new, except that whole chapters of what has been said about it [34] would have to be included in this programme, and would swell its paragraphs to unmanageable proportions.

2. When we were comparing the Christian priesthood[35] with the levitical, we found that there was at once continuity, rupture and fulfilment. If we now consider the pagan priesthoods, it is the contrast which is most striking. True, as nature is not wholly

either bad or false, there is still a certain aspect of fulfilment, but only if we first realise and state the need for a break and a radical correction.

'Pagan priesthoods', I said. Make no mistake about it: the subject, if it is understood in its fullest sense, is immense; I should have to distinguish many aspects and stages. I must make it clear that I am thinking chiefly of the pagan priesthood in the cultural world encountered by the gospel in its beginnings.

The established pagan religions were essentially a cult of forces acting in nature, aimed at making it favourable by certain minutely defined rites, the exact observance of which, reserved to an initiated priesthood, was essential.

I said a cult, not a belief. This clearly appears, for example, in a passage from Varro, quoted by Augustine:[36] 'There is a third kind of theology [that is, of mythology, the religion of the gods] which the people, and particularly the priests, in the cities ought to practise. It belongs to this theology to explain what gods should be worshipped in public and by what rites and sacrifices each one should do this.' It was essentially a matter of performing the sacred, sacrificial rites, not out of personal piety, or to attain a communion of a spiritual kind, but to pay a religious tax due, in the name of a community, more especially of the City (*in urbibus cives*). There were, of course, acts of divination and oracles in antiquity, and they were often included in the attributes of the priesthood. But that is something quite different from a faith in the living God and communion with his saving will, which was preached by the prophets of Israel and forms the content of the spiritual sacrifices of the New Testament.

This cult was a cult of the forces acting in nature and able to make man happy or unhappy in this present life. The different pagan gods are simply, at bottom, personifications of the elements of nature in so far as they are mysterious (fertility, water, wind, sun, the cycle of the seasons, days, nights, moons, etc.), or of the course of events (success, victory, an enterprise achieved, etc). Once again, we are the heirs of the prophets, who are as it were the first Christians. The prophets were fighting explicitly, not only against the idols themselves, but against every idea and practice of religion, even that offered to Yahweh, which made him a mere force of nature, a god of the springs, of fertility, of the sun or the moon, of the days and seasons, like Baal or Ashtaroth. The God of the prophets, who is our God and the God of the Christian priesthood, is the living God, who comes into man's life and history in order to assert his saving will in them, and who requires us, to that end, to give him our faith. The religion of the prophets is a religion of *faith*. The Jewish sacrifices first, and then the Christian sacrifice, aim above all at attaining a communion. This is so true that Augustine defines it as 'every work which brings about that we cleave to God in holy association.'[37] In the case of the Christian sacrifice we must add, of course, that this is only possible *per Christum et in Christo*, including its sacramental expression; eucharistic, public and visible. We must also add that the blessings expected from establishing or recovering communion with God are spiritual blessings, blessings of the world to come, which after all consist only in communion with God himself. [38] Here we may recall that at the very time of the birth and expansion of Christianity, and in the very heart of paganism, the mystery religions were offering, with some success, an ideal of communion and salvation which exceeded the horizons of popular paganism. That is true. But how to draw up a parallel between the Christian faith and the pagan mysteries is a question which needs special investigation, on the basis of strict chronology and comparisons. We would rather not embark on it here, nor on the examination of other forms of pagan religion.

In popular paganism the hidden forces had to be propitiated by carrying out certain definite sacrifices, special rites, which were the preserve of an initiated priesthood. We repeat, it was a cult, not a belief, and it was concerned with obtaining earthly benefits. It was necessary to propitiate certain powers which were sacred, that is, above human experience, and to influence them in one's own favour. The priest, as the depositary of the formulas or rites which had power to exorcise the hostile forces and to bribe the beneficent, was the intermediary between the sacred and the profane. In classical paganism, that was his essential function.

It is a melancholy fact that paganism is not historically or geographically confined, something external to Christianity. It exists in every child of Adam, attached as he is to his natural 'religious' instincts. Christianity encounters it, not only in the Græco-Roman world of the first century, or in the Africa and

Oceania of today, but in the hearts and minds of Christians themselves, just as the prophets found it rooted in the hearts and minds of the Jews. We suffer enough, yes, we priests of Jesus Christ, from being always taken for 'heavenly magicians', for ritual intermediaries between this earthly life and certain mysterious forces. The baby is brought to be christened, because 'it brings good luck'. The young couple come to be married, because 'in our family we like a church wedding'. The medal is brought to be blessed: we are expected to lead the procession to the well, to bless houses on Holy Saturday, and so on. In short, we are treated like priests of Hera or the sun, or Ceres or Baal, not like priests of the gospel.

The priest of the gospel is not a magician of the unseen world. From beginning to end the gospel has always meant substituting actions of faith for mere rites and things. For example, Christians have instinctively replaced the hired mourners of the pagan and even Jewish funerals, and musical instruments in the services, by the singing of psalms: worship in spirit and in truth. If my readers will not misunderstand me, I would even say that in the gospel there is no distinction between the sacred and the profane: all is sacred. What God asks from us is our life, our whole life, as Irenaeus says in his commentary on the story of the widow's mite.[39] It is our whole life, and even our death, something which no pagan religion ever thought of. 'Offer your *persons* as a living sacrifice, holy, acceptable to God that is the spiritual worship you owe him.'[40]

It is useless, then, to look in the Gospel or the apostolic scriptures for any trace of all that 'religious' material described, for example, in M. Éliade's admirable manual, and of which some traces may still be found in the Old Testament. The worship of the New Testament is a worship 'in spirit and in truth': *veri adoratores*. It consists of the offering of men themselves. The priests who celebrate it are neither pagan magicians nor even levites of the law of Moses. They are, they must be, priests and prophets, priests of faith in the living God, priests of the sacrifice of obedience offered once for all by Jesus Christ.[41] Here on earth its sacramental celebration exists simply in order that *it* may become fully our sacrifice, and the sacrifice of the whole Church.

D

NOTES

1. Published in the *Bulletin du Cercle S. Jean-Baptiste*, June–July 1957, pp. 193–204, and in *Évangéliser* (Brussels), 76, Jan.–Feb. 1959, pp. 288–304.
2. *Adv. Hær.*, III, 24. 1 (*PG*, 7. 166).
3. At least once, Acts 14:13.
4. Especially in Heb.
5. Revelation.
6. '. . . for the high priest has been allotted his proper ministrations and to the priests their proper place has been assigned, and on the levites their own duties are laid. The lay man is bound by the lay ordinances.' (Cor 40:5).
7. 8:1.
8. See 1 Pet 2:4–5, 9–10; Rev 1:5–6; 5:9–10; 20:6; 22:3–5; Rom 6:13f; Heb 12:28; 13:15–16; Eph 2:18, 22. And see Heb 4:14–16; 7:19; 10:19–22, the whole theme of *having access*.
9. Mk 10:41–5 and parallels.
10. Eph 4:11; 1 Cor 12:28.
11. 1 Cor 9:13–14; see 1 Tim 5:18, referring, this time, to Deut 25:4; then Mt 10:10; Lk 10:7.
12. 1 Cor 12:28; Eph 4:11.
13. Rom 12:1; author's translation.
14. See 1 Pet 2:4–10; Eph 2:13–22.
15. See 1 Tim 4:6.
16. Rom 15:27; 2 Cor 8:4; 9:12.
17. See Heb 10:4–10, which concludes with these words: 'We have been sanctified through the offering of the body of Jesus Christ once for all'.
18. Jn 3:13.
19. Rom 12:1–10, etc.
20. John Healey's translation, *Civ. Dei*, X. 6. *Hoc est sacrificium Christianorum: multi unum corpus in Christo. Quod etiam sacramento altaris fidelibus noto frequentat ecclesia, ubi ei demonstratur, quod in ea re quam offert, ipsa offeratur.*
21. See, among others, 1 Cor 12:13 (baptism); 11:23f (eucharist); Eph 2:16; a study by C. F. D. Moule, 'Sanctuary and Sacrifice in the Church of the New Testament', in *JTS*, 1950, pp. 29–41. In this perspective I agree with E. Lohmeyer (in *Theologische Rundschau*, 1937, p. 296) and E. G. Selwyn (*The First Epistle of St Peter*, London, 1947, pp. 294–8), that the passage in 1 Pet 2:4f, on the spiritual temple, sacrifices and priesthood, contains an implicit reference to the eucharist. I should say the same about Heb 10:19–22 and 13:10, 15–16.
22. We have not space to show how the other 'powers' of the ministerial, hierarchical priesthood have their place in this setting, flowing from the power to celebrate the eucharist: the power to remit sins, to govern and teach the mystical body.
23. *AAS*, 1947, p. 530.
24. As I have done in *Lay People*.
25. *Sum. Theol.*, Ia IIae, qu. 106, art. 1, the whole.
26. See Ex 19:5f.

27. Hos 2:19–20. Our Lord insists in the gospel that this was the spirit and meaning of the Law: Mt 23:23.

28. See Paul Claudel, *Introduction au livre de Ruth*, p. 96; '. . . those commentators on their own time, that living consciousness of Israel's vocation and destiny.'

29. See my article in *Festschrift f. Joseph Lortz*, vol. II, Wiesbaden, 1957, pp. 73–122.

30. *Sum. Theol.*, Ia IIae, qu. 102, art. 4, ad. 3 (English Dominicans' translation).

31. Jn 4:24.

32. Jos 1:1.

33. *In lib. Jesu Nave*, hom. 1. 3, (ed. Baehrens, pp. 296–7), or in *PG* (12. 833–4), hom. 2, n. 1.

34. Especially the authorised texts collected by P. Veuillot in *Notre Sacerdoce*, 2 vols, Paris, 1954.

35. Documentation can be found in Mircéa Éliade, *Traité d'Hist. des Religions*, Paris, 1949; E. O. James, *The Nature and Function of Priesthood*, London, 1955. But from a biblical point of view the comparative position inherent in this type of study is deceptive and seems to me to be most inadequate.

36. See *Civ. Dei*, VI, 5. 3.

37. *Civ. Dei*, X. 6. *Omne quod agitur ut sancta societate inhaereamus Deo*. See Aquinas, quoted in *Lay People*, p. 118.

38. The obtaining of temporal blessings is not excluded. Augustine, presumably in order to turn the tables on the pagans, emphasises the fact that the grant of earthly gifts depends on God, the same God from whom we hope for eternal gifts: *Civ. Dei*, X, 14; *En. in Ps. 34*, sermo 1. 7.

39. Here I quote the admirable passage of Irenaeus, which corresponds to Origen's: 'The rite of sacrificial offerings has not been rejected. There were sacrificial offerings then [in the Old Testament] and there are today. There were sacrifices among the [Jewish] people, there are sacrifices in the Church. But the type of sacrifice has been changed, for the present sacrifice is offered by free men, not by slaves. . . . The Lord is one and identical in either case, but the servile offerings have their own nature, the offerings of the free man have theirs. . . . They consecrated only the tenth of their possessions, but we, who have received our freedom, set apart for the Lord's use all that is ours . . . like that poor widow, the Church, who offered up all her life (*panta ton bion*, Lk 21:4) into the treasury of God.' *Adv. Hær.*, IV (Harvey, IV, 31: vol. II, p. 201).

40. Rom 12:1; author's translation.

41. Heb 10:5–10.

CHAPTER SIX

Notes on our Priesthood[1]

I. THE PRIESTLY CHARACTER OF
ALL CHRISTIANS

This priestly character is part of the general truth that everything belongs to God and is bound to glorify him, as we are reminded in so many passages of the Psalms. But whereas inanimate and merely animal creatures belong to him and glorify him without knowing it, men do so by a free and willing ratification of their relation to God.

This is true even of Israel, although it was chosen *as a body* to be the 'people of God'. The texts are familiar, and this idea of the people of God has again become both fundamental and common ground in our theology. It is on the basis of the Covenant[2] that Israel is constituted as the people *of God*, because it belongs to God and is consecrated to him. So we have the decisive decree of Sinai: 'Now therefore if you will obey my voice and keep my covenant, you shall be my own possession among all peoples: for all the earth is mine, and you shall be to me a kingdom of priests and a holy nation.'[3] This is the text quoted by Peter[4] in order to define the priestly character of all believers, who, 'like living stones', are 'built into a spiritual house, to be a holy priesthood, to offer spiritual sacrifices, acceptable to God through Jesus Christ'.[5]

This priestly character is asserted in other passages of the New Testament, especially in Rom 12:1: 'I appeal to you therefore, brethren, by the mercies of God, to present your bodies as a living sacrifice, holy and acceptable to God, which is your spiritual worship.' Paul speaks of presenting his body. Certainly we cannot deny a special emphasis on the body, defined even more clearly in other passages, but we must not forget that in semitic usage the body stands for the whole concrete person. Paul's idea is, then, that one must offer *oneself*: that is exactly what he means by a spiritual sacrifice. This point is of the utmost importance.

When Israel received from God, on Sinai, a priestly character, it received at the same time a law of worship which prescribed the offering either of the firstfruits of the earth or of animal sacrifices. But later, from the eighth century onwards, the prophets had to insist that God took no pleasure in such things.[6] It was not that the prophets were opposed to all outward worship, as some have held, nor that God no longer desires sacrifice. He says, through the same prophets, that he desires it still, and more than ever.[7] But he is not pleased with the offering of material *things*: he wants no sacrifice but that of man *himself*. Among numerous passages,[8] we quote only one, for it indicates most precisely the sense of the divine will:

Sacrifice and oblation thou dost not desire . . .
Burnt offering and sin offering thou hast not required.
Then I said: 'Lo, I come;
. . . to do thy will, O my God.[9]

This text is quoted by Paul in one of the most important passages of the Epistle to the Hebrews: 'Consequently, when Christ came into the world, he said, Sacrifices and offerings thou hast not desired, but a body hast thou prepared for me: in burnt offerings and sin offerings thou hast taken no pleasure. Then I said, Lo, I have come to do thy will, O God.'[10] We can now understand the nature of the spiritual sacrifices required of us. It consists in lovingly doing the will of God, and thus in returning to him *passibus amoris*,[11] in the beautiful words of Bernard. There is only one who has perfectly made this spiritual sacrifice: Jesus Christ. His sacrifice consists in nothing else, as regards his interior soul: it does not consist in his tortures—the impenitent thief suffered exactly the same—but in the obedience of love through which Jesus returns to his Father, by accomplishing his will. By this obedience he renders, once for all, the perfect adoration, the perfect sacrifice. The cross of Jesus Christ is the centre of the whole spiritual history of the world. All that came before it looked forward to it and drew its worth from it in advance; the text I quoted from Exodus, which spoke of priesthood, even then linked that consecrated character with Israel's obedience. All that has followed it flows from it and derives its religious efficacy from it alone. It is the plain truth that 'no man has ascended into heaven but he who descended from heaven, the Son of man who is in heaven'.[12] Jesus is the Son of Man precisely because he fulfils the whole destiny and the whole idea of the human creature. He fulfils it in the decisive act of his sacrifice, of which the suffering on the cross is only the outward aspect, but its soul is his filial obedience. 'Jesus, knowing that his hour was come that he should pass out of this world to the Father . . .'.

We can arrive at the same idea if we start from an analysis of the notion of sacrifice. We must not take too narrow a view of it by identifying it purely with what is painful.[13] Its aspect as a burdensome duty to be discharged is real, but second in importance, and even secondary. When a girl has not married and has passed marriageable age, in order to look after her old parents, we say that she 'sacrificed her life'. It may well be that inspired by daughterly affection she has been able to do this calmly and cheerfully. Or again, when a conscript leaves for his term of service he accepts the possibility of giving his life for his country. After the war, when I visited the families of my comrades who had fallen on active service, I was deeply moved to hear the wife of one of them say simply: 'Our life is given us to give.' Many young soldiers, many men in the resistance forces, made the sacrifice eagerly: 'the morning sacrifice . . .'. Sacrifice certainly involves a painful renunciation, but that is not its essential element. In essence it is the accurate expression of our relationship to someone or something greater than ourselves, and to whom we owe all that we are. It is the expression of our true position in regard to our parents, or our country, or God.

It is plain, then, that we do not discharge our duty to God by offering him in sacrifice 'some thing', however precious or costing, if it is anything, or even everything, except *ourselves*. 'For every beast of the forest is mine, the cattle on a thousand hills. . . . If I were hungry, I would not tell you: for the world and all that is in it is mine.'[14] The only thing God desires from us—because if we do not give it him he will not have it, having forbidden himself to take it without our consent—is our heart, our selves, living persons, made in his image.

It is plain, too, that our sacrifice can consist of the whole span of our life: that is the spiritual worship we owe to God. There may well be, indeed there must be, specially intense times of offering, but the actual matter of this offering is strictly co-extensive with our lifetime, *quamdiu fuero*.[15]

Of this spiritual sacrifice every one of us is the priest. Sacrifice and priesthood are indeed realities which exactly correspond, priesthood being simply the quality which enables us to stand before God and obtain his grace, and therefore his communion, by the offering of a sacrifice acceptable to him. The nature and quality of the priesthood correspond to those of the sacrifice. A liturgical and sacramental sacrifice requires a liturgical and sacramental priesthood; an interior, spiritual and personal sacrifice requires an interior, spiritual and personal priesthood.

The qualification which enables every Christian to stand thus in the presence of God is that he appears in God's sight as clothed in Christ: by baptism, by faith, by the holiness of his life. That is why the Epistle to the Hebrews insistently repeats that we can present ourselves boldly before God, having a high priest who, as forerunner of the whole body, has entered once for all into the Holy of Holies.

II. OUR PRIESTHOOD AS ORDAINED PRIESTS

First it must firmly be laid down that we, who are priests by a new title, are also in the first place, along with all Christians, priests of that spiritual sacrifice which is simply ourselves. We were at first, and we remain, Christians, who have to pray, to do penance, to love, to offer ourselves and all our life, to work out our own salvation. That is a truth we find in all tradition, from Augustine, saying, with his love of striking alliteration: *Vobis sum episcopus, vobiscum Christianus*,[16] to Abbé Huvelin, who was fond of quoting these counsels of M. Olier and de Condren: 'A priest, after finishing his functions at the altar or his ministrations of the sacraments, should, in some way or other, resume his place among the laity.' And Abbé Huvelin comments:[17]

When a priest . . . has offered up the holy sacrifice, administered the sacraments, preached the word of God, he should go
and resume his place; I mean he should become like one of his
hearers. Hence a priest, for instance, who preached on the
Gospel of the Sower should take his place in the congregation
to listen, in his own turn, to the parable, and ask himself if he
be not the soul on which the seed was wasted because it fell by
the wayside; or the soul hardened by routine, through frequent
repetition of the same acts, so that the seed does not sprout
within it, or even the soul that has stifled the good seed under
the thorns, the thorns of worldly occupations, or even if he be
not all three together. If the priest has given Benediction of the
Blessed Sacrament, after having assisted our Lord and done
the work of his Heart, he should kneel down among those
whom he has blessed, and ask our Lord for a blessing on
himself. After having heard confessions and given absolution,
he should take his place on his knees among the laity and ask
himself: *Numquid ego sum, Domine?*[18]

All this is of the utmost importance, both in theory and in
practice. We priests must never forget that we are in the first
place ordinary Christians, who have to build the Church in ourselves, by establishing the true religious relationship, which
means the sacrifice of ourselves: a sacrifice of which each one of
us is the priest.

But we are also priests in virtue of a function which is public
and therefore hierarchical. This is another fact which it is
interesting to view in a wider context.

Everything in the world is function, in the sense that nothing
we possess is for ourselves alone, but for the good of all as well
as for our own good. We have in fact received from God everything we have, for we are not the real creators, and therefore
absolute owners, of anything. All we can do is to transform and
set in motion the gifts which God has made to us. We are only
the stewards of goods which God has placed in the world, which
is his property, for the good of all mankind, which is his family.
That is the Christian idea of property and profession. The German language here uses the word *Beruf*, which means both 'profession' and 'vocation'. In Old French, moreover, *vocation* was

used for *métier*, and the latter word itself comes from the Latin *ministerium* (or sometimes *misterium*): it is a service, a *diakonia*, a ministry. And so a Christian economist (I think it was Ruskin) made the profound remark, that you should not say of a shoe-maker that he makes shoes, but that he keeps Christendom shod.

Between these two expressions there is more than a slight shade of difference. 'To make shoes' refers only to production and implies that the maker's only aim is his personal profit. The Christian idea is quite different. Of course it is legitimate and natural to live, in the first place, by one's profession, and to support oneself and one's dependents, comfortably if possible. But profession and property have a purpose beyond that. When they have provided a living suitable for a man and his dependents (there is no need to define this too narrowly), every profession, all property, all that can be described as what one *has*, must serve all men. I have money, or health, or strength; I have intelligence or knowledge; I have a house, a car, credit and influence. I can benefit from them with a clear conscience, but everything beyond my own needs belongs to others and must serve them. Everything is service, everything is function, because men are one single body and members one of another.

It is thus that the shoemaker 'keeps Christendom shod', the doctor provides the service of health, the teacher the service of knowledge, the officer or the soldier the service of security. One man makes bread, another builds houses, etc.

What is our place in this one world, what is our profession, our function? Those we have mentioned provide various services of the earthly city: they do the work of the world, if I may so put it, in its horizontal dimension. Our speciality as priests is to serve men in their vertical dimension, that by which they are citizens, not of the earthly city but of the City of God. Equally we might say, referring to an earlier paragraph, that our own function, our *métier* (ministry!) is—while working out our own salvation, our own return to God, which is also our spiritual sacrifice—to help men, not to be shod, to be cared for or to be amused, but to work out their salvation, their return to God, and to stand before him in their true relation: in short, to make the spiritual sacrifice which is that same salvation and that return.

I suggest that this is the sense (paraphrasing the translation without betraying the meaning) of that famous verse in the Epistle to the Hebrews (5:1): *Sacerdos, ex hominibus assumptus, pro hominibus constituitur in iis quae sunt ad Deum.* 'A priest is a man, chosen by God from among other men, and appointed for service in the things which represent their order or their return to God.' The text speaks of sacrifice, and our adaptation only gives the statement its full sense. Thus the priesthood of the ordained ministry is seen to be a divinely qualified and hierarchically appointed service of the aims of a body which is wholly priestly. The fourth chapter of the Epistle to the Ephesians represents the Church as a body alive in every part, in which the hierarchical functions of ministry are, precisely, organs of *movement*: joints, muscles and tendons, for service. Every cell in the body is priestly, in order to offer to God the spiritual sacrifice of its own life, but the body as a whole is organised. It is also *organically* priestly, and by the will and animation of its head, our High Priest, it includes members qualified by a priesthood of service, functional, ministerial and hierarchical—our own.

It is a fact that the New Testament never applies the words *hiereus* or *archiereus* to priests of our order. It uses them only to denote either Christ or all Christians. It is not my business here to deal with the historical problem involved, which is ultimately one of apologetics.[19] But it will throw much light on our subject if we recall two texts of Paul in which the use of definitely cultual and sacrificial expressions gives an interesting sense to the idea of the Christian priesthood. These are the two:

> Because of the grace given me by God to be a minister (*leitourgon*) of Christ Jesus to the Gentiles in the priestly service (*hierourgounta*) of the gospel of God, so that the offering (*prosphora*) of the Gentiles may be acceptable, sanctified by the Holy Spirit.[20]
> Even if I am to be poured as a libation upon the sacrificial offering (*thusia kai leitourgia*) of your faith. . . .[21]

Paul's priestly office consists in bringing about the spiritual sacrifice of the Gentiles, the consecration, that is, of their whole selves to God by faith, which is inspired by the preaching of the gospel. That is our vocation too, that for which we are consecrated, not only as ordinary members of the people of God, but as 'men of God', ministers of the return and sacrifice of others. We have to do God's work not only in and for ourselves, but in and for others.

But, perhaps you are thinking, where, in this vision of the priesthood, is the Mass? Have we not been ordained primarily and chiefly to say Mass 'for the living and the dead'? That is true, but the whole point is to realise the place of the Mass in all this, and the precise purpose for which we are ordained.

As we saw, Jesus took upon him, in his sacrifice, the sacrifice of all men. We ourselves return to the Father only in him and through him, and so he has instituted a memorial (an active celebration) of his sacrifice, under the form, both symbolic and real, of a sacrament, so that his sacrifice, celebrated and represented (made present) every day and in every place 'until he comes again', may become ours, and ours may be united even now to him. The eucharist has a meaning, and that meaning is the unity of the mystical body, offered together with Jesus: that is the theme both of the scholastics under the category of *res hujus sacramenti*, and of Augustine in the immortal pages of the *City of God*,[22] and in so many sermons to his flock, insisting that 'it is the mystery of yourselves which is on the altar'. We are, then, ministerial, hierarchical and sacramental priests of the one sacrifice of Jesus Christ, sacramentally celebrated throughout time and space, in order to consummate, in union with this sacrifice, the sacrifice of his mystical body: that is, of the faithful who have been turned to God by our ministry. We are not priests of a sacrifice external to man, like the Mosaic priests, and Jesus did not proclaim the transitoriness of the ancient ritual only to substitute a new ritual, analogous to the old. He abolished the law only by fulfilling it, that is, by bringing to fulfilment in men that which it had foretold only in outward things. We are indeed made priests in order to say Mass, but ultimately in order to unite the spiritual sacrifice of men to the sacrifice of Christ.

It must never be forgotten that the Church exists and consists supremely not in things but in men. 'Not walls, but the faithful, make the Church!'

The priesthood I have tried to describe is common to every priest. But we, like other men, are 'in situation', as the existentialists say. The actual priestly duties are not the same for all: some have a *cura animarum*,[23] geographically defined: I myself am a preaching friar, and as such I gladly range myself under the banner of Paul, who said: 'Christ did not send me to baptise but to preach the gospel.'[24] You, on the other hand, are army chaplains, each entrusted with a quasi-parish of persons, with the pastoral care of a unit and its personnel. With your permission, I should like to analyse this 'situation' of yours in its main lines. I shall pick out three principal facts, which will lead to some pastoral applications.

1. We represent an opportunity, for many men perhaps the last after their catechism, to meet a priest and hear about Jesus Christ. In France the great majority of men attend catechism; in very poor conditions, unfortunately, but still they attend it. The majority of the lads later pass through the barracks. There again, they meet us in very unfavourable conditions, but still, an opportunity is offered us. You have in your hands one of the opportunities of the Church and the Faith!

2. From that we must draw this conclusion, this resolution, to strive to be truly the ministers of Jesus Christ!

The conclusion is idealistic, I admit, for we are faced with the greatest difficulties. They spring not only from the apathy and indifference of the majority,[25] but from the conditions in which we are called to work.

We have too little time for anything more than the most superficial apostolic contact. There is only Sunday, at Mass, or the evenings, in the canteens or elsewhere. On Sunday we often have to celebrate several Masses, and we have barely time for a rapid celebration, none for more personal contacts. I remember my own period of service, during the first occupation, at Bingen. There was no resident chaplain. The chaplain came from Kreuznach, ten miles away, in a car: he arrived only to say Mass. After Mass he conducted a hasty catechism for the children. I never saw him personally, apart from confession, and I never heard that he came at all except for the Sunday morning Mass, said between a first Mass at Kreuznach and no doubt another elsewhere.

For soldiers, the evenings are a time for relaxation and recreation. We welcome them then, of course, but is it easy to find any opportunity for really priestly activity?

The danger is thus that we seem to be only official celebrants, or else just good fellows: now distributing sacraments, now dealing the cards. In short, as officials of worship who are at the same time 'good sorts', perhaps even 'nice types', good natured and kind—which of course has its value. All the same, we run the risk of missing what is most important, and that in two ways.

First, if we fail to put into practice one of the great rediscoveries of the modern pastoral movement: what has been well called the 'priesthood-laity pair'.[26] This means that the priest is not the sole agent in the Church's activities, though he alone has authority. As in the husband-and-wife pair, so in the Church between priesthood and laity, there is both association and inequality; union, but a union which is organic and does not abolish differences. It is the husband who decides (in principle!), but the wife's opinion and the children's wishes help to form the head's decision, which is thus equally the work of the whole body of the family. It is something like this with the priest and his people, at least his active workers. It is he who celebrates, but the whole body offers: it is he who teaches, but all bear witness and are active in the knowledge of the faith: it is he who has the care of souls, but all have the mission to the apostolate and all, moreover, have to share the charge of the cares and needs of men.

What are we doing to give practical expression to the truth that the life of the Church must be lived by all and that all the faithful are active in building and completing the Church?

The second way in which we might miss what is most important would be if we did not try seriously to be educators in the faith. This point is extremely important. We are drawing ever nearer to a situation in which Christianity will have to exist and be active by means of personal convictions, far more than by the support of institutions and laws: a Christianity no longer ritual and hieratic, but prophetic and lay. That is why we must devote ourselves to planting deep convictions in some souls. Collective action, of course, is necessary; we have to celebrate, preach, organise meetings for the many. But also we have to try to give depth to the good Christians, those who have already given something of their hearts to God, and to try to arouse fresh consciences to strive for a life of solid faith. My own belief is that a chaplain who, without neglecting the duties of his general ministry, has deepened the Christian convictions of four or five men in his year of service, has not wasted his time.

Here I should like to tell you of my experiences when first we were prisoners of war. To start with, I was the only priest in a rather small but also rather unpromising camp. For various reasons, including the lack of places to meet in, I was led to act chiefly on individuals or small groups. In particular, I gave a series of retreats for about ten men at a time (never more than a dozen). I have since learned, several times, that this unspectacular activity has borne fruit. If it were not disproportionate to the results I should gladly recall the rather cryptic but expressive saying of one of my old teachers: 'You must start from causes, not effects.' More simply, I should say: never forget that the Church exists above all in men, and must be built in souls.

Now in spite of the unfavourable conditions in which we have to work, we have nonetheless a certain number of means to our hand in the way of education: talk, and above all private talk, in the confessional or in conversation. Do we give the ministry of the confessional the care it deserves? Are we careful to speak of Jesus Christ, of prayer, of Holy Scripture, of life under the eyes of God? We can lend books, we can stimulate and enlighten the reactions which may be aroused by a novel or a film, or something reported in the papers, or occurring in real life. We can try to awaken or educate the sense of a Christian loyalty in the course of events. For this task we must ourselves learn to be quick to recognise the psychological moments, when the shock of an event, an idea or a play has put men's minds into a favourably receptive state.

3. Such a programme requires on our part a certain quality of life, a life which has both a high standard and a solid foundation. It is something more than deciding when to be the official and when the good fellow: we have to find a style of life which enables us to be both thoroughly 'with them' and thoroughly men of God.

It is a difficult problem, certainly, but it is not peculiar to us, as it faces all who are subject to certain demands of priestly and apostolic fidelity.

Like every attitude which is not artificial, this can only come from within. The only solution is to 'purify the source', to raise the interior level. Unfortunately that is made harder by the fact that chaplains live in an atmosphere which is anything but devotional. The conditions of their life also make it difficult to work intellectually, or to have their lives continually renewed in God, with all that this involves of retreat, silence and austerity.

One of the lessons taught by both experience and history—which is experience writ large—is that it is only possible to overcome these difficulties in a team, or at least by having contacts on that level. All the most alive and creative elements in the Church of today, especially on the pastoral and missionary level, draw their tonality from a community life, or at least from team action. That is true not only among the clergy but among the laity: just think of all the 'family groups' and the associations of the type of *Vie Nouvelle*. I don't know what exists in the way of priests' meetings. In any case, no external organisation can take the place of personal activity, born of a firm resolution to overcome the difficulties and conquer the tendency to routine and mediocrity.

I would therefore urge every one of you to look out for any influences within his reach which are alive, creative and uplifting, and to get into touch with them. It may be a priest, a religious house, a place of prayer, a group, a critical or fervent layman, a Christian home, an intellectual, perhaps even some cultural centre or institute. I would almost say: no matter whom or what, provided it forces you to aim higher. One must systematically stake everything on the things which challenge, which demand, which raise questions, which force one to give of one's best and to excel oneself. Might we not take as our own the motto of a mountaineering club: 'I can do more'?

But wherever we seek this stimulus or power to reach ever higher, we must always renew our lives from the one source. Never neglect mental prayer, which is to the soul like breathing and oxygen. It is utterly useless to make fine speeches and use fine words if we are not faithful to that elementary practice, daily mental prayer!

NOTES

1. Paper read at the Congress of Military Chaplains, Paris, 1952. Text published in *Cahiers de l'Aumônier Catholique*, May 1953, pp. 7–18.
2. 'I will be their God and they shall be my people'; Lev 26:4–12; see 2 Cor 6:16.
3. Ex 19:5–6.
4. 1 Pet 2:9.
5. V. 5.
6. See especially Is 50:11–15; Jer 7:21–3; Ps 50:10–13.
7. See Is 56:7; 66:20f; Jer 33:11; Ps 51:21, and the whole of Exk.
8. See Hos 6:6; Am 5:24–5; Is 1:16f; Mic 6:6–8; Ps 40:7, 9, 10; Ps 51:18f; Ps 69:31f; Ps 141:2, etc.
9. Ps 40:6–8.
10. 10:5–9.
11. 'By the steps of love'.
12. Jn 3:13.
13. 'Making little sacrifices'; something, by the way, we regard as reserved for children!
14. Ps 50:10–12.
15. 'As long as I live'.
16. 'For you I am a bishop, with you a Christian'. *Sermo* 340, n. 1. (*PL*, 39, 1483).
17. *Some Spiritual Directors of the Seventeenth Century*, London, 1927, p. 190.
18. 'Is it I, Lord?'
19. I have said something about this in *Lay People*, Part II, chap. I, and also in 'Un essai théologique sur le sacerdoce catholique: la thèse de l'abbé Long-Hasselmans. Textes et remarques critiques', in *Rev. S.R.*, 25 (1950), pp. 187–99 and 288–304.
20. Rom 15:16.
21. Phil 2:17.
22. Book X, 5 and 6.
23. 'Care of souls'.
24. 1 Cor 1:17.
25. 'It is not you they reject, but me', God said to the prophet Samuel: 1 Sam 8:7.
26. 'The apostolic authority which was formerly on the shoulders of the priesthood is now shared by a pair, the priesthood-laity pair,' Hasseveldt in *Masses Ouvrières*, July 1948, p. 28. See Cardinal Suhard, *Le prêtre dans la Cité*, pastoral letter, 1949, pp. 44–5 (*The Pastoral Letters of Cardinal Suhard*, London, 1955) and see my *Lay People*, p. 358.

CHAPTER SEVEN

The two Forms of the Bread of Life

In the Gospel and Tradition[1]

THE TITLE OF THIS ESSAY OBVIOUSLY REFERS TO the sixth chapter of St John's Gospel, and more particularly to the discourse on the Bread of Life, delivered by our Lord at Capernaum, perhaps in the synagogue which preceded, on the same foundations, that whose noble ruins no one can view today without deep emotion. That chapter of John has been the subject of innumerable studies.[2] It is evidently considered by many critics to be an expression of the theology elaborated by the Christian community, rather than a more or less reconstructed account of real episodes and a discourse really delivered by Jesus. But even those exegetes who accept the existing texts and admit the substantial historical authenticity of the words attributed to the master, differ in their interpretation. We are faced, in fact, with four principal opinions.

1. According to some, the entire chapter is concerned with eating *by faith* the bread of life, Jesus himself, as the means to eternal life. There is complete continuity of meaning between verses 32–47 (where this meaning seems to be certain) and verses 48–58, where Jesus speaks of eating his flesh and drinking his blood: for 'flesh' and 'blood' are simply a manner of denoting the concrete person of Jesus, sacrificed and living, and the need to be united to him by faith. As supporters of this interpretation they claim, among older writers, Cajetan and several theologians,

chiefly Dominicans, at the Council of Trent (but this needs, I feel, fresh examination).[3] They have even quoted Jerome, Augustine, Aquinas and Bonaventure, although, in my opinion, very wrongly. Careful reading shows that the Fathers neither saw nor taught any contrast between the eating by faith and the eating by the sacrament. This contrast is the work of the moderns, especially Protestants. It springs from a rather superficial spirit of dissociation and a system of rather materialistic literary analysis, foreign to the spirit of Christian realism which marked the ancients and the Fathers.

The moderns have read the texts of these Fathers and great schoolmen too cursorily in the light of the distinctions inherited from the sixteenth-century controversies. They have supposed that where Augustine, Aquinas or Cajetan spoke of *spiritualiter manducare* they were not thinking of the *sacrament* but of the purely pre-sacramental or extra-sacramental eating by faith. But these Doctors use not only two terms (faith or sacrament), but three: the purely spiritual eating by faith alone, the spiritual eating *of the sacrament* really received, and the carnal, purely physical eating of the same sacrament, which Aquinas also calls the (purely) sacramental eating.[4]

2. Others, among modern and contemporary authors,[5] have maintained an entirely eucharistic and sacramental interpretation of the discourses on the Bread of Life. For on the one hand the discourse follows the multiplication of the loaves, and eucharistic allusions are found in the chapter as a whole ('after giving thanks . . .', v. 11); on the other hand, the discourse is all given in one place, and therefore it all refers to what is clearly stated from verse 48; finally, the sacramental eating of the flesh of Christ is both spiritual and real: the opposition between spiritual and real, and the assimilation of the sacramental realism to the material betrays a false conception of things, to which Protestantism has often succumbed, but which it should now shake off.

On the exegetical level this interpretation roughly corresponds to the theological thesis according to which all saving *faith* already implies a desire for baptism, which itself implies a desire for the Eucharist: for it is impossible to have life without eating the body and drinking the blood of Christ.

3. A third group of exegetes sees in the discourse two suc-

cessive themes: from verse 26 (or at least 29) to verse 47, in which Jesus speaks of eating and drinking by faith in himself, and from verse 48, where he speaks of a sacramental eating and drinking, by the eucharist, of which his hearers, of course, could have no idea, but which St John's readers knew all about.[6]

4. Finally there is a fourth line of interpretation, which combines the most valuable elements in these three. In general it resumes the vein of the Fathers of the Church and especially of Origen and Augustine who, rightly understood, are often considered the most 'spiritualising'.[7] The whole discourse, from verse 35 to verse 58, is about the same thing, namely, feeding on Christ *himself*, the true spiritual food, in order to obtain *heavenly*, not bodily life. Psalm 78:24: 'Thou gavest them bread from heaven'[8] has been quoted about Christ: the subject was the manna. But the manna was only a heavenly *gift*, a gift of God. The true bread from heaven is God himself, it is heaven itself, come down to us, communicated to men in the person of Jesus.

The gospel message of salvation, delivered by the apostles, states the same thing in different terms. Jesus Christ is offered to men as a life, not earthly and perishable, but heavenly, imperishable, and even strictly divine. What Paul expresses in terms of the First and Second (or Last) Adam,[9] John expresses in terms of the Word of God made flesh, source of grace and truth,[10] proceeding, not from the world, not of human origin,[11] but from God, from the Father:[12] truly *from God* and truly *man*. It is on him that we must feed to obtain the life which must be a truly *eternal life*: 'As the living Father sent me, and I live because of the Father, so he who eats me will live because of me.'[13] Compare Paul: 'God . . . by whom you were called into the fellowship (communion) of his Son.'[14]

Hence it is equally true to say that the discourse on the Bread of Life is wholly concerned with the relation of faith, or that it relates to the eucharist, for these two parts are not strictly divided; they are, rather, continuous, the second taking back nothing from the affirmations of the first, but adding something to it in the line of its spiritual realism. One eats the bread of life under two different forms, so intimately connected that the first introduces the second, which assumes and consummates its aim: the perfect 'fellowship of his Son' is fulfilled for us in and by the eucharist.

Tradition, expressing and developing the apostolic testimony, which in essence has been fixed in the New Testament scriptures, lays down in the first place that the means, whatever they may be, are relative to the essential and unique way, the Word, incarnate in Jesus Christ. What supremely concerns the fathers is not the means themselves, whether Scripture or sacraments, but the union with the Word made flesh. In the writings of Ignatius of Antioch there is complete homogeneity and continuity between faith and charity (which are personal, spiritual acts or attitudes), the body and blood of Christ,[15] association with the cross of Christ[16] and Christ himself, in fact, who is perfect faith.[17] From beginning to end what matters is a *real* union with Christ, or with his mystery.[18]

The inscriptions of Abercius (180–200) and Pectorius (second to third century) imply the infinitely rich and simple idea that the believer feeds on the *IXΘΥΣ* himself, who of course is Christ, whom Pectorius also connects with Wisdom.[19] In both cases, it is in and through the eucharist that union with Christ himself is effected. In two fragments of the *Acta Pauli* (end of second century), published by A. Wilmart,[20] the eucharist is conceived as a pledge of the eschatological gift of Christ himself. Later theology retained this meaning of the sacrament. That which not only feeds but refreshes us is nothing less, it says, than the bread of angels, that is, Christ himself, in that his flesh is united to his divinity.[21] Of this bread the angels are the first to partake, and they do so fully, being united to the reality as it is in itself. Men do so in a still imperfect and therefore also unsatisfied manner, which gives them a yearning or aspiration to a more perfect state of communion, clearly eschatological.[22]

In the writings of Origen certain historians, projecting into them their own categories of thought, have lately tried to find something fundamentally anti-sacramental and anti-sacerdotal, but we know what they mean when they are read in their true perspective, which is that of the realism of union with the Word of God. It is that union which interests Origen: the method of it matters little in comparison with its reality. Whether it is by the sacraments or by the word and the Scripture, matters little, but the word has a sort of priority or preference, because it is more spiritual.[23]

Christ is thus considered as universal salvation, universal life. In him exists eternal life. He *is* eternal life, for his part, for all men. But as men are persons, as they cannot be saved unless they do something themselves to obtain life and salvation, they must personally apply this life and salvation to themselves. This they do by the *means* of faith and the sacraments of faith.[24] 'Means' is indeed the right word, for obviously the decisive agent of this application can only be God, and by 'appropriation' the Holy Spirit.

Faith and the sacraments are therefore the means by which every person is united to the reality of salvation and life which is, for every one, Christ. The rôle of faith and the sacraments is to establish a contact with him, and thus to enable him, the universal cause of salvation (especially in virtue of his Pasch), to communicate this salvation to us. Aquinas, with other great schoolmen, expresses this establishing of contact by the words *copulare*, *continuari*, *continuatio*.

Particularly and decisively he attributes this effect of *continuity* to faith.[25] Decisively, because the sacramental elements themselves would have no relation to Jesus Christ, God made man, if they were not related to him by faith. Western tradition is here especially indebted to Augustine, but L. Villette has clearly shown that Augustine's theology is fundamentally the same as that of the Greek fathers. What is the water of baptism, Augustine asks, if we consider it in itself and apart from the word? Water, nothing more. It is necessary, first, for the element to be appointed by an institution of the Lord, and second, for it to receive its present value as a means of salvation by (*a*) the word, which makes that value active, and (*b*) faith, which accepts that word. Whence the famous sayings of Augustine: (*a*) *Accedit verbum ad elementum, et fit sacramentum*; (*b*) *verbum, non quia dicitur, sed quia creditur*. In the sacrament there is wrought a double event, which constitutes, in the heart of the sacramental institution, the sacramental event: the *coming* of the word to the appointed element and that element's actuation by it; and the coming of man, by faith, to the word actuating the sacrament, at the same time as the sacrament gives effect to the word. 'The sacrament is not "the word" on the one hand and "the element" on the other, juxtaposed by a divine decree; it is *the actuation of the one by the other*, in such a way that this actuation entails an effective participation by God himself. It is the word *accedit* which is fundamentally the most important in our definition. . . .'[27]

We can see why the institution is decisive: there would be no sacrament if a bathe or a sprinkling with water or the consumption of the bread and wine were not, through the Lord's institution, part of the structure of his Covenant, that is, of his dwelling with men.[28] But it is equally clear why faith is decisive: without the word and without faith there would be no sacrament either. So Aquinas could write: *cum omnia sacramenta ex fide efficaciam habeant.*[29]

In its original unity, faith, we know, is altogether the act both of man and of God. It is thus that in the spiritual order it can *touch* God. It touches him because it is a movement of men to him, an opening, a gift of ourselves to him, because in it man embraces the mind and will of God: but it can only be that if God creates in us, here and now, the very possibility and the act of going to him, of joining him effectively and touching him.[30] On the basis of this gift, however, faith has chiefly the character of an opening of man to God: it is we who give ourselves to him, so that he may assert himself and reign as God in our life.

The Fathers and the theologians love to speak of this faculty that faith has, to let us *touch* God effectively, to establish a *contact* with the saving power of Christ. This is vividly illustrated in the story of the woman with an issue of blood.[31] A whole crowd is touching Jesus physically, since it is pressing round him, but only one has really touched him, the woman who has approached him, not only by motion but by the faith of her heart. So Augustine comments: *illa tangit, turba premit. Quid est 'tetigit' nisi credidit?*[32] He goes on to show that Christ wills to be touched, not in his mortal flesh, in his earthly, fleshly nature, but in his heavenly reality, in which he is one with his Father, equal to his Father.[33] It is thus that he is truly the object of our *faith*.

This is indeed the sense of John's Gospel, not only in the scene between Jesus and Mary Magdalene in the garden, but in this sixth chapter. All could eat the eucharistic bread materially, but only those who eat it with faith and love touch Jesus and are united to him. John shows in several ways that one can only reach Jesus, as one should, with faith, which exceeds the potentialities of the flesh and requires that we exceed them. It is the Spirit who gives life: the flesh is of no avail.[34] The flesh is concerned only to be refreshed with the multiplied loaves, not to perceive in them a 'sign'.[35] It sees Jesus as the son of Joseph, not as the Son of God;[36] it sees in the eucharist ordinary bread, bread for food, for which the stomach is the sufficient organ,[37] not the bread of the spirit, which is the sacrificed and risen Christ, living, in the presence of his father.[38] That, too, is why in his sixth chapter John shows that Jesus is superior to the conditions of the body or the flesh: the multiplication of the loaves, the refusal of an earthly crown, the walking on the water, the instantaneous crossing of the boat, arriving at once in the harbour. . . .[39]

The contact established by living faith is fundamental, indispensable. Not only has it its own efficacy, but this efficacy is a condition of that of the sacraments, to which, as we have seen, faith is truly integral. With a prophetic instinct of this truth, tradition has inserted, in the very words of the consecration of the chalice, as reported for us by the apostles, the words *mysterium fidei*, just as the Latin liturgy, at the moment when the true Body of Christ is about to be given to the faithful, repeats the prayer of the centurion, 'I am not worthy that thou shouldst come under my roof, but speak only a word and my soul shall be healed.' Yet the contact in and through the sacrament—penetrated by faith—adds to the contact effected by faith. That is what we must now try to understand.

Living faith, and whatever flows from it in our lives, is a movement of ours to God, though this movement, like all others but in a very special way, can take place only on the basis and in the power of an initiative of God in us. Living faith, our movement to God, has God for object and end: God, and Jesus Christ whom he has sent.[40] It carries us to them and establishes with them that contact which is part of the fact that they have effectively become our end. The union established between Christ and us by faith depends on the fact that he has become the end of our life. It may be called, in this sense, 'intentional'.

But the Lord has willed and founded another mode of contact, on the basis of another way in which he comes to us. For he has not remained simply 'word' for us. He has become flesh, he has lived, talked and worked among us.[41] During his earthly presence among us Jesus communicated salvation (or at least bodily health, prophetic image of total salvation) by the bodily touch of his person. Examples are legion. One could compose a list by consulting a Latin concordance on the verb *tangere*, or a Greek concordance on ἅπτω. We need not go to this trouble, but we shall recall certain passages, for that is necessary if we are to perceive the truth and solid foundation of the fact in question. In eighteen out of twenty-eight stories of cures recorded in the gospel, it is stated that Jesus *touched* the sick[42] or laid hands on them.[43] In several cases where this is not explicitly stated it can reasonably be presumed, as in the case of the ruler Jairus, who said: 'Lord, my daughter has just died, but come and lay your hand on her and she will live.'[44] Even before Jesus had approached the body of the little girl, a woman who had suffered from hæmorrhage for twelve years drew near and *touched* the fringe of his robe.[45] Jesus had cured so many that all who suffered from diseases crowded to him to touch him;[46] 'and all the crowd sought to touch him, for power came forth from him and healed them all'.[47]

The hands of Jesus! The laying on, the touching of the hands of Jesus! Already in the Old Testament the hand signified in man, and by analogy in God, the organ of action and strength, of possession and defence, of blessing and the transmission of a power.[48] It is the embodiment of power. The hand of God, which in the Old Testament was so often heavy with punishment, in Jesus Christ is the organ of his mercy and saving power: it is the very dwelling-place of his grace, in his son made flesh, terminating, as it were in fingers, in the mission and gift of the Holy Spirit, *Digitus Dei*.[49]

In the gospels, this bodily touch of Jesus requires, for its healing effect, faith and its spiritual touch. But wherever faith effects a movement of man towards God, the bodily touch of Jesus effects a descent of power, a communication of energy, from him to us.[50] It is a fact, a truth of sacred history of *Heilsgeschichte*: God has willed this way, this structure of his action.

We see it again in an event of that history of salvation, which seems to me of very great importance for the theology of that history itself; I mean the descent of Christ into hell.[51] The just who died before the coming of Christ had, implicitly or explicitly, faith and charity; they thus fulfilled the conditions which on man's side enabled spiritual contact to be established with Christ in his Pasch, that is, with the source of salvation.[52] But it was necessary for Christ to touch them, so that they might effectively receive the reward of their justice, namely, the vision of God.

This world of action through bodily touch is that of the sacraments. These continue, on their own level, the contact with the body of Christ, as it is, the source of salvation for us through his Pasch. That is why John shows us the water and the blood— baptism and the eucharist, or perhaps the Spirit and baptism, which represents all the sacraments, as in the Nicene Creed— flowing from the side of the dying Christ. 'The sacraments of the Church draw their virtue specially from the Passion of Christ: it is the reception of the sacraments which puts us in communication with the virtue of Christ's Passion. The water and blood, flowing from the side of Christ on the cross symbolise this truth, the water referring to baptism and the blood to the eucharist, for these are the most important sacraments.'[53] It is undeniable that this symbolism is in fact sacramental in John, and that it marks the continuity of the sacraments with the incarnation of the Word.[54] Many commentators have expressed the idea that the sacraments play a part in the era of the Church analogous to that played by the miracles in the time of Christ. That is true, but it would perhaps be better to say that the sacraments continue to fulfil a rôle, after the departure of the glorified Christ, analogous to that played in the days of his flesh by bodily contact with him, through which full effect was given to the saving word he proclaimed. The sacraments are a continuation, a supplement, of the presence of the *incarnate* Word and of the rôle of his body in the work of salvation. That is why, as Schillebeeckx acutely remarks, Paul, the thirteenth apostle, had to be baptised,[55] while the twelve, who had enjoyed contact with Jesus in his ministry,[56] had not.[57]

Aquinas well defines the respective natures of the spiritual contact of faith and the spiritual-bodily contact of the sacrament when he writes that the *continuatio* brought about by faith is effected *per actum animae*, whereas the other is effected *per usum exteriorum rerum*.[58] Of course, if these 'outward things' were determined only by men, they would be conditioned by the faith they express, which we have described as 'intentional'. But if these 'outward things' have been determined by Christ, whether formally and unquestionably,—the water of baptism, the bread and wine of the Eucharist—or more or less indirectly or implicitly, by saying or doing something which in some way implies them—as is the case with penance and marriage—their value is something more than that of signs of *our* movement to God; they belong to the order of God's movement to us, to bring about our salvation, that order of condescension by which he has truly come, come down in our flesh (Christmas, the beginning of God's *kenosis*!),[59] the order of the incarnation: not only because they are palpable realities, but because these realities *convey an action of God*, effecting the New Covenant in Jesus Christ.

Thus we must regard the sacraments, when they are now administered by men, as the place where the movement of men to God meets the movement of God to man. The movement of men, which is indispensable, is taken up by God, who consummates it. The faith of the catechumen, which he professes, is consummated in the sacrament which really makes him πιστός, *fidelis*: the Fathers often described that growth of faith, called to be consummated in the bodily act in which it is expressed and in which God perfects it.[60] The movement of penitence or conversion on the sinner's part, submitted to the power of the keys, and flowing out in the sacrament of penance, there meets the gracious act of God, which completes it and gives it its fruit. The consecration of himself to the ministry which a man makes on the basis of a preceding call, and which already has a rich moral and spiritual reality in him, is taken up by an act of God, which truly *ordains* him. The love of a man and a woman, which leads them to be joined to each other for life, is taken up and sanctified by an act of God, who enters as a third party into their contract of mutual love. The puny offering of bread and wine, which the Christian and the Church bring before God as the sign of their offering, is taken up, sanctified, changed into the perfect sacrifice of Jesus Christ himself, in the eucharist. Thus, from beginning to end, man's movement to God, entering into the structures of the Covenant which flow from the incarnation, and using sacramental things, is consecrated by a coming or action of God himself. Whenever, reaching out to God through the sacrificed and living

Christ, as the chief end of my life, I mould and express that movement in a sign, expressing and commemorating that paschal mystery of Christ, I set in action not only the order of finality, of my 'intention' to God, but the order of effectiveness flowing from the incarnation, which distributes its health-giving fruits in the structures of the Covenant.

There is a well-known saying of F. C. Oetinger, *Leiblichkeit ist das Ende der Wege Gottes*: 'corporeity is the end of God's ways'. Oetinger is not the source of the saying: he would be a doubtful source, for he has mingled a certain dose of theosophy and his personal views with revealed Christian truth. But we should like to point out how this structure, in which the spiritual is joined to the bodily and perfects its movement, is in conformity with the biblical sense of what we call bodily and spiritual. We know that the bible does not contrast body and soul as two independent realities, but sees the body as the actual reality of the person, manifesting itself and making itself active.[61] Man achieves his activities in bodily life and expression. 'For every idea and every ideal the Israelite demands a visible and perceptible incarnation, and favourable results: he is unwilling to recognise an ideal which has not the strength to conquer reality and to take bodily form in it.'[62] You will find no theology in the bible without an anthropology and a cosmology. Biblical faith quite naturally takes bodily form in an action; the man who believes is baptised. . . .

Thus the sacrament adds to the movement of faith, though it is only owing to faith that it exists. We may say that the sacraments have efficacy only through faith, but we must not say that they have no efficacy except that of faith. Faith is indispensable if the sacrament's value as a channel of grace, which it derives from the divine institution, is to be realised in action, but God's action does not pass through faith alone; it is effectively exerted through the sacrament itself.

The Protestant reformers have tended to reduce all the means of saving action to the word. Treating of the means of grace, H. Strohl recently wrote: 'The Reformers basically admitted only one; the word.'[63] They certainly make frequent mention of the sacraments, and even include them in the definition or description of the true Church: *Ut hanc fidem consequamur, institutum est ministerium docendi evangelii et porrigendi sacramenta. Nam per verbum et sacramenta tanquam per instrumenta donatur Spiritus Sanctus. . . .*[64] *Est ecclesia congregatio sanctorum in qua evangelium pure docetur et recte administrantur sacramenta.*[65]

These two things are constantly noted as the outward elements by which God wills to gather to himself a people.[66] One could fill several long pages with passages of this sort. Accordingly, contemporary Protestant theologians who wish, out of loyalty to the scriptures, to give the sacraments their true value, have no difficulty in quoting texts from the reformers and the confessions of faith or credal documents.[67]

And yet, precisely in the interests of such an endeavour, we must pursue the enquiry further. For we also find texts which create difficulty. Perhaps they can be clearly explained, or perhaps they have simply been misunderstood: we must see how it is.

We often find in Luther that he reduces the ways of God's grace to the word: *solum verbum est vehiculum gratiae.*[68] The Church is constituted by the word, it is the word that does all.[69] Therefore the ministry, or what we should call the priesthood, is defined only by reference to the word. As early as 1512, in the first sermon of Luther's we possess, he explained that preaching is the most characteristic activity of the priesthood and that neglect of it is the only sin which is peculiar to the priest and causes him to sin as a priest.[70] He expounded the same idea, more systematically, in *De Captivitate Babylonica.*[71] And one must, of course, make allowance for a reaction against a situation in which the 'thing' aspect of religious practices, even the sacraments, had developed to excess. The reformers reacted against the idea that the sacraments worked by themselves and that the movement of faith could almost be dispensed with.[72] But has the reaction not gone too far?

We find, too, that they constantly and deliberately assimilate the sacraments of the New Testament to those of the Old, because they think that, like the latter, they are purely signs, to which is added, in the New Testament, connection with a promise of God, confirmed by the sacramental signs.[73] In the sacraments themselves the reformers insist so strongly on the word and on faith that the latter is, *in the sacrament itself*, the sole principle in the communication of grace.[74]

Once again, we have here a theme of Augustinian and even Thomist theology pushed to extremes, in reaction against a possible reliance on things (*chosisme*) or a possible distortion in the direction of magic, dangers which are attributed, quite wrongly, to Catholic doctrine[75] or to the Thomist theology[76] of the sacraments, more especially to the *ex opere operato*. This regrettable error has persisted to this day in the minds of good Protestant theologians, to say nothing of the average Huguenot.[77]

Incidentally, it is this same Augustinian theology of necessary faith which, applied univocally, seems to be the real ground of the Calvinist idea of the eucharistic presence: does not this theology confuse the conditions of the sacramental presence with the conditions of spiritual reception? Luther, for his part, distinguished the two: he admitted that even the wicked eat the body of Christ sacramentally.[78]

On the other hand, both Luther and Calvin, with the reformed theology, reduce everything that happens, even in the sacraments, to the word. The sacrament is defined as 'added to this (word) as an appendage ordained to signify, confirm and even more strongly certify it to us'.[79] Its value and rôle are in the order of testimony, of knowledge: it is 'a revealing addition'.[80] In Calvin's commentary on John 20:23, the mission of remitting sins is entirely confined to the preaching of the gospel of reconciliation.[81] Farel, the French Swiss reformer, wrote: 'All is but poison save the heavenly bread which is the word of God.'[82]

When we turn to contemporary Protestant theologians, we find the same doctrine. According to A. Lecef, the sacraments are a *verbum visibile*, a word of God expressed in symbolic actions: their only value for salvation is as seals and pledges of the blessing of Christ and the operation of the Holy Spirit, promised to those who add faith to the promise.[83] The same idea is found in T. F. Torrance,[84] and of course in Karl Barth.[85] The latter's son, Markus Barth, has pushed to extremes something which with Calvin and his followers was a tendency, somewhat tempered by acceptance of the traditional sacramental *fact*. To Markus Barth, baptism is not a sacrament, that is, a symbolic rite which brings something about. It is a mere action by which a man expresses his faith, his obedience, his prayer, in expectation of a purification, a sanctification, which is wrought by God alone.[86] Never before

had anyone pressed so far the idea of a mere sign, a mere an-
nouncement of the wholly inner reality which, on man's part, is
his faith and, on God's part, the coming of the gift of the Spirit.
Everything is reduced to the faith-word relation: God's action
has no other method; the 'sacrament' exists only in the noetic
order, it is only an expressive sign, conveying nothing of its own
in the order of effect. We should add that the exegetes have
emphasised the arbitrary and unsound elements in Markus
Barth's treatment of the biblical texts.[87] A recent monograph by
H. Mentz on the connection between the Church and baptism
fully admits, against Markus Barth, the sacramental character of
baptism, but in the Calvinist line, reducing it to a *Verkundigungs-
form*,[88] just as the baptism of our Lord is represented as an
Offenbarungsakt.[89]

This radicalism has at least the advantage of bringing us to the
heart of the problem, which we can state as follows: in the relation
of union with God as constituted by the new and eternal Covenant, does the use of a bodily element, directly or indirectly
instituted by Jesus Christ, convey something of its own, in addition to what is effected by the presence of the word of God, and
of the faith which responds to it on our side? To this question the
Catholic tradition of east and west answers in the affirmative, it
being always understood (though it is sometimes in danger of
being forgotten) that the presence of the word and of faith is
absolutely fundamental, and forms part of the reality of the
sacrament as such.

Some contemporary Protestant theologians give an equally
affirmative reply, whether imprecisely (from a certain feeling for
reality, rather than a really elaborated theological analysis)[90] or
lucidly and formally, as with H. Asmussen,[91] Leslie Newbigin,[92]
and F. J. Leenhardt.[93]

This 'something in addition', added to the spiritual act of faith
by the use of an outward element ordained by Christ, was precisely what the Council of Trent meant by *ex opere operato*. The
Council wished to reject the error of holding that grace is given
through faith alone and regarding the sacraments only as signs,
occasional or concomitant, with no efficacy. Peter Bertano, Bishop
of Fano, had wished to keep the original version proposed: *per
ipsa sacramentorum opera*, because these were Luther's own

words.[94] The Canon as finally adopted substituted for these words *ex ipso opere operato*, now classic in theology.[95] The purport of this expression is not at all to assert a work of *man*, still less an intrinsic capacity of any element, even blessed or consecrated, to convey a divine energy (= magic). It is to assert that the celebration of the sacraments brings something to the work of grace which the act of faith alone does not bring: and this is *because* the sacrament belongs to the structures of the Covenant, to which God has freely and graciously bound himself.[96]

There are thus two modes by which men have access to the Kingdom of Christ our glorious Saviour. To make the sacramental mode a mere appendage to the 'intentional' mode of faith, even with the proviso that, being also willed by God, it commands our loyalty, is in my opinion to assimilate the conditions of the New Covenant to those of the Old. For the whole movement of the biblical revelation is one which advances from signs to reality, from the God who speaks by the prophets to the God who comes and gives himself.[97] It is in full conformity with the first verses of the Epistle to the Hebrews that the fathers understand in this sense the text of Isaiah[98] in the Vulgate translation: *Ego qui loquebar, ecce adsum.*[99] To assimilate the sacraments of the New Testament to mere signs of attestation like those of the Old Testament —the rainbow, circumcision, even the Passover[100]—is to be blind to the fullness and originality of the gift God made us when he took flesh in Jesus Christ. In him, the Word was made, not simply word, but flesh.[101] God has come and given himself in an original manner, which is precisely the incarnation.

The consequences and applications of all this theology are considerable and many-sided. They chiefly concern ecclesiology, and the doctrine of the ministry.

Ecclesiology: is the Church simply the assembly of disciples or believers, *congregatio fidelium*, or is she the Body of Christ in a real sense (not physico-natural, of course), a sense indicated when we use the adjective 'mystical'? *Congregatio fidelium*, the 'People of God', adequately describes the Church of the Old Testament. 'Body of Christ', in the real sense referred to, can apply only to the Church of the incarnate Word, really communicating eternal life (albeit in a pledge) to the faithful who have become his members. The Church accomplishes her integral mystery in three successive stages, the first two of which are historical and earthly, and coexist now in her.[102] She is first of all a community of disciples, the Church of John the Baptist, the Church of the catechumens. Next, she is a sacramental community, feeding on the body and blood of Christ, called to be a communion of glory, that is, of the perfect, dazzling presence of God, who sacramental in all.[103] To fail to recognise the full reality of the shall be all communion is to remain, from the point of view of ecclesiological ideas, at the stage of the Old Testament or of John the Baptist.[104]

This Church, a sacramental community, is herself sacramental. She is built up, indeed, by the word, but over and above the word, presuming and including it, as we have seen with the sacraments, she is built up by the action of the sacramental powers of the ministry, received from Christ.

From these positions a certain concept of the priesthood necessarily follows. We have briefly seen[105] how the Reformers thought of ordination as essentially a vocation, and the ordained ministers as essentially ministers of the word.[106] Against this misunderstanding of tradition the Council of Trent made this definition:

> If anyone says that there is not, in the New Testament, a visible and external priesthood, or that there is no power of consecrating and offering the true body and blood of the Lord, and of remitting or retaining sins, but only a function and a bare ministry of preaching the Gospel, or that those who do not preach are in no wise priests, let him be anathema.[107]

Catholicism is not anti-Protestantism, nor is it what remains of Christianity when Protestants have separated from it whatever they can claim for themselves. It would not be difficult to collect Catholic testimonies from after the Council of Trent which preserve all the wealth of the gospel and tradition on the idea of the priesthood. Bossuet, for example: 'What is order? It is a sacrament instituted by Jesus Christ to give the Church preachers of the word and ministers of his sacraments.'[108] We must admit, however, that there has often been a tendency among us to be rather blind to the inclusion of faith in the sacrament, or to the nature of what Aquinas calls, with significant emphasis, 'the sacraments *of faith*', with the result that we have not sufficiently

emphasised that the function of the word is *interior* to the priesthood, if we mean the priesthood of the New Testament, of the
Gospel. It has too often been regarded as belonging to the priest
in virtue of his authority, but as something added to the function
which alone seemed to define his priesthood, namely, the sacramental function, directed to the sacramental offering of the sacrifice of Jesus Christ. Now the sacrifice itself ought to be seen as
a sacrifice of *faith*, proceeding essentially from the obedience of
faith.[109] And for this there is no need to look outside Tradition,
but rather to return to it, for it is full of the most formal testimonies, governed from the start by a very definite biblical
groundwork. Many recent studies, both theological and biblical,
have helped us to realise afresh the fullness of the values pertain-
ing to the priesthood in its gospel reality.[110] Obviously we cannot
here launch into an exposition which, to be both balanced and
supported, would have to be developed at length.[111] A full restoration, in sacramental theology, of the rôle of faith[112] and, in the
theology of the priesthood, of the function of the word, would
have very considerable pastoral consequences.

We may expect the theology of the missions to be equally
concerned, especially as regards the laity. Lay people can both
start the Church and maintain her, in so far as she is an assembly
of the faithful, *congregatio fidelium*, for that is within the terms of
their testimony as disciples. But they cannot perfect the Church
in her character as the body of Christ, which can only be consummated by real communion in the body of Christ, and therefore requires the public priesthood, to whom it pertains, in the
line of the apostles and the ministers instituted by them, to celebrate the eucharist. Only the priesthood of the sacrament of order
can feed the people of God, under the dispensation of the new
and eternal Covenant, with the fullness of the bread of life as it
has been given us in Jesus Christ, according to the twofold truth
of the word and the body.

We should like to complete this all too sketchy study by quoting
some testimonies from tradition, which clearly illustrate one or
more aspects of the two forms of the bread of life. It is, of course,
only a selection of examples, to which fresh texts could be added
indefinitely. As such, however, it will serve to mark the links
between the biblical theme, the chapter of sacramental theology

E

and the idea of the Church's ministry which we have sketched in the preceding pages.

The earliest evidences of tradition combine the statements of duality with the affirmation of unity so closely together that they are somewhat obscure. About 107, Ignatius of Antioch writes to the Trallians: 'Refresh yourselves in the faith, which is the flesh of the Lord, and in charity, which is the blood of Jesus Christ.'[113] The spiritual means of faith and the bodily means of the sacrament are here united and as it were mingled, in the same realism of union with Jesus Christ. In fact the eucharistic allusion seems unmistakable,[114] but the spiritual disposition which is completely expressed in the sacrament and is its fruit, is so interior to that sacrament that it is represented as if it were the same thing.

It is with a similar sense of the connection between the two that faith and baptism, in Tertullian, in Augustine and right into the Middle Ages, are often taken for each other.[115] Faith and baptism are two distinct realities, but they are so connected that one (baptism) is, so to speak, the body of the other, or its consummation. Faith is not baptism; it is not the eucharist, but they are as it were its clothing and its consummation. This was surely what Abercius of Hierapolis meant, about 200 or a little earlier, when he had these words engraved for his epitaph:

> I had Paul for my companion,
> Faith led me everywhere,
> and everywhere served me for food a Fish from the spring,
> Very great, pure, caught by a Virgin;
> Faith ceased not to give it to her friends to eat.
> She has a delectable wine: she gives it with bread.[116]

This text, too, which no one with any knowledge of Christianity can deny to be Christian, well expresses the duality of the communications and the unity of what is given. Faith gives for food the fish (*ichthus*), that is, Jesus Christ, son of God, saviour. She gives it first by herself, drawing on scripture and especially on Paul. She gives it a second time, in the bread and wine. But it is the same food, the same divine fish.

This is a common idea in early Christianity. In Origen, the first great systematic genius, it took a systematised form, in his wide view of the comings or incorporations of God the Word. He came,

and he can be found, in the world, as the creative Word and
wisdom, immanent in things. He came, he comes, he is heard in
the spoken word and the scriptures. He comes, and we can feed
on him, in the eucharist.[117] That is why Origen begins the series
of texts connecting the eucharist and scripture with the use the
faithful ought to make of them and the reverence they ought to
show them: 'You know, you who are accustomed to assist at the
divine mysteries, with what religious care, when you receive the
Lord's body, you watch to see that not the smallest particle may
fall. . . . You would feel guilty, and rightly so, if that were to
happen by your neglect. Then, . . . how should it be a less grave
fault to neglect the word of God than to neglect his body?'[118]

From the days of the apostles, the Sunday assembly comprised
a first part, consisting of readings from the holy writings and of
teaching, and a second part, the sacramental celebration of the
eucharist. This structure, attested by Justin,[119] is still that of our
Mass. From beginning to end of it we receive the gifts of God in
order to praise him, *de tuis donis ac datis*. We praise the Father,
in the Holy Spirit, through the Son, who has been given to us
both as the word in the scriptures—from which the liturgy is
born and of which it is woven—and as the incarnate Word, in the
sacrament of the bread and the wine, which he has given us to
offer in his train.

The two comings of the Word are beautifully expressed in the
eastern liturgy, in the two 'entries'. The Little Entry is the climax
of the liturgy of the catechumens: the deacon comes into the
church, carrying the gospel-book. This is the coming of Christ as
wisdom. The Great Entry opens the liturgy of the faithful, in an
atmosphere of intense recollection. The priest enters the church,
carrying the oblations, to the chant of the Cherubikon, expressing
the unity of the earthly celebration with the heavenly. It is the
coming of Christ in his flesh, called to be sacrificed and glorified.

This union of the word and the sacrament, of the enlightening
of minds and the transforming action of Christ in the very core
of our lives, is not only written into the structure of the liturgy:
it is the law of the whole liturgy, as A. Chavasse has so clearly
shown.[120] In every liturgical celebration, Christ is made present to
us as the utterance of God and as the inner principle of the transformation of our hearts. The whole liturgical cycle is full of the

same truths; it is inseparably biblical and sacramental, an almost mimed reproduction of the history of salvation and an unveiling of its mysteries, the fruits of which are communicated to us by Christ himself. 'Patristic and theological tradition does not regard evangelisation and sacramental action as two successive stages in the Church's apostolic action, but as two simultaneous components, complementary and inseparable from the action of God and the Church in the conversion of men.'[121]

This sort of double polarity of an action which is basically one has also been evident on the plane of the liturgical celebration, ever since Christians have been able to arrange their churches. These were designed as the place of assembly of the *ecclesia*, grouped round the bishop's throne (raised up in the apse), and the altar, erected somewhat lower, in the heart of the sacred area.[122] From his *cathedra* the bishop distributed the bread of the word: from the altar, the bread of the eucharistic sacrament. And since Christ is the supreme bishop,[123] it was only natural that he should be depicted in the apse of the church, himself presiding over the twofold but single celebration, and then in the ninth century, in the illuminated gospel books, in glory, holding in one hand a book and in the other a host.[124]

Such were, and always have been, the two great acts of the ministry. A whole catena of texts speaks of them in combination.

We have Hilary, speaking of the *mensa Domini*, where the faithful receive the bread of life, and the *mensa lectionum domincarum*, where they are given the teaching which will help them to receive worthily the divine food.[125] Primitive Christianity and the Fathers attached the greatest importance to the knowledge of God. In the midst of a world still full of paganism, faced with a culture and a philosophy all but pagan, it seemed to them that this knowledge, communicated by the Holy Scriptures and supremely by Jesus Christ, was a benefit as inestimable as it was new. To receive into oneself the *doctrina spiritualis* was to be nourished with the bread which is Jesus Christ. So says Ambrose, quoting a eucharistic text of Paul, and so continuing the series of passages in the style of Origen, which seem to 'spiritualise' the sacrament.[126] Jerome says the same, in almost identical terms.[127] He adds that since the flesh of the Lord is the true food and his blood the true drink, we can transpose this statement and say that on earth we have this boon only if we eat his flesh and drink his blood, not only in the sacrament but in the reading of the scriptures.[128] To be ignorant of the scriptures is to be ignorant of Jesus Christ.[129] So we see again that always, through one or other of the two forms of the bread of life, it is union *with Jesus Christ himself* that really matters.

It was obviously natural to connect teaching with nourishment. This is a *topos* no doubt universally received, and in any case often invoked in the scriptures, where the themes of hunger, eating, nourishment, are often applied to the word.[130] The Fathers and the ancient authors made frequent use of this *topos*, citing the manna, or the feeding of the five thousand,[131] or the profoundly moving episode of Emmaus, when Christ expounded the scriptures and broke the bread. At bottom, it was the same thing, for 'breaking' is opening, revealing, explaining the mystery. . . .[132]

To Augustine too, without doubt, the word of God was the bread of souls.[133] But it is not so by itself: we are spiritually born, born in the Holy Spirit, by the word and by the sacrament.[134] Moreover, Augustine defines the object of the priestly ministry, and of the episcopal ministry in the first place, by the twofold service of the word and the sacraments.[135] The idea is evidently not peculiar to him: it may be considered traditional, but he has given it his personal stamp.

St Caesarius of Arles is as pastoral as Augustine, but in a more moralising line. In a sermon handed down under the name of Augustine, included in many canonical collections, and therefore made part of the training of the clergy throughout the Middle Ages, St Caesarius developed the idea that the word of Christ, being invested with the same dignity as the body of Christ, ought to be the object of the same reverence: to let a crumb of it be lost is as bad as to let a particle of the host fall to the ground.[136]

The pastoral and spiritual tradition is firmly rooted. Bede writes that the Christians have not only the eucharist for food, but also the books of the New Testament, warmed by the flame of the Holy Spirit, to nourish their priestly souls, which are united to the members of the eternal priest.[137] The faithful look to the Church for the Mass and for preaching, according to Theodulph of Orleans,[138] or Florus of Lyons, who writes: *Quicumque societatem cum Deo habere desiderant, primo Ecclesiae socie-*

tati debent adunari, illamque fidem addiscere et ejus sacramentis imbui, quam apostoli ab ipsa praesente in carne Veritate perceperunt.[139] We have the same idea in that very interesting Council held at Arras in 1025: *Cur conveniat populus ad ecclesiam: unum ex antiqua traditione ut judicia rerum et cognitiones accipiat; alterum ex novo testamento, ut manducet corpus Christi. Utraque enim quaerimus ad ecclesiam, scilicet ut in ea audiamus judicia nostra mala, sive bona, et cognitionem Dei, et ut manducemus corpus Christi.*[140]

We can follow the series of similar testimonies further still. There is Peter Damian (*Habet Christus ministros verbi, habet ministros nihilominus sacramenti*),[141] and Bernard.[142] That brings us to the twelfth century when, largely owing to Hugh of St Victor, 'Faith and the sacraments of faith' became the actual title of the content of theology and the priest's field of action.[143] When Innocent III reconciled a group of 'Humiliati' in Lombardy in 1201, he gave them license to preach, on condition that they did not treat *de articulis fidei et ecclesiae sacramentis.*[144] Francis of Assisi, who has his own unique place in the history of movements of poverty, often mentions and combines, in his short works and letters, the eucharist and the scriptures, the letter of which was for him a sort of sacrament of the presence of Christ.

In the thirteenth century there are many texts which attribute to the priests, at least to those with a cure of souls, the double ministry of the word and the sacraments.[145] About 1253, Henry of Segusa (Hostiensis) gave this definition of the parish church: *in qua dantes (decimas) divina audiunt et recipiunt sacramenta.*[146]

In this sort of classic definition of the ministry by the service of the word and the celebration of the sacraments, it was also quite traditional, with reference to Matthew 28:19, to emphasise that the duty of preaching was prior to that of giving the sacraments. This had been the teaching of Tertullian,[147] Athanasius,[148] Jerome[149] and Augustine.[150] Thus spake in their turn the churchmen of the Carolingian era, then Rabanus Maurus, whose texts were reproduced by the twelfth-century canonists.[151] Thus again Aquinas: *Salvator noster discipulos ad praedicandum mittens, tria eis injunxit. Primo quidem ut docerent fidem; secundo, ut credentes imbuerent sacramentis. . . .*[152]

Aquinas could not be satisfied with reproducing a traditional statement on the object of the priestly ministry:[153] he had to give it a formal value in his system of thought, the fruit of a powerfully synthetic mind. To Aquinas, who is here the heir of Hugh of St Victor, the whole subject-matter of theology can be summed up as *fides et fidei sacramenta*.[154] These two realities in conjunction constitute the foundation of the Church, that on which and with which the Church is constructed.[155] That, in the first place, is what Christ has done for her.[156] It was in view of these two activities of his ministry that he was anointed with the Holy Spirit and that the same spirit was sent down upon his apostles after him.[157] The apostles planted the Church *per modum doctrinae et administrationis sacramentorum*.[158] These are the two means through which the salvation won for us in the passion of Christ is conveyed to us.[159] The two are analogous in structure and belong to that field of signs which corresponds to the structure of man—a mind bound to the world of sense, and to whom a certain use of the world of sense, beyond the purely physical aspect, restores the possibility of accomplishing his metaphysical vocation.[160]

Aquinas quotes these classical statements and adds to them a reflection of his own, depending rather on his Aristotelian sources and a philosophy of causality. The word, or teaching (*doctrina*) on the one hand, and the effective aid given by the sacrament on the other, correspond to the two modes by which one man can act on another, *per modum operationis, per modum doctrinae*.[161] In the writings of Aquinas there is a general scheme, founded on a philosophical interpretation of things, which adds, to the traditional teaching expounded in the preceding pages, a value of correspondence with a certain structure of things. The two forms of the Bread of Life have a certain connection with the two lines of causality which appear in the world as a whole.

It is not so much this philosophical aspect of the question as its moral or 'spiritual' aspect that we next find developed, for the use of the clergy or religious persons.[162] Rudolph of Biberach, a Franciscan, alluded to the theme of the two tables, of scripture and of the eucharist, at the beginning of the fourteenth century.[163] But it is to Thomas à Kempis and his immortal work that the theme owes its widest diffusion:

Now I see in this life two things to be chiefly necessary for me, without which this miserable life would be unbearable to me. Whilst I am kept in the prison of this body, I acknowledge myself to be in need of two things, to wit, food and light. Therefore hast thou given me in my weakness thy sacred body for the refreshment of my soul and body; and thou hast set thy word as a lamp to my feet. Without these two I could not well live; for the word of God is the light of my soul, and thy sacrament the bread of life. These also may be called the two tables, set on either side in the store-house of the Church. The one is the table of the holy altar which hath the holy bread, that is, the precious body of Christ: the other is that of the divine law, containing holy doctrine, teaching the right faith, and leading securely even within the veil, wherein is the holy of holies.[164]

M. Olier made only some brief allusions to the scripture-eucharist theme, especially in his chapter on the Order of Lectors, where he quotes (under the name of Augustine) the text we have already quoted from Caesarius of Arles.[165] But some twelve years earlier, Bossuet had given to the Carmelite nuns, in the presence of the queen, that wonderful sermon of 13th March 1661, the memory of which will serve to conclude this enquiry.[166] One must seek in the pulpit, he says, the truth of the word, as one seeks at the altar the truth of the body of Christ. The priest himself must enter the pulpit to celebrate the mystery of the word, in the same dispositions as those in which he approaches the altar to celebrate the mystery of the body—a theme which was to be resumed by Lacordaire (another Burgundian!) and a past master of the word.[167] Just as the eucharist is for the heart, not the mouth, so the word must go by the ear to the heart: it must be attended to by the heart. And here is a final connection 'between sacred doctrine and the eucharist. The eucharist comes to men to discern between consciences with the authority and the eye of a judge:[168] some it crowns, others it condemns. So the divine word, that bread of the ears, that spiritual body of the truth, judges those who are not touched by it;[169] whom it does not convert, it condemns; whom it does not nourish, it kills.'[170]

NOTES

1. Article published in *Parole de Dieu et Sacerdoce, études présentées à Mgr Weber, Archev.-év. de Strasbourg*, 1962, pp. 21-58.
2. Besides the commentaries: F. Cavallera, 'L'interprétation du chap. 6 de S. Jean. Une controverse exégétique an Concile de Trente', in *Revue Hist. eccl.*, 10 (1909), pp. 687-709; T. Philips, *Die Verheissung der hl. Eucharistie nach Johannes*, Paderborn, 1922; E. Janot, 'Le pain de vie', in *Gregorianum*, 11 (1930), pp. 161-70; W. Goossens, *Les origines de l'Eucharistie, sacrement et sacrifice*, Paris-Gembloux, 1931; P. Gaechter, 'Der Form des eucharistischen Rede Jesu' in *ZKT*, 1935, pp. 419-41; J. Schneider, 'Zur Frage der Komposition von Joh., VI, 27-58(59)', in *In Memoriam Ernst Lohmeyer*, Stuttgart, 1931, pp. 132-42; O. Cullmann, *Les sacrements dans l'évangile johannique*, Paris, 1951; J. Jeremias, 'Jo. 6, 51 c-58 redaktionell?' in *Zeitschrift f. Ntl. Wiss.*, 1952-3, pp. 358-63; G. Bornkamm, 'Die eucharistische Rede in Johannesevangelium', *ibid.*, 1956, pp. 161-9; J. Leal, 'La promesa y la institucion de la Eucaristia. Sus coincidencias de forma y fundo', in *XII Sem. Bibl. Espan.*, Madrid, 1953, pp. 339-58; E. Ruckstuhl, 'Wesen und Kraft der Eucharistie in der Sicht des Johannes-Evangeliums', in *Das Opfer der Kirche*, Lucerne, 1954, pp. 47-90; E. J. Siedlecki, *A Patristic Synthesis of John VI, 54-55*, Mundelein, 1956; D. Mollat, 'Le chap. VI de S. Jean', in *Lumière et Vie*, no. 38 (1957), pp. 107-19. W. Wilkens, 'Das Abendmahlzeugnis im vierten Evangelium' in *Evangel. Theol.*, 18 (1958), pp. 354-70; H. Schürmann, 'Joh. 6, 51 c, ein Schlüssel zur johanneischen Brotrede', in *Bibl. Zeitsch.*, N.F. 2 (1958), pp. 254-62; X. Léon-Dufour, 'Le mystère du pain de vie', in *Rech. S.R.*, 1958, pp. 481-523; F. J. Leenhardt, 'La structure du chap. 6 de l'Évangile de Jean', in *RHPR*, 1959, pp. 1-13; H. Schürmann, 'Die Eucharistie als Repräsentation und Applikation des Heilsgeschehens nach Joh. 6, 53-58' in *Trierer Theol. Zeitsch.*, 18 (1959), pp. 30-45 and 108-18; R. Schnackenburg, 'Herrenmahl und Lebensbrot' in *Amt und Sendung*, Freiburg, 1950, pp. 300-12; *Idem*, 'Die Sakramente im Johannes-evangelium', in *Sacra Pagina, Miscellanea Biblica Congressus intern. cath. de re biblica*, Paris, 1959, vol. II, pp. 235-45; B. Gärtner, *John 6 and the Jewish Passover: Coniectanea Neotestamentica*, XVII, Lund-Copenhagen, 1959; A. Feuillet, 'Les thèmes bibliques majeurs du discours sur le pain de vie (Jo. 6)' in *NRT*, 82 (1960), pp. 803-22, 918-39, 1040-62. Many of the preceding references are due to this study (p. 803).
3. Among modern or contemporary authors, F. Godet, B. Weiss, K. Bornhaüser, H. Odeberg, A. Schlatter and H. Strathmann.
4. Here are some characteristic passages from Augustine's commentary: *Ut quid paras dentes et ventrem? Crede, et manducasti*; this refers to the spiritual eating of the flesh and blood, even in the sacrament (*In Ev. Joann.*, tr. XXV, 12; *PL*, 35, 1602); Moses, Aaron and others, *qui Domino placuerunt*, (ate the manna) *et mortui non sunt. Quare? Quia visibilem cibum spiritualiter intellexerunt, spiritualiter esurierunt, spiritualiter gustaverunt, ut spiritualiter satiarentur. Nam et nos hodie accipimus visibilem cibum; sed aliud est sacramentum, aliud virtus sacramenti ...) Videte, ergo, fratres, panem caelestem spiritualiter manducate*: that is, eat the

Eucharist also on the plane of the *Spiritus* (tr. XXVI, 11, col. 1611); the same in n. 12, col. 1612, in terms of *qui manducat intus, non foris, qui manducat in corde, non qui premit dente,* and all that follows.

Aquinas (*Sum. Theol.,* III, qu. 80, art. 1 et par.), distinguishes two manners of receiving the eucharist; the 'sacramental', which is carnal, and the 'spiritual', that *qua homo Christo conjungitur per fidem et caritatem,* or again, *particeps fit eccelesiasticae unitatis, quae fit per caritatem* (*Comm. im Ev. Joannis,* c. 6, lect. 7, n. 2).

It is precisely *this* distinction which Cajetan reproduces in his commentary on Jn 6. The sense of this commentary is not to deny that Jn 6—at least from v. 48— has a eucharistic application, but to say that it envisages the *spiritualis manducatio,* not a purely *sacramentalis manducatio*: see *In IV Evangel. Comm.,* Lyons, 1558, fol. 381, v s., in particular this comment on *Nisi manducaveritis: Triplex igitur sensus dicitur hujus litterae. Primum est de fide mortis Christi. Secundus sensus est de fide sacramenti eucharistiae.* . . . *Et hic sensus est verus in se; quia spiritualiter manducare et bibere sacramentum eucharistiae quo ad rem sacramenti nihil aliud est quam manere in Christo* (. . .) *An autem sit intentus, non clare apparet, imo si perspicaciter fuerit consideratum, apparet quod sermo formalis non est de sacramento, sed de re sacramenti, sed de fonte sacramenti* (. . .): *Tertius sensus est de manducatione sacramentali, digne tamen* . . . (f. 387 v. – f. 388 r): this third sense is the great argument of the Bohemians in favour of communion in both kinds: Cajetan refutes them at length. He is certainly guided in his expressions, on the one hand by considerations of theology (concerning the *res sacramenti*) or polemics (against the Calixtines), on the other hand by philosophical and theological categories (*Animae autem cibus constat ex vero et bono,* f. 381 v.; *manducare vere Jesum vivum, hoc est pasci in intellectu et affectu de Jesu vivo,* f. 390 v.). But in my opinion the question of Cajetan's exposition of Jn 6 requires reconsideration. Cajetan's little work, *De erroribus contingentibus in Eucharistiae sacramento,* 1525, recently re-edited by Fr A. von Gunten, Rome, 1962, shows without question that our interpretation is correct.

5. For example, Corluy, A. Loisy, O. Cullmann, T. Philips, E. Janot, W. Goossens, D. Mollat (pp. 114f), cited above, n. 2; H. van den Bussche (in the symposium *L'Évangile de Jean, Études et problemes,* Paris-Bruges, 1958, pp. 94–6); etc.

6. This is the thesis of Ruch, in the article 'Eucharistia' in *DTC* (vol. V, 1913, col. 989–95), Fr Lagrange, Abbé Villette, MM. E. Gaugler, E. Schweizer and P. Menoud. *Foi et Sacrement,* I. *Du Nouveau Testament à St Augustin,* Paris, 1959, pp. 83f, 91f.

7. For Origen, see Urs von Balthasar, *Parole et Mystère chez Origène,* Paris, 1957; H. de Lubac, *Histoire et Esprit, L'Intelligence de l'Écriture d'après Origène* (*Théologie,* 16), Paris, 1950. For Augustine, see E. Hocedez, 'La conception augustinienne du sacrement dans le Tract. LXXX in Joann.', in *Rech. S.R.,* 1919, pp. 1–29; T. Camelot, 'Réalisme et symbolisme dans la doctrine eucharistique de S. Augustin', in *RSPT,* 31 (1947), pp. 394–410. From the exegetical point of view, see A. Feuillot, *op. cit.,* n. 2.

8. See Wis 16:20.

9. 1 Cor 15.

10. 1:17.

11. Flesh and blood, Jn 1:13; Mt 16:17.

12. Jn 1:13; 1 Jn 1:1–2.

13. Jn 6:57.

14. 1 Cor 1:9; see Phil 3:10f.

15. *Trall.*, 8. 1.
16. *Smyrn.*, 1. 1.
17. 10.2.
18. His Pasch: *Magn.*, 9. 1.
19. See art. 'Abercius' in *DACL*, vol. I, col. 70, and G. Bardy, *La Théologie de l'Église de S. Clément de Rome à S. Irénée* (*Unam Sanctam, 13*), Paris, 1945, pp. 72–3; art. 'Pectorius' in *DACL*, vol. XIII, col. 2892–3.
20. 'Extraits d'Acta Pauli' in *Rev. Bénéd.*, 27 (1910), pp. 402–12; see pp. 410 and 411.
21. Bread of angels: Ps 78:25; Wis 16:20; Aquinas, *Comm. in Ev. Joann.*, c. 6, lect. 3, n. 5; *Caro Christi est cibus in quantum conjuncta est verbo Dei, quod est cibus quo angeli vivunt.*
22. See Sum. Theol., IIIa, qu. 80, art. 2, ad 1; see St Bernard, *In Cant.*, sermo 33, 3 (183, 952); Postcommunion of the votive Mass *Pro quacumque necessitate*: *Ut ad superni plenitudinem sacramenti, cujus libavimus sancta tendamus.*
23. See H. de Lubac *op. cit.*, pp. 355–70, esp. 366. Whence follows the interpretation of the Bread of Life in John 6 as the teaching or the word, in Clement of Alexandria (*Paedag.*, I, 6, 46–7) and Origen (see Joann. Comm. VI, 431 X, 17; XX, 41–3, and again *DTC*, vol. XI, col. 1558–9. In St Gregory of Nyssa the manna is seen as a figure of the word, not of the eucharist: see *Life of Moses*, *PG*, 44, 368 C; French trans., J. Daniélou (*Sources chrét.*, 1. Paris, 1945), p. 100.
24. A point constantly repeated by Aquinas: III Sent., d. 19, qu. 1, art. q. 1, ad 4; *De verit.*, qu. 27, art. 4; qu. 29, art. 7, ad 8 and 11; *Sum. Theol.*, IIIa, qu. 39, art. 5, ad 3; qu. 49, art. 3, ad 1 and art. 5 c.; qu. 62, art. 5, ad 2 and art. 6; qu. 79, art. 7, ad 2; *in Hebr.*, c. 3, lect. 3; *Expos. in Symb.*, art. 10; and see below, n. 155.
25. See *IV Sent.*, d. 1, art. 4, q. 3 sol., ad 1 and 3; qu. 2, art. 6, sol. 1 and q. 2, ad 3; d. 4, qu. 3, art. 2, q. 2, ad 2; d. 25, qu. 1, art. 2, ad 4; see *Sum. Theol.*, IIIa, qu. 62, art. 5, sol. et ad 2; art. 6 sol.; qu. 64, art. 2; etc.
26. *In Ev. Joann.*, tr. LXXX, 3 (*PL*, 35, 1640): the passage is taken from the commentary on Jesus' words: 'You are pure, because of the word . . .', see E. Hocedez, quoted above, n. 7.
27. M. L. Guérard des Lauriers, *Dimensions de la Foi*, Paris, 1951, vol. I, p. 387.
28. See *Sum. Theol.*, IIIa, qu. 60, art. 5, sol.
29. *IV Sent.*, d. 1, qu. 2, art. 6, q. 2, ad 3. Many similar texts: d. 1, qu. 1, art. 5, q. 5; art. 5, q. 3; *De Malo*, qu. 4, art. 8, ad 2, or, on the subject of baptism, *Sum. Theol.*, IIIa, qu. 38, art. 6; qu. 39, art. 5. See J. Gaillard, 'Les sacrements de la foi' in *Rev. Thomiste*, 1959, pp. 5–31, 270–309; L. Villette, *op. cit.*, p. 225; E. H. Schillebeeckx, *Christ, the Sacrament of the Encounter with God*, London and New York, 1964.
30. See Jn 6:37, 44 and 65.
31. Mk 5:28–34; Lk 8:43–8; Mt 9:20–22.
32. *In Ev. Joann.*, tr. XXVI, 3 (35, 1608); see Tr. XXVII, 7, *per fidem copulamur* (col. 1618); tr. XLVIII, 3, *accedere est tangere* (col. 1741); *Serm. Mai* 5, 95, *credere, tangere est.*
33. *Ibid.*, and in his commentary on *Noli me tangere, nondum enim ascendi* (*in corde tuo*) *ad Patrem meum.* tr. CXXI, 3 (col. 1957): *Sic in se credi voluit Jesus, hoc est, sic se spiritualiter tangi, quod ipse et Pater unum sint. Ejus quippe intimis sensibus quodammodo ascendit ad Patrem, qui sic in eo profecerit ut Patri agnoscat aequalem: aliter non recte tangitur, id est, aliter non recte in eum creditur.* The important thing is to see Jesus with the eyes of the heart, then he is truly present: *Serm. Guelf.*, XXI, 3 and *Denis* 17, 1 (ed. G. Morin, *Misc. Agost.*, pp. 509 and 81.

34. 6:63; see 1:12–13; 3:6–8; Mt 16:17.
35. 6:26.
36. 6:42.
37. 6:52, 'Capharnaism'.
38. Vv. 57 and 62; see 5:26; 10:15.
39. An aspect specially considered by J. Leenhardt in the article named above, n. 2.
40. Jn 17:3.
41. Jn 1:14; 1 Jn 1:1; Heb 1:1–2.
42. Mt 8:3 and par; 8:15 and par; 9:20f and par; 20:34; Mk 3:10 and par; 7:33f; 9:26f; Lk 7:14; 14:4; 22:51; Jn 9:6f. See M. Kaiser, *Die Einheit der Kirchengewalt nach dem Zeugnis des N.T. u. der Apostol. Väter*, Munich, 1956, p. 10.
43. Mt 9:25 and par; Mk 6:6a; 8:23 and 25; Lk 4:40; 13:20.
44. Mt 9:18 and parallels.
45. 9:21 and parallels.
46. Mk 3:10.
47. Lk 6:19, see Mk 6:56 etc.
48. See H. Lesêtre, art. 'Mains' in *Dict. Bibl.*, vol. IV, col. 581f; W. Bauer, art. Χείρ in his *Griechisch-deutsches Wörth. zu den Schr. des N.T.*; M. Kaiser, *op. cit.*, p. 104, and the monographs on the imposition of hands (J. Coppens, E. Lohse, etc.). One must also remember the symbolism of art and gesture, no doubt already known to prehistoric man (cave-paintings). See *DACL*, art. 'Bénir', (III, 746–58); 'Impos. des m.' (VII, 391–413); 'Main' (X, 1205f), etc. From the dogmatic point of view, we may refer to what Charles Journet says on the action of Christ by contact, in *The Church of the Word Incarnate*, vol. I, New York, 1959, pp. 9, 43, 184; *La sainte Messe ou la permanence du sacrifice de la Loi nouvelle*, Freiburg, 1950, p. 26.
49. See Lk 11:20, compared with Mt 12:28.
50. See *passim* and Mk 5:30; Lk 6:19; 8:46.
51. See my *Le Mystère du Temple*, (*Lectio Divina*, 22) Paris, 1958, pp. 324ff (English translation *The Mystery of the Temple*, London and Westminster, 1962) and *The Wide World my Parish*, London, 1961, pp. 99f.
52. See Aquinas, *III Sent.*, d. 19, art. 3, q. 3, ad 1; *Sum. Theol.*, IIIa, qu. 52, art. 1, ad 2.
53. *Sum. Theol.*, IIIa, qu. 62, art. 5. Texts which explain the ecclesiological and sacramental symbolism of the water and the blood are innumerable: see S. Tromp, 'De nativitate Ecclesiae ex Corde Iesu in Cruce', in *Gregorianum*, 13 (1932), pp. 488–527; *Corpus Christi quod est Ecclesia*, vol. I, 2nd ed., Rome, 1946, pp. 33f, 104f.
54. See O. Cullmann, *op. cit.*, n. 2; F. M. Braun, 'In spiritu et veritate', in *Rev. Thomiste*, 1952, pp. 245–74, 485–507; R. Brêchet, 'Du Christ à l'Église. Le dynamisme de l'Incarnation dans l'Évangile selon S. Jean', in *Divus Thomas*, 56 (1953), pp. 67–98; P. Menoud, 'La définition du sacrement selon le N.T.', in *RTP*, N. Sér., 38 (1950) pp. 138–47; 'Miracle et sacrement dans le N.T.', in *Verbum caro*, 6 (1952), pp. 139–54. Aquinas sees the sacraments as a kind of extension of the Incarnation; *Sum. Theol.*, Ia IIae, qu. 108, art. 1; IIIa, qu. 61, art. 4; qu. 62, art. 5 et 6; qu. 64, art. 3; qu. 80, art. 5 (*sacramenta humanitatis ejus*).
55. Ac 9:18.
56. 1:21–2.
57. *Op. cit.*, p. 71–2. The work of purification for Christians effected by baptism

was effected for the apostles by the word of Jesus (Jn 13:10b; 15:3; Schnackenburg, in *Sacra Pagina*, p. 249). Tertullian wrote '(For the apostles) the privilege of being the first to be called and then of living in personal intimacy with Christ could well take the place of baptism' (*De Bapt.*, 12). He then speaks solely of the apostles' faith, and envisages baptism as the 'seal of faith'. Refoulé admits (Introd., p. 49) that this passage might be understood in a somewhat Calvinistic sense (the sacrament a mere sign), but he shows (pp. 45, 47, 52) that on the other hand Tertullian makes statements in favour of a real sacramental causality. Compare *De Resurrectione carnis*, c. 37 (*PL*, 2. 847), where eating the flesh of Christ is equated with accepting the word (with quotation from Jn 6:64 and 5:24).

58. *Sum. Theol.*, IIIa, qu. 62, art. 5, ad 2 et art. 6.

59. The Fathers and the Eastern Liturgy regard it from this angle: see 'Dum visibiliter Deum cognoscimus: Méditation théologique', in *Maison-Dieu*, no. 59 (1959), pp. 132–61.

60. See especially Basil, *Treatise on the Holy Ghost*, 12. 28 (*PG*, 32, 217 BC; *Sources chrét.*, 17, Paris, 1947, p. 157); other texts in J. Mouroux, *L'expérience chrétienne* . . . (Théologie, 26), Paris, 1952, pp. 58f, and in chap. 1 of my *La Tradition et les traditions* II, *Essai théologique* (Paris, 1960 and 1963; English trans. *Tradition and Traditions*, London, 1966).

61. On the biblical meaning of these things, read J. Pedersen, *Israel, its Life and Culture*, London and Copenhagen, 1940; T. Boman, *Das hebräische Denken im Vergleich mit dem Griechischen*, 2nd ed., Göttingen, 1952; C. Tresmontant, *Essai sur la pensée hébraïque*, Paris, 1953; J. A. T. Robinson, *The Body. A Study in Pauline Theology*, London and New York, 1952; etc. Also some profound pages from V. Soloviev, *Le judaisme et la question chrétienne*; French trans. in *Foi et Vie*, Sept.–Oct. 1955, pp. 406–9.

62. Soloviev, *op. cit.*, p. 408, which speaks of 'religious materialism'.

63. *La Pensée de la Réforme*, (*Manuels et Précis de Théol.*, XXXII), Neuchâtel-Paris, 1951, p. 225.

64. *Confession of Augsburg*, 5 (*Die Bekenntnisschriften der evangel.-Luther Kirche*, 2nd ed., Göttingen, 1952, p. 58).

65. *Ibid.*, art. 7 (p. 61).

66. *Articles of Schmalkalde*, III, 8 (*id. op.*, pp. 453f); etc.

67. See, for example, J. J. von Allmen, 'Les sacrements d'après le Catéchisme de Heidelberg', in *Etudes théol. et relig.*, 1944, pp. 74–89.

68. *Com. in Galat.*, 1519, Weimar. II, p. 509, 1. 14–15.

69. *Wider die himmlichen Propheten* (W. XVIII, p. 202, 1. 37f); *De Captivitate Babyl.*, Bk VI (W. VI, p. 560); *Ad libr. . . . Catharini . . . Responsio*, 1521 (VII, p. 721, 1. 9f); *La liberté d'un homme chrétien*, no. 5.

70. Weimar, I, pp. 10–17.

71. Bk VI, p. 564, 1. 15f. *Ex quibus fit, ut is qui non praedicat verbum, ad hoc ipsum per Ecclesiam vocatus, nequaquam sit sacerdos, et sacramentum ordinis alius esse non possit quam ritus quidam eligendi Concionatores in Ecclesia* . . . See also M. Rade, *Das Priestertum der Gläubigen und seine Forderung an die evangel. Kirche unserer Zeit*, Tübingen, 1918, pp. 26–7. If we are not mistaken, modern Protestant historians interpret the laying on of hands, already described in the Acts, as a symbol of mission for the ministry of the word.

72. This is connected with the criticism (worthy of study for its own sake) directed by the Reformers against the theology of the *obex*: thus Luther, *Vorlesung über d. Hebraerbrief*, 1517–18, Corollary to the scholia on 7. 12f; Calvin, *Institution*, 1541 edition, ch. X (ed. Coll. Budé, vol. III, pp. 212–13); etc.

73. See Luther, *De captiv. Bab.*, Bk VI (W. VI, p. 532): 'Error est sacramenta novae legis differri a sacramentis veteris legis penes efficaciam significationis: utraque aequaliter significabant (. . .) In hoc ergo differunt legales figurae a signis novis et vetustis, quod legales figurae non habent annexum verbum promissionis, quia non sunt sacramenta fidei, quae sola justificant, sed sunt sacramenta operis tantum.' Calvin, *Inst.*, *ed. cit.*, ch. VII and X (vol. III, pp. 228f, 238f, 243f). And see my *Vraie et fausse réforme dans l'Église*, Paris, 1950, pp. 406, 431, n. 145, pp. 433f, 479f.

74. *Non sacramentum, sed fides sacramenti, justificat: Pro veritate inquirenda et timoratis conscientiis consolendis* (1518, W., I, p. 631); *Ein Sermon v. d. Sakr. der Buss* (1519: vol. II, p. 715, I. 30: *sacramenta non implentur dum fiant, sed dum creduntur*). Here Luther adopts the Augustinian principle, *non quia fit, sed quia creditur*; and he holds this principle to be 'vulgatissimum et probatissimum': *Vorles. über Hebraerbrief* (1517), ed. Hirsch-Ruckert, 1929, p. 173. But is it consistent with this principle, is it even faithful to Luther, to interpret the Lutheran notion of the sacrament by thus transposing the Augustinian formula quoted above: *Accedit testamentum* (the virtue of the word) *ad sacramentum* (= *signum*) *et fit revelatio*, as E. Roth does, *Sakrament nach Luther* (*Theol. Bibl.*, 3), Berlin, 1952? If this were indeed the Lutheran position (which is denied by such men as W. Stählin and H. Asmussen), it would part company with Catholic and even Augustinian realism, in order to join hands with the Calvinist thesis of the value of the sacrament as cognitive and pure sign.

75. See *l'Apologie de la Confess. d'Augsbourg*, IV, 63 (*Die Bekenntnisschr.*, p. 172); the *Confession* itself, in the 1st edition art. XIII (*ibid.*, p. 68). See Luther, *Vorles. über I Mose* (1535–43; on Gen. 25. 21; W. XLIII, pp. 383–8).

76. *Articles of Schmalkalde*, III, art. 5 (*ibid.*, p. 450).

77. We may quote, among others, A. Vinet, *Théologie pastorale*, Paris, 1889, p. 376: 'The error of *opus operatum* must be firmly opposed, the error which attributes a merit to outward works and especially to outward participation in the sacrament . . .' Merit has nothing to do with it here. R. Will, *Le Culte . . .*, vol. II, Paris, 1929, p. 194: 'By transubstantiation the elements of the Supper become divine substances containing and discharging supernatural forces, which may be called magical, since scholasticism has declared the theory of the efficacy of the sacraments ex opere operato'; K. Barth, *The Teaching of the Church regarding Baptism*, London, 1948; R. Mehl, in *Foi et Vie*, Jan. 1949, p. 55; etc.

Fortunately, some no less expert Protestant theologians have now restored the true meaning of *opus operatum*. Karl Barth himself, *Kirchl. Dogmatik*, I, 1, p. 70: 'Protestant controversy must be earnestly recommended to avoid the word "magic". There is in fact no sensible definition of magic which could apply to the genuine Catholic position' (in a note, Barth quotes an article by D. Winzen in *Catholica*, 1932, pp. 19f); L. Hodgson, in the *Introduction to the Report of the Theological Commissions* of the Faith and Order Conference at Lund, 16th Aug. 1952, pp. 4–5; P. Y. Emery, in *Verbum Caro*, no. 50 (1959), pp. 173–4; F. J. Leenhardt, *Ceci est mon corps . . .* (*Cah. théol.*, 37), Neuchâtel-Paris, 1955, p. 55: 'The point which men have always tried to emphasize in speaking of the efficacy of the sacramental *opus operatum* is that the efficacy of the sacrament depends exclusively on the action of Christ who acts in it, sole source of the sacramental grace'; various contributors in the review *Una Sancta*, Aug. 1958, pp. 121–35 (H. Hennig, 'Die Lehre vom opus operatum' in *d. Luther. Bekenntnisschriften*); May 1959, pp. 34–9; Dec. 1959, pp. 316–18; etc. The subject is well worth a 'dissertation'.

78. *Articles of Schmalkalde*, III, art. 6 (*Bekenntnisschr.*, pp. 450–1).

79. *Inst.*, edition of 1561 or 1562, IV, xiv, 3 (*C.R., Calvini Opera*, IV, col. 879); ed. 1541, ch. x (ed. Coll. Budé, vol. III, pp. 199f, 205, 214, 235). See R. S. Wallace, *Calvin's Doctrine of the Word and Sacrament*, 1953. See the *Confession of La Rochelle*, 1559, art. 34: 'We believe that the sacraments are added to the word for fuller confirmation; to be pledges and seals of the grace of God, and by this means to aid and comfort our faith' (*Bekenntnisschriften u. Kirchenordnungen d . . . ref. Kirche*, ed. by W. Niesel, Munich, 1937, p. 74); art. 35, baptism = a testimony of adoption; art. 36, the Eucharist = a testimony of the unity which we have in Jesus Christ. See also *Catechism of Heidelberg*, qu. 66; *Catechism of Geneva*, sect. 46 and 54; etc.

80. H. Clavier, *Études sur le Calvinisme . . .*, Paris, 1936, p. 38.

81. *C.R., Opera Calvini*, vol. XLVII, 1892, col. 440f.

82. *Du vrai usage de la croix* (1560), Geneva, 1865, p. 45.

83. *Notes dogmatiques*, Fasc. II; *Des moyens de grâce*, Edit. *Revue Réformée*, No. 22 (1955-2), pp. 31f.

84. See *Calvin's Doctrine of Man*, 1952, pp. 131f; 'Le sacerdoce royal', in *Verbum caro*, No. 47 (1958), p. 298.

85. *Die kirchkl. Lehre v. d. Taufe* (see n. 48 above); *La Confession de foi de l'Église (Cah. théol. de l'Actual. prot.*, 2), p. 10: 'The sacraments are the means ordained by God to testify sincerely and visibly to our faith and service.'

86. *Die Taufe, ein Sakrament? Ein exegetischer Beitrag zum Gesprach über die kirchliche Taufe*, Zollikon-Zurich, 1951.

87. See P. Benoit in *Rev. Bibl.*, 1953, pp. 620-3 and (without naming M. Barth), H. Schlier, in *Evang. Theol.*, 1948 and in *Theol. Literaturzeitg.*, 1947 (reproduced and translated in *Le Temps de l'Église*, Tournai-Paris, 1960, pp. 59-67, 116-39, 172 n. 5); also from the Protestant side, E. Schweizer, in *Kirchl. Blatt f. die reformierte Schweiz*, 1952, fasc. 6; C. Masson, in *RTP*, 1953-1, p. 21; E. Barnikol, from a personal and disputable point of view, in *Wiss. z. Halle-Wittmeberg Univ.*, 1956-7, p. 4.

88. H. Mentz, *Taufe und Kirche in ihren ursprünglichen Zusammenhang*, Munich, 1960, pp. 91, 93, 95. Hence, to *baptise* is an act *of the Church* and a duty for the Church (like preaching) but *to be baptised* is not necessary and contributes nothing to salvation (pp. 95, 106, 107-8).

89. P. 98.

90. Thus, for example, in very different climates of thought, R. Will, ('Parole et sacrement' in *Études théol. et relig.*, 1947, pp. 192-200; two aspects of the presence of God, who is at once revealed and mysterious, known and transcendent, object both of an experience based on faith and of a mystical experience); R. Chapal, in *Positions Protestantes*, Paris, 1944, p. 68.

91. *Die Kirche und das Amt.*, Munich, 1959, pp. 162-3.

92. *The Household of God*, London and New York, 1953, pp. 52f.

93. *Op. cit.*, n. 48, p. 13: 'The question these pages will in the first place attempt to answer is: what relation has Christ willed to establish with us? Or, more precisely: since Christ has wished his disciples to preach his gospel, he has established that link with us which is the preaching of his word: "He who hears you hears me." The question is, then, whether he has willed to establish, by another means than the word, another relation of a different kind.'

94. General congregation of 1st March 1547: *Conc. Trident.*, ed. Goerresges, vol. V, 2, 1911, p. 988, 1. 38. Text first proposed for eighth canon, p. 884, 1. 21-2: 'Si quis dixerit per ipsa sacramentorum opera nullo modo conferri gratiam, sed solam fidem divinam promissionis ad gratiam consequendam sufficere, A. S.'

95. Denz.-Bann., 851.

96. On this last point, see J. de Baciocchi, 'Les sacrements, actes libres du Seigneur', in *NRT*, July 1951, pp. 681–706.

97. See H. M. Féret, 'Peuple de Dieu et Pâque eucharistique', in *La messe et sa catéchèse*, Paris, 1947, pp. 205f (p. 215); L. Bouyer, *La Bible et l'Évangile. Le sens de l'Écriture: du Dieu qui parle au Dieu fait homme* (*Lectio divina*, 8), Paris, 1951; Congar, *Vraie et fausse réforme*, pp. 466f; *Le mystère du Temple* ..., Paris, 1958, App. III; J. de Baciocchi, 'Présence eucharistique et transsubstantiation', in *Irénikon*, 32 (1959), pp. 139–60.

98. 52:6.

99. There is also the *agraphon* (= unwritten saying) 'He who spoke in the prophets, I am there'. (A. Resch, *Agrapha* (*TU*, 30, 3–4: Leipzig, 1906), p. 207.

100. Examples given by Calvin himself (*Inst.*, ed. Coll. Budé, vol. III, pp. 215f.

101. See K. Thieme, 'Die gegenwärtige Dialektik des Deutschen Protestantismus,' in *Frankfurter Hefte*, 5 (March 1950), pp. 253–62: 'The fundamental question is the same as that which concerned the Amsterdam Conference. Is the true purpose of the Church to give salvation, as Asmussen said, and thus the necessary consequence of the Incarnation of God the Son, or is God-in-Christ merely the Word come into existence (*Wort geworden*)?'

102. See P. Liégé, 'Théologie de l'Église et Problèmes actuels d'une Pastorale missionnaire', in *La Maison-Dieu*, no. 34 (1953), pp. 5–19.

103. 1 Cor 15:28.

104. See Ac 19:1–7.

105. N. 70.

106. See n. 81.

107. Sess. XXIII: Denz.-Bann., no. 961 and see 957, 960. The Goerresges edition gives, as references to the positions condemned, Luther, *De captiv. Babyl.*, (W., VI, p. 560); Bucer, *Comment. sur S. Jean*, c. VI; Calvin, *Inst.*, IV, 19.

108. *Catéchisme de Meaux*, 1687, 1st Catechism, lect. 13 (*Oeuvres*, ed. Vives, vol. V, 1862, p. 15).

109. See Rom 15:16; Phil 2:17.

110. E.g., E. Masure, *Prêtres diocésains*, Lille, 1947; L. M. Dewailly, *Jésus-Christ, Parole de Dieu*, Paris, 1945, pp. 106f; K. H. Schlelke, *Discipleship and Priesthood*, New York, 1964. I have myself touched on the question (*Lay People*, pp. 166f), but have only really dealt with it in an unpublished work (*Mission. Sacerdoce-Laïcat*, 1953), in many conferences and retreats, and finally in a brief article, reproduced as no. 5 in this book. ('The Different Priesthoods').

111. I do not despair of doing it some day!

112. See notes 2 and 29.

113. *Trall.*, VIII, 1. On this subject, the following passage of Clement of Alexandria has been quoted (by A. Lelong, in the collection of Hemmer and Lejay): 'The Lord said, Eat my flesh, drink my blood (John 6. 54), evidently signifying the symbol of faith and hope ..., by which the Church is watered and grows, corporally by faith, spiritually by hope, by which faith is maintained, as if by its soul' (*Paedag.*, I, 6: *PG*, 8. 296).

114. See P. Camelot, (Introd., p. 38), with reference to Rom 8:3.

115. Tertullian, *De Pudic.*, 18, *passim*: 'post fidem lapsis' (*PL*, 2, 1016); St Augustine, *Epist.*, 98, 9 (*PL* 33, 364). See the opening question of the rite of Baptism: 'What do you ask of the Church?' 'Faith'. Some medieval rituals here give *baptismum* instead of *fidem*.

116. See above, n. 19.

117. See above, notes 7 and 29.

118. *In Exod.*, hom. 13. 3: ed. Baehrens, G.C.S., *Orig. Werke*, VI (1920), p. 274. See also H. Urs von Balthasar, *Geist und Feuer*, 2nd ed., Salzburg, 1938, pp. 121f, 160f, 364–77.

119. *I Apol.*, 67 (*PG*, 6, 429).

120. 'Le cycle liturgique, cycle biblique et eucharistique', in *Les questions lit. et paroiss.*, 36 (1955), pp. 111–18.

121. A. Chavasse, art. quoted, p. 111. In the same line of thought, see J. Daniélou, *Essai sur le mystère de l'Histoire*, Paris, 1953, pp. 74f (English translation *The Lord of History*, London and New York, 1958). (Marxist history and Christian history); W. Kahles, 'Glaubensverkündigung aus dem Geist der liturgischen Erneuerung' in *Archiv. f. Liturgiewiss.*, 6 (1959–60), pp. 417–54.

122. See A. G. Luike, *Cathedra en mensa. De plaats van preekstoel en avondmaalstafel in het oodchristelijk kerkgebouw volgens de opgravingen in Noord-Afrika*, Franeker, 1955; Ed. Stommel, 'Die bischöfliche Kathedra im christl. Altertum', in *M nchener Theol. Zeitschr.*, 3 (1952), pp. 17–32; F. Van der Meer, *Saint Augustin, Pasteur d'ames*, Mulhouse-Paris, 1955, vol. I, pp. 57f (Eng. trans., *Augustine the Bishop*, London and New York, 1962).

123. 1 Pet 2:25; 5:4.

124. See art. 'Évangéliaires', in *DACL*, vol. V, e.g., nos. 106, 108, etc.

125. *Tractatus in Ps.*, 127, 10 (*PL*, 9, 709); see *In Ps.*, 68 (col. 842), *mensa sacrificiorum* and *mensa scientiae, cum vel praescripta legis vel prophetarum voces ab Ecclesiae viris ad revelationem divinii concilii tractantur.*

126. *Com. in Luc.*, Bk VII, nn. 187–91 (*Sources chr.*, 52, Paris, 1958, pp. 78f), on the parable of the woman who put the leaven in three measures of meal. *Sancta Ecclesia, quae typo mulieris istius evangelicae figuratur, cuius farina nos sumus, dominum Jesum in interioribus nostrae mentis abscondat* (n. 187: *PL*, 15, 1749); *Bene enim fermentum doctrina dicitur Christi, quia panis est Christus et apostolus ait*: quia unus panis, unum corpus multi sumus (1 Cor 10:17; n. 191, col. 1751).

127. *Tractatus in Ps.*, 145: *Panis Christus et caro eius sermo divinus est, et doctrina caelestis* (ed. G. Morin, *Analecta Maredsol.*, III, 2, p. 291). See *in Ps.* 147, *ego corpus Iesu evangelium puto* (p. 301); in *Ezech.*, 4. 16 (*PL*, 25, 149).

128. *Com. in Eccles.*, c. 3: *Porro quia caro Domini verus est cibus, et sanguis eius verus est potus, iuxta ἀναγωγὴν hoc solum habemus in praesenti saeculo bonum si vescamur carne eius et cruore potemur, non solum in mysterio, sed etiam in Scripturarum lectione* (*PL*, 23, 1039 A).

129. *In Isaiam*, prol. (*PL*, 24, 17).

130. See Deut 8:2–3 (Mt 4:4); Am 8:11; Jer 15:16; Ps 119:103; Wis 16:26; Ecclus 24:18–22 (wisdom is eaten); Prov 9: Ezekiel eats a book (3:3; see Rev 10:9). A. Feuillet (*op. cit.*) shows on p. 1040 how a disciple, who is more than a pupil, has in a way to feed on his master, and how this theme, known to the O.T. and Judaism, finds its full truth in the gospel message of the Bread of Life. See also J. Audet, 'La soif, l'eau et la Parole' in *R. Bibl.*, 66 (1959), pp. 379–86; H. de Lubac, *Exégèse médiévale*, 1/2 (1959), pp. 567, 570–1, 617; vol. II/1 (1961), p. 111.

131. See Origen, *In Genesim*, hom. 12. 5 (*Origenes Werke*, VI, 112). In the Middle Ages, *Sententiae Parisienses* (ed. A. Landgraf, p. 42); Baldwin of Canterbury, *Lib. de Sacr. Altaris* (*PL*, 204, 762 D).

132. Thus St Ivo of Chartres, commenting on the breaking of the host at Mass, *in qua fractione possessionem suam designavit mox futuram, et sigillum veterum scripturarum, sub qui spiritualis intelligentia supersubstantialis animae panis claudebatur, aperuit*; Master Hermann (under the name of Abelard), *Epitome theol. christ.*, c. 29 (*PL*, 178, 1742). See Jerome, *In Is.*, XVI, c. 58 (*PL*, 24, 567 B);

Bede, *In Marc.* 6 (*PL* 92, 194 B): Ps.-Bede, *In Mat.* 14 (92, 72 C); Hildebert of Lavardin, *Panis significat Scripturam; frangere panem est exponere Scripturas* (*PL*, 171, 1278 B). See H. de Lubac, *op. cit.*, I, pp. 674 and 407.

133. *Et verbum Dei quod quotidie praedicatur, panis est: Serm.* 59, 3 (*PL*, 38, 401).

134. *Spiritualiter ergo nascimur et in Spiritu nascimur verbo et sacramento: In Ev. Joan.*, tr. XII, 5 (35, 1486).

135. Some texts: *Epist.*, 21, 3, at the beginning of his priesthood, *Qui populo ministrat sacramentum et verbum Dei* (*PL*, 33, 89; *CSEL*, 34, 1, p. 51); *Epist.*, 228, 2, at the end of his life, *Ministri verbi et sacramenti* (33, 1014; *CSEL*, 57, p. 485); *C. litt. Petil.*, III, 54, 66 and 55, 67 (*PL*, 43, 384: *Minister verbi et sacramenti evangelici*); *C. Crescon.*, II, 11, 13 (43, 474: *Neque enim episcopi propter nos sumus, sed propter eos, quibus verbum et sacramentum dominicum ministramus*); *Quaest. in Ev.*, II, 39 (35, 1353); *Sermo* 296, 1. 1 (38, 1353); 351, 3, 5 (39, 1540: *dispensatores verbi et ministri sacramentorum*); *En. in Ps.* 109, 1 (37, 1445: *Qui nos ministros verbi et sacramenti sui*); *Ps.* 126, 2 (col. 1668: *Qui sunt qui laborant aedificantes? Omnes qui in Ecclesia praedicant verbum Dei, ministri sacramentorum Dei*); *Serm. Denis* 17, 7; *Serm. Bibl. Casin.*, I, 133, 1; etc.

136. *Inter Opera Augustini, sermo* 300, 2 (*PL*, 39, 2319); *S. Caesarii Arelat. Sermones*, ed. G. Morin, vol. I, Maredsous, 1937, Serm. LXXVIII, 2, pp. 309–10; *Interrogo vos, fratres et sorores, dicite mihi quid plus esse videtur corpus Christi, an verbum Christi? Si vultis verum respondere, hoc dicere debetis, quod non sit minus verbum Dei quam corpus Christi. Et ideo quanta solicitudine observamus, quando nobis corpus Christi ministratur, ut nihil ex ipso de manibus nostris in terram cadat, tanta solicitudine observemus ne verbum Dei, quod nobis erogatur, dum aliud aut cogitamus aut loquimur, de corde nostro depereat, quia non minus reus erit.*

Quoted by Ivo of Chartres, *Decr.* II, 106 (*PL*, 161. 189 AB); *Coll. tri. Part.* III, 2 (3) 21; *Caesar.* XIII, 45; by Gratian, *Decr.*, c. 94 C.I., qu. 1 (Friedberg, col. 391–2).

137. *In Sam. Proph. alleg. expos.*, Bk III, c. 8 (*PL*, 91, 652 B).

138. *Capitul.*, 46 (*PL*, 105, 206 A).

139. *Opusc. de act. miss.*, n. 54 (*PL*, 119, 49 D).

140. Cap. 3: Mansi, XIX, 437 E.

141. *Liber gratissimus*, c. 13 (M. G. H., Libelli de Lite, vol. I, p. 34).

142. *In festo omnium Sanctorum sermo* i, 3: *Ipse vos pascit, et ope ribus et sermonibus etiam et carne Filii sui, quae est vere cibus. . . . Ergo nunc quidem cibari habemus factis eius et verbis; post haec etiam illibatum Dominici Corporis sacramentum in altaribus mensa sacrosancta, ipso propitio, percepturi* (*PL*, 183, 454).

143. See n. 154, below, St Thomas. The school of Abelard, on the other hand, is characterised by the trilogy 'Fides, Caritas, Sacramentum'. Texts collected by H. Denifle in *Archiv f. Lit. u. K. des MA.*, i (1885), pp. 419f.

144. See H. Tiraboschi, *Veter. Humiliatorum Monum.*, vol. II, 134.

145. See the texts in 'Aspects ecclésiologiques de la quérelle entre Mendiants et Séculiers dans la seconde moitié du XIIIe siècle et le début du XIVe' in *Arch. Hist. doctr. littér. du Moyen Age*, 1961, pp. 35–151.

146. *Summa aurea*, Bk III, De Decimis, Ed. Basle, 1573, col. 861.

147. *De bapt.*, c. 14: 'The first thing is to preach, then to baptize after one has preached.' (*Sources chr.*, 35, Paris, 1952, p. 87).

148. *Oratio 40 contra Arianos*, 42 (*PG*, 26, 237).

149. *In Matt.*, 28. 19 (*PL*, 26, 218 BC): *Primum docent omnes gentes, deinde doctas intingunt aqua. Non enim potest fieri ut corpus baptismi recipiat sacramentum, nisi ante anima fidei susceperit veritatem.*

150. See Migne's Tables: *PL*, 46, 110.

151. References in A. Landgraf, *Dogmengesch. d. Frühscholastik*, III-i, Ratisbon, 1954, p. 283.

152. *In Iam Decretalem: Opera*, ed. Vivès, vol. XXVII, p. 422; *Opusc.*, ed. Lethielleux, IV, p. 325.

153. *Sacerdos quodammodo constituitur sequester et medius inter populum et Deum, et ideo ad eum pertinet divina dogmata et sacramenta exhibere populo*, *Sum. Theol.*, IIa IIae, qu. 86, art. 2.

154. *De art. fidei et sacram. Ecclesiae: Cum omne theologicum studium versetur circa dubietates contingentes articulos fidei et Ecclesiae sacramenta* (Vivès, XVII, 170; Lethielleux, III, p. 1).

155. *Ecclesia fundatur in fide et sacramentis* (or, *constituitur, fabricatur per fidem et sacr.*): *IV Sent.*, d. 17, qu. 3, art. 1, sol. 5; d. 18, qu. 1, art. 1, sol. 1; d. 27, qu. 3, art. 3, ad 2; *Sum. Theol.*, IIIa, qu. 64, art. 2, ad 3; *instituitur* (Ia, qu. 92, art. 3); *consecratur* (*In Joan.*, c. 19, lect. 5, n. 4). See also *IV Sent.* d. 17, qu. 3, art. 1, qa 5; *Sum. Theol.*, IIIa, qu. 48, art. 6; qu. 56, art. 1, ad 3; qu. 64, art. 2, ad 3. Natural priority of faith: Ia IIae, qu. 107, art. 1, ad 3; qu. 106, art. 1; qu. 108, art. 1.

156. The double relation of Christ to grace: *ut eam faciens, ut eam docens*, *In Joan.*, c. 1, lect. 11, pr.; c. 4, lect. 4, n. 1: *primo docuit veritatem, invitando et vocando ad fidem . . .; secundo consummavit ipsam veritatem, aperiendo per passionem suam in nobis januam vitae, dando potestatem perveniendi ad consummatam veritatem. . . .*

157. To the two forms of the Bread of Life corresponds the double mission of the Holy Ghost: *a)* on Christ, at his baptism, for the sacraments, and at the Transfiguration, for teaching; *b)* on the apostles, for the sacraments on the evening of Easter Day, and for teaching on the day of Pentecost. *I Sent.*, d. 16, qu. 1, sol. 3; *Sum. Theol.*, Ia, qu. 43, art. 7, ad 6.

158. *I Sent.*, d. 16, qu. 1, art. 2, ad 4.

159. A point already highly developed by Augustine (see L. Villette, *op. cit.*; D. Zähringer, *Das kirchliche Priestertum nach d. hl. Augustinus*, Paderborn, 1931, p. 144). For Aquinas, see *II Sent.*, d. 9, qu. 1, art. 3; *Sum. Theol.*, qu. 60, art. 5, c et ad 1; qu. 62, art. 1, tertia ratio, etc.

160. For a reflection on the theme, see J. Maritain, *Quatre Essais sur l'esprit dans sa condition charnelle*, Paris, 1956; M. M. Davy, *Essai sur la Symbolique romane*, Paris, 1955, pp. 40f, 212f.

161. I have developed this view of Aquinas and the application he makes of it to the various moments of the economy of salvation, in ' "Traditio" und "Sacra Doctrina" bei Thomas v. Aquin', in *Kirche und Ueberlieferung. Festgabe J. R. Geiselmann*, Freiburg, 1960, pp. 170–210.

162. This moral aspect was obviously not strange to the Fathers or even the great Schoolmen. Aquinas, accordingly, after showing that the manna was only a figure of the Body of Christ, whereas the eucharist contained its reality, says that those who received either could avoid or incur spiritual death, according to what they sought in it. *Potest sumi dupliciter: vel quantum ad signum tantum, id est quod sumatur ut cibus tantum, non intellectu significato, et per hoc non tollitur more spiritualis seu corporalis.* It is the same with the word of God. See *In Joan.*, c. 6, lect. 6, n. 3.

163. In his *De Septem donis Spiritus Sancti* (Pars 2, sect. 3, c. 4: De mensa divinae scripturae, sive scientiae), published in the Works of St Bonaventure, ed. Vivès, vol. VII, Paris, 1866, pp. 611–13.

164. *Imitation of Christ*, Bk IV, c. 11. Trans., London, 1933.

165. *Traité des saints Ordres* (1675): Part II, c. 12, ed. J. Gautier, Paris, La

Colombe, 1953, p. 153 (ed. Chernovitz, Paris, 1896, p. 277). Saint-Cyran exploits the parallel between the Eucharist and the word, from the moral point of view of the standards of the ministry, in *Lettre XXXI* to M. Rebours: 'Preaching is a mystery no less formidable and to be dreaded than that of the Eucharist. It seems to me that preaching is much more formidable, for it is thereby that one engenders and revives souls for God: whereas in the Eucharist one simply feeds them, or rather, cures them. To make oneself worthy of this function, one must labour to put great restrictions on oneself, and having reduced the heart to desiring nothing of this world, to reduce the tongue to a perfect silence. . . .'

165. Second sermon for the 2nd Sunday in Lent: ed. Lachat, vol. IX, pp. 112f (he dates it 1663); ed. Labarcq, *Oeuvres Oratoires*, vol. III, Paris, 1891, pp. 566–91.

166. Second sermon for the 2nd Sunday in Lent; ed. Lachat, vol. IX, pp. 112ff. (he dates it 1663); ed. Lebarcq, *Oeuvres Oratoires*, vol. III, Paris, 1891, pp. 566–91.

167. *Panégyrique du Bx Pierre Fourrier*, 1853: 'There are two caskets in the hands of the priest, the book of the Scriptures and the tabernacle of the altar: both contain, under inanimate signs, eternal life; both are waiting to be opened to the multitude, starving for the bread of the word and the bread of life!'

168. See 1 Cor 11:27–9.

169. See Jn 15:22.

170. Ed. Labarcq, p. 590.

CHAPTER EIGHT

A 'real' Liturgy and
'real' Preaching[1]

AFTER KEEPING IT BY ME A LONG TIME I AM
sending you today a letter which I actually wrote three years ago,
during a course of sermons in a good, splendid parish in the east
of France. But its essential theme took shape in my mind in 1943,
behind the prison-walls of Colditz, when I learned, to my great
joy, of the creation of the Centre de Pastoral Liturgique. Its
subject may be summarised as the quest for a liturgy and for
preaching which shall be *real*.

What do I mean by 'real'?

'Real' is in no way contrasted, in my mind, with 'intellectual'.
There are real ideas and equally real abstract representations.
Nor do I mean to contrast it with 'notional', which involves an
interpretation of human knowledge and experience. I do not
understand 'real' in the sense of 'realist' literature or painting. In
demanding 'real' preaching, I am not for a moment asking anyone
to treat of profane themes, or to present 'slices of life', hot and
raw, and still less to adopt a profane or coarse style of speech. The
realism I have in mind, and which I apply to the liturgy as well
as to preaching, is not confined to a question of literary form. In
comparison with what I want to say here, all these senses of the
word 'real', interesting as they may be, are still rather superficial.

On the other hand, I believe that when theology speaks of the
res of the sacraments, it enables us to give the word 'real' a very
full and precise meaning, highly serviceable to the purpose of

these remarks, and giving them a foundation in one of the most central and profound doctrines of classical theology. I hope that the ensuing explanations will make it clear that by 'real' liturgy and preaching I mean those which are *really capable of bearing fruit in the consciences of men*. But to understand this rather vague and perhaps enigmatic pronouncement it would be well to stand back a little and look at matters from above and farther off: approached in this way it will be clear that the quest for 'real' liturgy and preaching is bound up with the deepest essence of God's design, of Revelation and the Church.

God's plan, as it is revealed to us in the bible, may be described as a progress from the outward to the inward, from figures and means in the sense-world to a reality situated in man himself. We are familiar with the classic schema of the Fathers, which is also that of iconography and the Christian liturgy, and was the central idea of the New Testament before either: that the Old Testament rites had the value of figures, a forecast, a promise, a stage. Their true meaning lay beyond themselves: *Sacramenta Veteris Testamenti*, the Fathers used to call them.[2] More precisely we can say that everything which in the prophetic, preparatory stage of the Old Testament is still *something outward*, must be made spiritual and interior in man himself, under the new and final Dispensation. We can easily show this by reviewing the notions which the Epistle to the Hebrews connects and contrasts, as to their situation under the Old Covenant and the New: the notions of law, priesthood, sacrifice, the temple, or the presence of God. Let us now consider simply the idea of sacrifice.

From beginning to end of the bible, God demands worship and sacrifice. Under the Old Covenant, worship and sacrifice are legally regulated and expressed in a certain number of appointed outward actions: in particular, the Old Testament is familiar with animal sacrifices. Yet we read of the prophets bitterly criticising these sacrifices and even proclaiming that God abhors them. Some historians have been carried away by this and have thought that it was a condemnation of the cult as such.[3] But the very prophets who thus repudiate the sacrifices invite men to a perfect sacrifice, which the ancient law was powerless to produce, being unable to bring anything to perfection.[4] In Louis Bouyer's *The Paschal Mystery*, or in the writings of the Anglican theologian, the late Gabriel Hebert,[5] will be found some very illuminating pages, showing how in the Old Testament God demanded sacrifices and at the same time declared that he did not desire them. There we have a typical example of the prophetic function in the divine economy. Sent to initiate and serve the development of the religious institutions and the fulfilment of God's plan, the prophets say: 'It is that', and at the same time: 'It is not that': 'God wills it', and 'God does not will it'. He wills it, but not in the way you believe and practise it: he wills it, but in another form, another manner, than that which you now hold. Thus God desired a sacrifice, but not that which the Old Law, in its imperfection, ordered men to offer him, the blood of bulls and goats: he desired a sacrifice, but no other than that of man *himself*. What God wants in his worship is no ceremony, no offering, nothing outward, but man himself, the opening, the conversion and the gift of the heart of man. Here as everywhere, the 'fulfilment' of the law by Jesus does not mean adding to the Mosaic commandment some supplementary and more perfect commandment, a new, more rigorous and universal obligation. It means distinguishing and reaffirming, in the law, the fullness and purity of meaning which it had, from the beginning, in God's intention, and which was the perfection of love: it means unfolding a fullness which was always confined by the historical conditions within which, in each of its stages, God's people carried out the design entrusted to it.[6] From the point of view of sacrifice, fulfilment means that what is sacrificed should not be any outward thing, but man himself. This takes place in Jesus Christ and then, after him and through him, in us who unite ourselves to him.

This is the idea behind a passage of Augustine, almost unsurpassed for depth and beauty, which is translated by Louis Bouyer in his book *The Paschal Mystery*.[7] Augustine there develops the theme I have outlined, and he does so all the more completely in that he can connect it with the general scheme of his thought, namely, conversion to *true* reality, which is also a conversion and a passing from without to within, from the sense-world to the inner reality, from signs to the truth. To this scheme —not in fact originated by Augustine, for resemblances to it can be found in Irenaeus, Tertullian and Cyprian—we ultimately owe the famous synthesis of the sacraments, systematised by the

Scholastics in three categories: *sacramentum* (the rite, the outward sign); *res et sacramentum* (the effect produced, though not the final fruit, the final reality which is the goal of the sacred process actuated by the sacramental rite); finally, the *res* (*tantum*), that is, the final fruit of the sacrament, the spiritual reality signified by the sacred rite and mysteriously produced by it.

This analysis as it stands was not formulated by Augustine, who was content to analyse the *sacramentum* in its order as sign, as a reality of signification, and to say that every (sacred) sign depends on a *res* which gives it its reality. The *res* of all *sacramenta* is Christ. Augustine does not transpose this analysis into the order of the efficacy of the strictly sacramental rites.[8] But when the Scholastics proceeded to this transposition and followed up the analysis in the direction indicated by Augustine, they naturally made the *res* of the sacraments to be the reality of grace produced by them in souls. The analysis thus elaborated eventually recovered (in spite of its systematised appearances) the profound meaning of God's plan as it is developed and unveiled in Scripture and can be formulated thus: every 'sacrament' is made for its *res*, which is a spiritual reality *in man*. So the liturgy, worship, the Church herself (a sort of greater sacrament), ought to have their fulfilment and reality *in man himself*. To be 'real', we may say, means to reach its reality, to attain its truth: a reality and a truth which are a spiritual fruit in man himself. It means genuinely to achieve its *res*, its fruit of spiritual reality, light or grace, in the conscience of a spiritual person.

Application to the liturgy

The liturgy is not a thing 'in itself': the worship of God is not fully accomplished if it is performed only in a celebration, however perfect, of rites, even sacramental rites. It is not accomplished until it achieves its *res*, its reality, in men themselves. That is the full meaning of the axiom, *Sacramenta propter homines*. The sacraments are for men, not only from the point of view of their purpose, which may govern and direct a whole system of their 'administration', but in the sense of their reality, of the accomplishment of the spiritual action which they are meant to be. Once we understand that, we know that no liturgy is really worth while unless it will finally be accomplished, or can actually be accomplished, in the minds and hearts of men. Paul said that he would rather speak five words with his mind than ten thousand in 'a tongue';[9] he also speaks of a 'reasonable' worship, which is precisely the offering of oneself.[10] A living liturgy does not mean an impeccable performance of ceremonies, or a restoration of all the outward forms of worship, however perfect,—though all this may be the first stage, of great educational value, in restoring to the liturgical action all its truth and 'reality'. Neither does it mean initiating *a few* persons while the multitude remain generally and incurably indifferent. A liturgy which could only become 'real' to a côterie of oblates, people who have undergone a long and detailed special education, is not what we are looking for. A 'real' liturgy is one which is capable of really producing its fruit in the soul of the faithful people, of being received and made personal in the conscience of men. So long as we only obtain *something which is displayed*, externally to the hearts of the faithful, we are still at the stage of the sacrifices criticised by the prophets, we are continuing the worship of the synagogue.

We must therefore get away from all ideas of archaeology or ritualism, and seek for a liturgy which can really be fulfilled in the hearts of men: and of men as they are, all of them, in our country and our time. That means, men who are no longer living a settled, limited life, within the narrow horizons of a purely agricultural, closed community, like our forbears in the ages when the liturgy was being created. The type of men conditioned and fashioned by the life of those times had dispositions which can hardly, if at all, be those of men conditioned and fashioned by industrial work, standardisation, the concentration of population, the intensity and rapidity of exchange, the bitterness of competition and the struggle for existence. It is no longer in the men of the late Roman empire, nor in those of post-Carolingian feudalism, that our liturgy has to be received and fulfilled. For the psychological and moral type of such men no longer exists, except in circles which are protected, closed or very exceptional.

The difficulty of a liturgical movement which aims at being popular and fully pastoral will always be a certain ritualism. For it must first strive to give value to texts and actions which have symbolism as their essential law, and were fixed at a certain epoch, now long past, according to a system of ideas and symbols, then accepted and even popular, but whose meaning is now forgotten or terribly remote.

The most important of these symbols are, of course, still thoroughly valid, but they are sometimes still difficult to understand, requiring a preparation which the Christian people itself no longer possesses. Some are simple, close to the commonest human experience. A great many of the significant actions or texts taken from the bible are of this type. They are infinitely rich in themselves, and proceed from a providential, divine pedagogy. But they need explanation, and even when understood and remembered they require an intellectual effort of memory and application. Other actions and texts are more subtle: they reveal their meaning only at the cost of a historical explanation which itself requires much learning: this or that is done because in olden days the popes or the emperor, on certain days, performed such and such acts, with such and such an historical explanation. It is obvious that certain subtle symbolical systems, and nearly all those actions which need a rather elaborate historical explanation to make sense, are unsuited to the spiritual needs of the men of our time. For those who have the necessary leisure and education to understand and appreciate them, these things are very meaningful, very fruitful. The study of symbols is attractive and even rather exciting. The discovery of harmonies, of correspondences, of the logic existing between words, symbols and texts, is something very moving and enriching. I admit that I have devoted myself to it and drawn enough benefit from it to realise its great value. But the problem is not one of very special circles, of men whose conditions of life allow them the necessary historical culture to understand the liturgical symbolism and derive nourishment from it. There will always be such men, whose conditions of life have withdrawn them from the movement of the age, which is mechanical, not contemplative. To be frank, it is already doubtful whether the training given to us priests of the apostolic ministry, which introduces us to a world in the main technical and industrial, does not tend to cut us off utterly from those for whom we ought to be the spiritual leaven. It may be, of course, that the concrete conditions of the Church require this, in order to ensure more effectively the continuity of the tradition which is her fundamental law, while adaptation to the movement and situation of the world is rather the province of the laity . . .? But the problem we are considering is that of the masses, to whom our ceremonies mean less and less; who, by and large, understand them not at all and are, in fact, incapable of understanding them.

Take, for example, the liturgy of Palm Sunday (I write just after celebrating it in a packed church). It is one of the days of the year, in many regions *the* day of the year, when the largest number of men come to church. The prayers of the palm-blessings are most beautiful. But no one in the congregation understands them, and scarcely anyone can even make the necessary effort to follow them. Then what are we doing there? Why are we doing it, and for whom? *Whose* worship and prayer is it? Is it *anyone's* prayer? The Church's, you say, and that is true, and no small matter, I am sure. But must we admit that the praying Church is really something else, and not this community of the faithful assembled here, today? When I am present at liturgical functions in the parishes, or think about these problems, I am often haunted by the memory of the following incident which happened to one of my fellow-preachers, who told me of it soon afterwards. It happened in 1927 or 1928, in a small town in the east of France. My friend was preaching the Lent course, giving in turn the retreat for the men, the retreat for the women, etc. Then came the retreat for domestic servants. The old rector said to the preacher: 'Your instructions are at five o'clock. But I warn you, there won't be many there. It's a time when they can't come.'

It seems to me that when we commit priests to the ministry of the word and sacraments of Jesus Christ for the people of God, we might sometimes say to them: 'You will perform certain actions according to the rubrics, you will sing the epistle and gospel in Latin. But I warn you, you will have nobody there. . . . These are things they can't understand.'

As a loyal minister of Christ in his Church, which is the Holy Catholic and Roman Church, when I celebrate the holy mysteries as they are ordered to be celebrated (I am not thinking only of the Mass), I cannot drive from my mind the words of our Lord: 'You have taken away the key of knowledge, . . . you hindered those who were entering.'

Is there not, in many of our ceremonies, something unreal,

unadapted, I mean, for bearing their spiritual fruit in the men for whom, after all, those sacraments are made?

However that may be, for the time being we have to find a liturgical 'realism' within the framework imposed by the Church, a framework whose immense value and invaluable treasure nothing I have said is meant to deny. A liturgical 'realism', that is, spiritualising the worship liturgically celebrated by men: producing in their conscience a fruit of prayer and love. The meaning of the liturgical action must therefore be developed and made relevant, not only by a good historical and theological explanation of the symbols, but by an explanation of the meaning the worship has for *men*, in their lives, in connection with the problems and facts of those lives. Generally speaking, liturgists hardly develop this aspect of things: I sometimes have the impression that they work for the liturgy itself, rather than for men, and that they miss the pastoral contact with souls. On the contrary, the liturgical movement, rising above all cult of the liturgy itself and for itself, ought to be dominated and haunted, as it were, by the concern for reaching real men and achieving the 'reasonable' worship of their own concrete lives.

This can only happen if the element we may call 'prophetic', that is, the element of the *word*, is constantly active to make the sacramental celebration inward and personal: if the rite is explained, not only in terms of history (even biblical) or of symbols of the past, but in terms of attitudes, of personal choices and of life, representing something real in the conscience of men, in the life of men as it is. To take an example, we believe that the exorcisms of baptism can represent something real to men of our time, to whom they are applied, only if we explain them precisely in terms of their experience, their problems and their needs. Only by dint of this effort can we obtain the 'interiorisation' to which we must attain.

Clearly, the celebration of a 'real' liturgy is bound up with preaching, and more precisely with the presentation of preaching which is equally 'real'.

Application to preaching

Practically everywhere, among the more exacting Catholic circles, criticisms are heard on the subject of our preaching. It is accused of being too 'ready-made'. Not that Christian doctrine ought to be 'made up', in the sense that it should not be essentially a deposit handed down, a dogma of the Church, originating substantially from the apostles. No one questions this in the least, and that is what differentiates the present current of reform from the Modernism of fifty years ago. What the Christian people of our day desire is much rather to be put in contact with the apostolic and patristic sources of the dogma. But our preachers are criticised for offering a bookish teaching, concerned first and foremost with canonically correct propositions and the handing on of authorised documents (sometimes by a mere reading of them), but not delivered in the form of a living response to the needs and questions of men. They are blamed for not speaking as religious men, themselves living by the things they preach,—not so much in their lives, on the moral level, as in their thought. They present a doctrine which is correct from the point of view of orthodoxy, and no one minds that. But they express themselves rather as licensed purveyors of an orthodox doctrine than as pastors and fathers of souls, enlightening and nourishing them for the needs of their lives, as these have to be lived day by day. In the pulpit, as in the sacristy and at the altar, they are 'administrators' rather than ministers (at the head of their people and in communion with them) of a word of God which should be a living response and food. Here as there, they continue to represent a religious system which exists *in itself and for itself*, but is not sufficiently a religious reality of human life. Religion, of course, ought to be transcendent, but ought it to be transcendent *in this way*, as something exterior, a quite peculiar order of things, not so much the vertical dimension of human realities as another world, apart, set over against the world of men?

In short, the complaint against our preaching is that it is often itself a *rite*: a more or less brilliant statement of what it is agreed we ought to say, and must say in the special place which is the church, from the special tribune which is the pulpit, in the course of a special ceremony and in a language which is often something special too. Once at a Confirmation I heard the expression: 'the septiform Spirit'. What could this represent? To me, a priest and a theologian, much: to the ordinary Christian, who had not had the special education of the clergy, absolutely nothing. It formed part of the rite, that was all. Now, as Abbé Michonneau has so truly said,[11] when anything has become *only* a rite, it means nothing and changes nothing in the lives even of those who still practise it. In our preaching the statements are generally correct: that is not my complaint. They are *sacramenta*, in which everything is perfect from the point of view of the validity of the *sacramentum*, but they scarcely produce their *res*, and can scarcely do so, the *res* being the fruit in the consciences of men, of which I spoke above. They are still too much of a *rite*, and do not obtain the fullness of that for which the rite is made, apart from which it has no *raison d'être*. For if the sacraments are made for men, what must we say of the word?

What I mean by 'real' preaching is not in the least the kind of preaching which is non-intellectual, nor even necessarily non-notional. It is preaching which:

(1) deals with real problems and gives real food to souls;

(2) is addressed, in a way they can understand, to an audience of men, who earn their own living, are married, have children and also concrete responsibilities in the world of men; which therefore presents things that are true and can be said, face to face, to a normal man, and not only to women and children, or 'the good nuns';

(3) is capable, in short, of producing its *res*, its fruit, in the mind, conscience and heart of such a man.

This theme is infinite, and I could develop it still further, but I have accurately expressed what I think. I would only add that the normal precondition for such a 'real' preaching is 'real' *studies*. As things are, a great many priests who want to preach in this way are forced, at whatever cost, to do again that part of their studies which should inform their preaching. That is not natural. I do not believe that clerical studies should or can prepare *directly* for preaching. To attempt that, to impose on them a purely practical orientation, would be to deprive them of something essential and irreplaceable for the very end we propose: I mean, recollection, disinterestedness (condition of all real culture), scientific seriousness, and therefore a fullness of truth. I do not think that clerical studies, to attain their end, should be less intellectual: in the criticism of scholasticism which is current in some quarters there is, I think, a very real problem, but also there is often something superficial and frivolous, which spoils what could be of value in other suggestions. What we need are not less intellectual, less scientific and strict, less traditional studies, but studies which will lead us to think about real things, to respond to the real needs of men, and not only enable us to handle, more or less brilliantly, a conventional language, of bare *sacramenta*, in fact, and therefore of rites.

About real things, I said: that is, about *true* questions, which (while preserving what is necessary to guard the heritage of the thought of centuries, not without its grandeur) include the *real* questions of men and try to provide them with real answers, answers which can be accepted in the mind and conscience of real men, earning their living in the world of today.

This will by no means result in making it a matter of 'modern' philosophy, political economy or literature. These answers are the answers of God, of the gospel, of the apostolic tradition living in the Church. We are ministers of the word of God, not agents for modern civilisation. But the word of God, and the doctrine of the Church in which it is applied and developed, must be studied by us and delivered by us to men, in order to provide them with spiritual food, fit to sustain them. Along with the liturgical celebration, and like it, the ministry of the word must aim at producing its *res*, that is, its spiritual fruit in the conscience of men. It is in this precise and, I think, very rich sense that I speak of a 'real' liturgy and preaching.

NOTES

1. Article published in *La Maison-Dieu*, no. 16 (1948), pp. 75–87.
2. To grasp this idea of the sacrament in the wide sense, the reader will find Henri de Lubac's *Corpus Mysticum* (Paris, 1944) the most helpful work.
3. See for example, A. Lods, *Les Prophètes d'Israel et les débuts de Judaïsme*, Paris, 1935, pp. 74f, 94 (for Amos), 106 (for Hosea); etc.
4. Heb 1:19.
5. L. Bouyer, *The Paschal Mystery*, London, 1951, pp. 166–8; 329–32 (translation of St Augustine, quoted below); G. Hebert, *The Throne of David*, London, 1941, pp. 111–22.
6. On this meaning of the fulfilment of the law, see W. Vischer (Protestant), *Das Christuszeugniss des Alten Testamentes*, vol. I, (6th ed.), pp. 309f.
7. See pp. 329–32 (from *De Civitate Dei*, Bk X, 5 and 6).
8. See the study by Féret, 'Sacramentum, res, dans la langue théologique de saint Augustin', in *RSPT*, 1940, pp. 218–43.
9. 1 Cor 14:19.
10. Rom 12:1.
11. One should read pp. 257f, in *Paroisse, communauté missionnaire*. (English translation, *Missionary Spirit in Parish Life*, Westminster Md. and London, 1952).

CHAPTER NINE

The Mission of the Parish[1]

THE THEME OF OUR CONGRESS IS DEFINED AS 'Social structures and the pastoral work of the parish'. Within this immense theme, Abbé Courtois, with his invincible optimism, has persuaded me to tackle the no less immense theme of the 'Mission of the parish'. I am not a parish priest, not even a parishioner in the Church. But before entering the seminary I led a fully parochial life, and since then I have known a good number of parishes and parish priests. I am a professor of theology and my special subject is the theology of the Church. So I shall try quite simply to repay the confidence of the organisers of this congress, and your attention, by setting before you a sort of theology or ecclesiology of the parish. I shall do this both in connection with the social structure of the Church and with social structures of the most general kind, and I hope to draw from them at least some skeleton conclusions on the level of the pastoral work of the parish.

The liturgists, I think, have spoken most, and no doubt best, about the parish.[2] Also, wherever the liturgical movement has developed, and especially where it has encountered parishes which are still alive, as in Belgium, it has proved remarkably effective in stimulating parochial communities. The liturgists have generally developed the idea that the parish is a realisation in miniature of the very mystery of the Church: which mystery is simply that of her relation to Christ as his spouse and his body. In its own order the parish is an original realisation of this two-fold relationship: it is the spouse and it is the local embodiment

F

(realisation) of the body of Christ. It is thus an objective reality (Pinsk) and a 'mystery' (Wintersig).

The liturgists like to regard this twofold relationship of spouse and body hierarchically, that is, by the hierarchical mediation of the priesthood, itself distributed hierarchically on the three levels of the universal Church, the diocese and the parish. The faithful are organically united to Christ by the work of the priesthood, which is exercised on these different levels, the priest being to every Christian the minister and the image of ecclesiastical unity. We know the support the liturgists can draw from the writings of St Ignatius of Antioch and St Cyprian about the unity of the local Church around its bishop. They extend the application of these texts both above and below the diocese: above, to the universal Church and the Sovereign Pontiff (I shall discuss later this manner of regarding the pope); below, to the parish and the parish priest. They represent him as bound to his parish in a stable manner, somewhat as a bishop to his diocese, father of souls by the celebration of the sacraments. Faithful and pastor form a community of worship, of life, through the sacraments: the parish is thus, in the words of Wintersig, 'a liturgical person', of which the pastor is the 'leitourgos', or the mystagogue, that is, the one who celebrates the mysteries or introduces men to them.[3] The Christian community is fully actualised in worship round the altar,—and here they draw on the passages and actions which express the great traditions of the single altar; first, around the episcopal priesthood and altar, then around the parish priest, the parochial priesthood and altar. Emphasis is laid on the close tie between the episcopal and presbyteral priesthoods, a tie which is indispensable, for the priesthood of the parish priest derives from that of the bishop as the parish derives, historically, from the single episcopal parish of primitive times; a tie which is attested in many ways by history and even by our modern discipline. Further, as we shall see later, the priestly functions of the parish priest are dependent on the bishop and have to be perfected by him.

In this liturgical concept, as we may call it, the parish is something else, and more, than an administrative unit. It is regarded in the light of the mystery of the Church and in her framework; especially in the light of the priesthood and the sacramental, cultural life of the Church. It is regarded as a community of the faithful round the altar, in order to feed on the holy mysteries and to praise God. It is not surprising that the liturgical movement claims to be effective in fostering the parochial spirit and the Christian spirit at the same time. All this aspect of things seems to me to be genuine: it is generally admitted and I shall not return to it.

I have a remark, however, to make on this subject. I find expositions of this sort completely in place at liturgical congresses or in liturgical reviews—which is where they are actually found. At the same time they seem to me insufficient to express an adequate theology of the parish. This liturgical view of the parish seems to me rather narrow. The documentation on which it is based, authentic though it is, seems equally narrow. It is hard to see, on this view, what difference there is between a parish and a monastery. Parishes have been and are, or ought to be, units of the faithful round the altar, but they have been and are something else besides.

The liturgists' temptation is to see the parish and, in a general way, the Church as *only*, or at least primarily, a community of worship.[4] By way of preamble they have usually outlined a Christological synthesis from a point of view almost exclusively of the priesthood of Christ, the worship, the satisfaction. . . . Thus they point to an element which is essential, but partial. This may well have some effect on the practical idea to be formed of the parochial ministry and of the parish itself, a notion which might easily be limited to what goes on inside the church, in the sacred enclosure. To be a Christian could mean to be grouped around one's parish priest, to obey him, to bring one's contribution to the cultural life of the Church. That may suffice for the function of a monastery: does it suffice to define the mission of the parish, and the priest in charge of a parish? Ought not the priest to inspire and support the faithful in *all* their human life, in their concrete situations and responsibilities? Because of this too exclusively cultural notion of the priest's functions, have we not allowed a certain gulf to be set between the first commandment, which looks to God, and the second, which concerns our neighbour? Have we sufficiently reacted against the type of 'good parishioner' who never misses his religious duties, goes to church and communion, but seems to worry very little about his duty to his neighbour or even his private responsibilities? And we priests, worthy celebrants and careful catechists—which is a great thing, of course—have we been sufficiently the spiritual educators of men? I shall return to this point later.

Thus the liturgical notion of the parish, though inspiring and true in its own sphere, seems to me to need supplementing. With your approval, I shall look for this supplement by considering the parish in relation to the social structures of human life and the Church, in these two pairs of notions: family and city; community formed from above and community formed from below.

Family and City

The parish, as an organism distinct from the diocese, is not something essential and indispensable to the life of the Church, which could exist, and has existed at least for a time, without parishes. This was true when she was confined to the single apostolic community of Jerusalem, but was yet more perfectly the Church than ever since, and also when, dispersed throughout the *Oikoumene* (the inhabited world, the empire), she still knew only episcopal parishes, 'dioceses', as we should now call them.[5] Our parishes were constituted only in order to make the holy mysteries and the Christian teaching available (at least in the ordinary circumstances of life) to a population scattered among the towns and, of course, the countryside. We may note that even for this practical purpose the parish in the strict sense, as something distinct from the diocese, was not an absolute necessity. The number of bishops could have been increased and only dioceses retained. This solution was tried, in fact, especially in the East, with the institution of the *chorepiscopi* or bishops of the country-side,[6] who received their maintenance sometimes from only a hamlet or large farm. If in the end a dualist structure grew up, I mean a duality of organisms, the parish *and* the diocese, this did not derive from the essential nature of the Church, but from a sort of social or human nature of things, a certain structure of the spiritual needs of the faithful. The parish therefore represents *both* a historical though not essential fact of existence, *and* a reality corresponding to an elementary and profound structure of life.

That structure is the natural grouping of a certain number of independent families in the solidarity of everyday life. The parish corresponds to the grouping of men who are united by neighbour-hood, in order to make joint provision for the elementary tasks of human life: the elementary education of children, and all those simple relationships and services which ensure an ordinary degree of development for a truly human life. It is not merely a question of proximity of residence (some have rightly spoken of the 'residential unit',[7] the community of neighbourhood); there is the community of those who serve one another and need one another in day to day life; and it would be a noble task for a parish priest to lead his parishioners to have a Christian awareness of this solidarity.

No doubt that is why some have compared the parish to that type of human community, the family, comparing the diocese to the city; Aquinas, for example, and Pius XI.[8] In Thomist socio-logy[9] the family (which must be understood on the pattern of the ancient 'house', including servants as well as the community of parents and children) is the human association which meets the needs of everyday life, in which men find the necessary bed, bread and hearth. The house is essentially the unity of the table, the hearth and the dwelling; it groups together those who share the same bread, obtain light and heat from the same fire. There is inequality between members of the same family, but not such as to make them aliens and strangers to one another. Properly speaking, there are no subjects in the family; all are, as it were, something belonging to the father. And so its authority is not like that which governs a society. The father governs the house as an extension of himself: he does not give it laws in the strict sense, nor does he exert compulsion or repression as we find them in societies where men are united externally, by a purpose, under the authority of rulers and laws, properly so called.

The city is the sphere of the full flowering of human life, the community which corresponds to that higher degree of humanity made possible by civilisation, which is the product of city life. As a fact, if men wish to rise above everyday life, to develop human potentialities to a certain level and quality, there must be a wider setting, allowing varied exchanges, providing the necessary re-sources for creating and maintaining more creative institutions, guaranteeing a security which itself requires resources, etc. This is verified by human experience in all ages.[10] On this level, there is a distribution of functions which presupposes or creates not only differences between men, but genuine inequalities: the authority governs subjects in the proper sense, makes laws and can use coercion.

To what extent can these categories of family and city, thus defined, apply to the parish on the one hand, to the diocese and the universal Church on the other?

We may remark at the outset that the Church, *in all her being*, is both family and city. She is a family up to her highest level, and not only at that of the parish, just as she is a city in her most elementary manifestations, as Aquinas briefly indicates.[11] The Church is a family up to her highest forms, because authority, in her, is never *only* a political type of authority, but is always paternal, generative, educative. That is why in the gospel the hierarchy is sometimes represented as a princedom, a judicature, sometimes as an economy, a provision for the family.[12]

The Church has members rather than subjects. Though she unites them under an external law and authority, it is far more true that she looks in the first place to man himself: she strives to form man, to model and perfect in him the divine likeness, as Pius XII said so well, when distinguishing the work of the Church from political imperialism.[13] On the other hand—and this is perhaps even more important—the Church is a city, because in her is realised the fullness and perfection of life made possible in a city, even at her most elementary levels, that is, in the parish and in her existence in the individual soul. This is one of the senses in which is verified the fairly frequent claim of the Fathers and ancient theologians, that every soul, each soul, is the Church. For the Church is a very special society, whose final common good is nothing less than communion in the life of the three persons of the Trinity. That good, which is obviously supreme perfection and supreme fullness of life, is not found by human co-operation, like the good of civilisation: it is communicated from above by faith, hope and charity. In that supreme and decisive order of the good of the divine life, existence in the body of Christ, even in its humblest degree—that of the parish or even the solitary life—suffices to obtain perfection. The recluse who receives communion at his grille mystically receives the gift of all his heavenly heritage. That eucharist, which the humblest priest can give him, is as divine as that celebrated by the pope: and in this respect the hierarchical scheme of certain liturgists is not theologically accurate.[14] It transposes what is valid in the order of jurisdiction into the sacramental order, in which every priest depends directly on Christ. As far as the celebration of the eucharistic mystery is concerned, the pope has no higher power than a simple priest.[15]

The fact that there are organisms in the Church corresponding respectively to the city and the family in human life, results not so much from the essence of the Church herself as from a kind of reflection in her of the nature of human affairs, of the social structure spontaneously assumed by the life of man. It is natural, and there are many things like that in the Church, because she is not purely a descent or communication of heavenly things: she is made up of men, she requires an action on the part of those men in order to be incorporated in the second, heavenly Adam, and to share in the treasure of reconciled life which is in him. That is why, founded in heaven and as it were suspended from heaven, she yet adheres to the human 'dough' in which she has to insert the leaven of the spirit of Christ, which will raise it up to heaven. That is why the Church, family and city in all that she is, more specially takes on the structure of a family in the parish, and of a city in the diocese. As regards the communication of the common spiritual good, heavenly and inward, the parish provides the essentials, but in so far as the Church involves an exercise of external resources, and a properly social kind of co-operation, she is differentiated in a manner analogous to a human community.

The parish is the milieu in which the Christian is generated and formed. As the family is the formative milieu of man, not in any special qualification or specialisation, but simply in his fundamental quality as man, the parish engenders and forms man simply in that new life and character as members of the Second Adam, without special qualification. From this point of view, in fact, all are equal and alike. St Paul says that in Christ there is neither male nor female, Jew nor Gentile, slave nor free.[16] The parish is the milieu of the basic engendering and forming of the Christian. It is the place of the baptismal fonts: the cathedral church itself has no font unless it is also a parish church, and monastic churches have no fonts. It is the place where the Christian conscience is formed, by the catechism and the Sunday instruction: like the family, it is the home where the basic person is formed, that with which we have to live and react all our lives.[17] It is the place of the ordinary sacramental life, where we receive the sacraments which are given to all, whereas those which place us in a particular state or dignity are reserved to the bishop.[18] It is the home of all and of the equality of all, something really common to all. As Abbé Michonneau so truly says, it imposes no 'spirituality', it demands nothing else and nothing more than what the Church demands. In this respect it really corresponds to the family, the house, or that simple grouping of families and houses which is the community of the neighbourhood, the community of mutual aid and services on the level of ordinary daily life.

The priest's powers correspond exactly to this function. He is the ordinary minister of solemn baptism, where men begin to exist in Jesus Christ,[19] he is the ordinary minister of the word,[20] he presides over the family's prayer *in persona ecclesiae*.[21] Finally, he celebrates the eucharist, and thus, as I have already noted, gives all that the Church can give in the order of inner and personal sanctity, but not so as to confer a particular distinction or appoint to a special state.[22] Sublime as all this is, in the Church it is still part of the daily family life. In the same way, for the pardon of sins, the ordinary priest is the minister of reconciliation for what we may call the ordinary, the private, that which has no strictly social character or repercussion, whereas crimes or sins of greater gravity are reserved to the bishop. The parish priest has very great powers in the sphere of interior personal life, 'private life', we might say, if the term were not so ambiguous. But from the strictly social point of view, he has only a private, not a public power and authority.[23] He is father far more than he is head. The hierarchical head of the parish is the bishop, not the parish priest.[24] The parish priest, like the father of the family, can administer his community, give precepts, not laws: he can rebuke and correct paternally, but cannot coerce or punish.[25]

The diocese and the bishop's power provide for other needs. In the parish, the Church puts forth scarcely more than her motherhood: she gives children to God, forms their consciences, nurses them for daily life. In the diocese and the bishop she puts forth also her royal power.[26] The parish, providing for a limited and relatively homogeneous milieu—I shall return to this point in a moment—see simply to the birth, the basic, unspecialised formation of the new man. On the diocese and the episcopal power depend all matters concerning differences, the regulation of responsibilities, the distribution of duties: all the things which require larger, richer, more varied resources, and a real authority, of the 'princely' kind, corresponding to a community of the city type. The authority included in it is a fully 'public' authority, 'political' in the sense of Aristotelian-Thomist sociology.[27] But I have no desire to plunge here into a theology of the episcopate. . . .

We can thus form an idea of the things which lie outside the proper functions of the parish. Whenever Christian action, whether in the field of the apostolate, of organisations, or of thought and teaching, passes from the private to the public order, we move from the plane of the family to that of the city, from the parish to the diocese, or to some organisation on a similar level. This is most fully the case when it is a matter, not simply of appointing a cantor or a president of some association, for example, but of 'ordaining' a Christian for a public ministry, in which he will act *in persona ecclesiaie*. This is true even in the order of the apostolate, when one passes from a private apostolate (though it may be collectively practised) to an 'instituted' apostolate, of a public, official, hierarchical status. Catholic Action in the proper sense depends, in itself, on the Church as a city and on the episcopate, even if (as often happens) it is organised at parochial level and within the parochial framework.[28]

Whatever requires the employment of large and varied resources and extensive co-operation, or concerns a particular way of Christian life, should be taken out of the parochial framework. If it is a matter of action on the scale of society itself, action 'on the structures', as they say, this is again something beyond the proper order of the parish, and it is certainly right to take account of this and to arrange the work and its management on another level.

It is not surprising that the first beginnings of the 'works' and then, even more, the 'movements', particularly from 1925 to 1935, presented parishes with so many problems, the memory of which is preserved in the reviews and congress reports of those arduous years, and which to many priests are something far more concrete and contemporary than a memory. What must be emphasised from our point of view is that, even for those who work on a level or in a framework which transcends it, the parish must remain the place where spiritual nourishment is sought and found. There are serious problems of organisation and harmonisation, but the main problem is to ensure that the parish should really provide spiritual nourishment to Christians, wherever they are engaged.

This brings us to a point where many of you have no doubt forestalled me, and where we cannot escape criticism of the idea of the parish as a family. We may wonder, indeed, how far this idea is shaped to a state of things, both in the family and in the parish, which is no longer what we have to deal with. Is the idea of a community, of ordinary needs and services, of the family type, still true today? In our social structures there is a considerable margin of changes and adaptations. It has been shown that, even in antiquity, domestic ties and paternal authority were relaxed in rigour in proportion as external and distant relationships were multiplied by the increase of commercial exchanges.[29] What then should we say of today? The socialisation of life, or at least man's awareness of its implications, its social pressures and commitments, is a phenomenon already considerable in extent, and no doubt on the increase. Modern life, especially in our analytic and rationalising west, tends to break up human life and distribute it according to social groupings of activity and occupation. Where, in all this, is the simplicity of the 'house'? Where is the community of neighbourhood and mutual aid for the needs of daily life? Nowadays these needs bring into play something quite different from an undifferentiated society, such as I mentioned in connection with the parish. The community of neighbourhood is too poor and narrow a reality, in many cases, to cope with the diversity and wide extent of the areas and social groups involved, as we emphasise, in this daily, ordinary existence to which the parish corresponds.

We have already seen that, in order to keep up with the actual current of life, the 'works' and the 'movements' very often had to be organised outside the framework and regular scheme of the parish. Some went even further: they suggested that, at least in the big centres, the parish should adapt itself to the different human categories: they spoke of bourgeois parishes, working-class parishes, parishes for fishermen, and so on.[30]

This idea has not become widespread and has encountered some criticism.[31] In fact, I think it is somewhat unfortunate. Not only is it based on a frail foundation (namely, a number of fluctuating sociological data which from the human point of view are not the most profound), but it entails a certain failure to understand a truth which is absolutely capital in the mission of the parish: its vocation to bring men to be born with a new birth and to unite them in Christ, beyond all their differences, natural or sociological. The Church, as I said, is the meeting-place between the first Adam and the second, the place in which the first passes mystically, spiritually, into the substance of the second. She exists both by a communication of the common gift of the divine life realised in Jesus Christ, her heavenly head, and by human co-operation. She cannot unreservedly accept the human differentiations and structures, because she is the body of the second Adam. As the place where Christian life is engendered and formed, the parish must preserve undifferentiated its transcendence with regard to human diversities: of man or woman, Greek or barbarian, slave or free. The pure and simple gathering together in the communion of the Lord represents, from the Christian point of view, *a value in itself*. That is beyond all question of *methods*. It is this that *effects* the Church.

Shorn of its exaggerations, however, the idea has a truth in it. Granted that the mission of the parish is to form Christian consciences, or Christians pure and simple, *sine addito*, they have still to be formed in accordance with what they are and what they are called to do, in the real, concrete conditions of their lives. They have still to be enlightened, inspired and upheld *for the exercise of their real responsibilities*. Now it cannot be denied that these responsibilities take men more and more, *in their daily lives*, right outside the undifferentiated framework of the family and the community of the neighbourhood. They involve them in all sorts of groups or detailed activities, which abound at all levels between the undifferentiated entity of the house and the supreme entity of the nation and the state. The priest whose mission it is to engender and form Christians *sine addito* cannot be a guide, a support, a spiritual encourager of these Christians in the real conditions of their life and for their real responsibilities, if his ministry remains common to all and undifferentiated. As Canon Guérin said to me recently, the loss of faith in a great many individuals and circles is chiefly due to a lack of realism and effort on this point: personal Christianity can only remain alive in a Christianity that is specific.

Our awareness of this fact need not, I think, lead us to conclude that the undifferentiated parish is on the way out. But I think that we may have to admit an increasing disengagement of the priestly ministry from the strictly parochial framework. More and more, —I mean, where this is in place, chiefly in the towns—we shall have to analyse (by means of a method of which Fr Lebret has given us the elements, and which has been so well inaugurated by the monographs of Godin and Boulard) the sectors of life, the sociological commitment, in which the concrete responsibility of our Christians is involved, and to organise an adapted pastoral scheme, in order to enable our priests to follow up, to guide and support the faithful, precisely where their life is spent and their Christian responsibilities are actually exercised.

If there is to be specialisation, it will not be in the parishes, but in the priestly ministry, the local spiritual organism, adapted to the residential unit and the community of neighbourhood, combined in some way with spiritual organisms specialised according to occupations and surroundings. The appropriate organism of the Christian life of a population will still be the parish, or a number of parishes, but also, I think, it will be more and more the *priestly team of the spiritual inspirers of the different sectors of life*. I repeat expressly, the priestly team. That is absolutely vital.

Vital but, you may say, not very new. How many parish priests there are who have for long been forming a team with their curates! That is true, I know. I have often observed it myself, and it enables me once again to bear witness: I have often observed that parishes generally reflect the communal life of their clergy, and that where there was understanding and friendship, even frankly human friendship, between the parish priest and his curates, the whole parish reflected their understanding and joy and experienced a real forward drive. But if we have often seen a happy team of a parish priest and his curates, how often have we seen the parish priests form a team themselves? The priestly team I am speaking of can be parochial, it can be inter-parochial, it can be based on a district, it can be mixed. It can embrace, besides the clergy of one or more parishes, the religious and the chaplains. The essential thing is that there should be a priestly team, an apostolic community of those who have the spiritual charge, not only of an area but of a definite population. Everywhere the complexity and intermixture of affairs leads men to group themselves, to combine in measures which are beyond the powers of individuals in isolation. It is also a fact that wherever there is missionary or apostolic realism, communities appear; or, if you prefer it, there is full apostolic realism where there is a community or a team, because the basis of such realism or of such teams is the common awareness—not just made once for all but constantly renewed, revised or reviewed—of the composition of the real needs of that portion of mankind for which the team is responsible, *in solidum*, under the direction of its leader.

The mission of the parish thus continues to be the engendering and forming of Christian souls *sine addito*, in everyday life and by ordinary means. That mission, if it is that of the parish, is incumbent on the clergy in charge of it. But the clergy will only be able to fulfil it if it is not purely parochial, in the narrow and impoverished sense of the word. Was it not one of the conclusions frequently repeated at the Besançon conference and after it (by Cardinal Feltin, for example), that to avoid a sort of sclerosis the parish must succeed in avoiding self-sufficiency?

From the pastoral point of view these considerations lead us to the following conclusions: the parish has an essential function—the education of the inner man, of the Christian animated by charity in his whole life, as it is, with his own concrete responsibilities. A parish is not only a collection of organisations which are administered. Pius Parsch draws attention to the error of supposing the *organisation* of works and groups, however useful, to be the aim and content of pastoral work.[32] The aim of pastoral work exists only in living souls.[33] The parish priest must try not so much to govern as to educate, for he works, in the Church, at the level of the family.

This idea, that we ought to become educators, far more than we are now, is one that I have encountered whenever I have studied the conditions of apostolic work. When, for example, during the campaign of 1946-7, I gave conferences to the priests of Paris on Christendom, its past and present conditions, I remarked then that a new Christendom, lay and prophetic in style, was only possible on the basis of inner, personal convictions, no longer on that of institutions; that is, on the basis of an essentially educative pastoral work. Again, having reflected with you on the mission of the parish and the task of the parish priest, I have found that their chief function is to form Christian souls, *sine addito*, in ordinary life and for their concrete responsibilities.[34]

Let us devote ourselves, more than we have yet done, to being spiritual educators, always offering a doctrine, promoting a religion, who have their fruit and their reality in the consciences of living men! But I do not wish to embark on a theme which involves both liturgy and preaching, and hence the studies which prepare for them.

A community constructed from above and from below

For certain questions now confronting pastoral theology, and especially for that major question of the laity, it is important to realise that the Church is constructed both from above and from below. There are, in the life of the Church, two different logics, so to speak, a sort of dialectic in which neither of the two terms must be sacrificed.

This presence of the two logics derives from the fact, already noted above, that the Church is the place where the second Adam and the first Adam meet, to be united together. The first Adam is all of us men. The second is Christ, 'delivered for our sins and raised again for our justification'.[35] He represents in himself the whole shared boon of reconciled life: in the strictest sense of the word, he is our peace.[36] From this point of view, everything has been done for the Church; all that remains is to communicate from above a treasure, fully established on the cross, and now in heaven. The first Adam, who has grown, multiplied and filled the earth, is all men. But they have to make their own the gift which is in Christ, to make it their own on the basis of faith, by a personal action, and collectively by an action all together, a co-operation with God and with one another. From this point of view, everything has still to be done in the Church.

That is why, by essential principle and constitution, the Church is built from above, and yet, in order to be effectively herself, she is also built from below.

She is built from above and hierarchically: the profound meaning and reason of the hierarchy, which is of the very structure of the Church, is to show and ensure that in the Church everything comes from above and is a communication of a supernatural gift already made real in Christ. There is a hierarchical mediation of truth (dogma) and grace (sacraments), because grace and truth exist in Jesus Christ.[37] These gifts come to us from above and outside us, as something already made.

In this respect the Church is very different from temporal society, which is constituted wholly from the base. It is made up of families. It is a moral person, ordered by nature and choice to an end, and it has in itself the capacity to attain that end, and so to order and administer itself. In temporal society public authority is the organ which the body politic gives itself, to organise and administer itself for the attainment of its end.[38] But the Church is not, structurally, made up of parishes, and her power is not a sort of product of the body, giving itself limbs from within. The power comes to it from outside and above. That is the meaning of apostolicity and the fact of the hierarchy. The Church is a homogeneous body, made up of dioceses.

But the parish itself is hierarchical: it is constituted by means of powers received from above. Here the liturgists are in their element, and it is they who are in the right. Fundamentally, the Church, from end to end, is built on the image of the Three-in-One, on the double principle of hierarchy and communication, as Gréa has so well shown in his book *De l'Église et de sa divine Constitution*.

But essential as this point is, we cannot leave it at that. The Church is not only an apparatus of hierarchical mediation, an administration of doctrine and sacraments, or means of salvation considered objectively. It is that, of course, but not only that. It is also a community of believing men, living actively on the foundation of this communication of salvation. I have quoted elsewhere those words of Bismarck, cruelly false, but enlightening: 'The two Churches, Catholic and Protestant, have very different foundations. The Catholic Church draws its being from its clergy; it exists and fulfils itself through them; it could exist without a community; the Mass could be said without a community; the community is a useful object for affirming the Christian function of the Catholic Church, but it is not in the least necessary for the Church's existence. In the Protestant Church, on the contrary, the community is entirely the foundation of the whole Church. . . .'[39] Whether Protestantism is ignorant of the fact of the hierarchy and of apostolicity in the sense I have earlier defined, does not here concern us: but we ought to take careful note of the fact that the Church in general, and the parish in particular, are not built solely from above, by hierarchical mediation of the means of salvation, but equally from below. The Church is also the community of men who have in them the fruits of that mediation, the life of the heavenly Adam, and are active in virtue of that life, *plebs adunata sacerdoti et pastori suo grex adhaerens*, as Cyprian put it.[40] By essential right, the Church comprises a people, an active people. As the Fathers and medieval theologians never tire of repeating, she is *societas fidelium*, the society, the community, of those who believe. The Church is an institution, an apparatus, of salvation; she is also a community of saved men.

Just as she is, from top to bottom, a family, but particularly so at her base, in the parish, so she is from top to bottom a community, but she can and ought to be so especially in the parish.

In the movement of self-criticism which has been evident in the Church, at least in France, since the war, and (where it is loving and reverent) can open so many possibilities for good, the complaint is sometimes made that the Church presents too much of the ready-made. I think that in this complaint there is a fact worthy of attention, which may not only provide a clue to many of the aspirations found among both clergy and laity, but may also reveal one of the reasons for the shortage of recruits to the priesthood, which in many regions is tragic. The root of the matter here, as I see it, is to complete the construction of the Church from above (that is, by the hierarchical transmission of given realities) by a construction of the Church from below, as a reality with its roots in men, in the religious individual, and nourished *equally* by what they contribute to it.

It is especially complained that the parish is ill-adapted, that it provides little help for a religious life, that it is a collection of ready-made things, of 'rites', a mere setting for ceremonies, and for that reason it no longer interests men.[41] Of course that is not true everywhere, far from it. But after all, I have not invented these complaints . . . and they directly concern our subject.

All the studies on this question, and especially those emanating, not from the theorists, but from those with practical experience,[42] envisage only one issue, that the parish should be a living community. It is certainly easier to say this than to do anything about it, but who would maintain that it is useless to speak of it, and to try to see what has to be done?

A community is not just a juxtaposition or even a bundle of individual Christianities. Nor is it just a formation, biddable to the decisions and initiatives of a head. It is a collectivity, where all are active and interested, in which (though all is done in orderly fashion) everything is done *with* all. To act *with*, together, is the law of the community.

No ecclesiastical body can be defined apart from this quality of community, but the parish least of all. Canonical definitions are certainly necessary, but a purely canonical notion of the parish, defined as an area within which a priest exercises certain rights and duties, is clearly a notion inadequate to the facts. The parish is a community, and whatever remains to it of strength and vitality is largely derived from its correspondence to a certain human reality, its basic contact with the actual life of men. Let us never despise this trump card we hold, that we can build from below, from a human soil of solid reality and consent. (This is one of the advantages, for example, of our schools and 'works' over other organisations created from above.) I said that the Church does not grow limbs from below, like the body politic. She is not just a mass of parishes, each made up of individual believers.[43] But there is indeed a sense, a point of view, in which she is community and people, in which the Church is made of parishes, somewhat as the nation is made of families.

Whenever we have analysed the component principles of the parochial community, the same conclusions have emerged. Community of prayer or spiritual life, community of mutual services, community of Catholic action—so said my friend Mgr Lacroix at Besançon.[44] Liturgical community, fraternal community, missionary community—so Cardinal Feltin wrote later.[45] Thus, under the pressure of Christian realities, they both found the characteristic traits of the first Christian community, type of all the rest of which we read, in Acts 2:42, that it was devoted to the teaching of the apostles, to the fellowship, to the breaking of bread and to the prayers. It is by all these elements that the parish must form a community, that is, must live and act *with*, live and act *together*.

There is an idea often found in the best nineteenth-century pastoral theologians,[46] and repeated, I think, in various pastoral studies today,[47] and it is this: that the 'subject', that is, the bearer, the person both beneficiary of and responsible for the Church's activity, the pastoral activity in fact, is not the priest alone, not the parish priest by himself, but his whole people with him; the faithful too, with their priest. That implies that he is not only priest and pastor *over* them, but priest and pastor *among* them, *with* them, *their* priest, *their* pastor. It is not, of course, from the faithful that the priest receives his priesthood nor the pastor his powers. That error, held to some extent in the parochialism of the fifteenth and eighteenth centuries, and even by some episcopalists of the eighteenth and early nineteenth centuries, has now been quite eliminated. The priest and the pastor are not an emanation from the parish and an expression of the community. The universal priesthood, which is something very real and profound in the Church, has not this constitutional quality. In the Church, powers come from above: they themselves give birth to the ecclesiastical community: we have seen what a profound truth this fact reflects. But when this community exists through the apostolic ministry of the word and the sacraments of the faith, it is itself living and active. It is not a secular thing *over* which sacred powers are exercised. It is a Christian thing, the body of a head who is himself prophet, priest and king. The Church's work is the community's work: it is wholly responsible for that work, although it cannot perform all the acts involved in it. Thus the parish, with a pastor who is really *its* priest, ought to be a community of prayer, of mutual services, of apostolic action.

This is difficult to put into practice. Yes indeed, and it will always be difficult, much more difficult than to talk about it. But I don't hesitate to talk about it, one of the Church's general staff and a man of the schools though I am, before you, the infantry of the line: because I am more and more convinced that in pastoral matters and particularly on this point, the first effort to be made, the first victory to be won, is one of ecclesiology.

In this matter of creating real community at the level of the parish, there is a final point to be noted before I conclude. Especially when the parish is rather large, or when it exists among varied and scattered human groups, it will be found that smaller and more differentiated groups are being formed. The fact is very marked in these days, and arises from several causes. First, there are groups linked by Christian responsibility and formation, or by mutual help in facing the responsibilities we have mentioned: these support the 'works' and 'movements'. Then there are small voluntary communities, which abound nowadays, at least in the big centres, and meet the need, I think, to construct the Church from below, that need for the Christian life, very loyal and sometimes very fervent, to take root and be fostered in the religious individual. I am thinking of certain evangelising groups, of those family circles, of missionary or unionist circles, of those groups of teachers, among which some very apostolic priests give of their best.

The danger is that such groups may form small parishes, as it were, within the larger one, or rather alongside it, and so deprive it of their vitality, which is often considerable. There is clearly a danger here, and I hope that all may be aware of it. But we must see the positive, constructive side of this state of affairs. First, I think that these little communities, if they are really communities, if they are moved by a spirit which is true to the name, if they live by the pooled contributions and efforts of the persons themselves, will be a help and source of energy to any parish which itself really wants to form a community. I am not alone in thinking so: such seems to me to be the lucid conviction of Abbé Michonneau, in particular.[48] Further, one could show that the older parishes attracted men chiefly by groupings.[49] I believe that the two things, the parish as a real community, and these groupings of affinity, respond to the same profound logic, that of an awareness and a construction of the Church from below, in both cases. On a certain scale, our parishes seem too anonymous, too administrative: and what shall we say of the diocese or the universal Church? To many men of our time the Church, appearing to them as a ready-made mechanism, anonymous and rather overwhelming, obscures God, obscures even her own mystery. She does not interest them, they see her from outside with a tinge of fear and distrust. They leave her to live and get along without them. Men who approve such sentiments will understand her and join her only if they start from below: by themselves forming cells of the Church, little communities, in the heart of which the priest can be fully with them, in the midst of them, before he is over them.

Finally, is there not here a way by which the faithful can be organically integrated into the body of Christ, and the whole Christian community? It is a way which may help to bring about the marvellous programme formulated by Pius XII in connection with democracy, when he himself sketched its application to the Church—that men should be treated, not *en masse*, as a passive and inorganic collectivity, but as a *people*, a living and organic collectivity.[50] Does not this formula wonderfully sum up what I have been saying about the parish as a community, constituted not only from above but from below, not merely a flock ruled by a hierarchy, but a faithful people animated by its priests?

The pastoral conclusion of this last section can be formulated thus: just as from the idea of the parish-as-family we drew the conclusion that the parish priest ought to be supremely an educator, an educator of Christian life, so from the idea of the parish-as-community, forming itself from below, we draw the conclusion that the priest ought to be the priest *of his people*, the man of God in the *midst* of men and *with* men, the man of God providentially placed among a small people *for* that people. Not an external authority, dealing with the ready-made, administering alien things for the sake of a great anonymous machine, but acting *with*, making men act with him.

Allow me to sum up. What is the mission of the parish? It is to form men, united by neighbourhood and mutual service, for a Christian life, *sine addito*, and to do so in harmony with a priestly work which, in order to follow men up on the ground of their real responsibilities, sometimes goes outside the strictly parochial framework. Next, both in that framework and in the various groups of affinity, to make the most of that aspect of the Church in which the faithful act together, in which they make the Church, after being made by her.

What a programme! I, who have an easier life than many of you, realise how very sublime and how very difficult it is. I know some priests who are sometimes tempted to be discouraged. To them I would say, I would exclaim with a sincerity they could find no cause in me to doubt, that always and everywhere, in the Church, a magnificent work is being done: always and everywhere, by the Church, that is, by you, a magnificent work is being done. And if I may be allowed, I should like to end with the words of General de Castelnau, addressing the seminarists at Issy: 'You've chosen a ghastly job!'

EXCHANGE OF VIEWS

(A few days after the Congress, Fr Congar received the following letter from Abbé Pécréaux, assistant curate at Paray-Vieille-Poste (Seine-et-Oise). This, with Fr Congar's reply, gives a clearer statement of the issue than was possible in the oral discussion at Lille.)

From Abbé Pécréaux: Allow me to send you a few reflections on your conference at Lille.

I have before me only a few notes taken down on the spot, but, if I understand you rightly, you think that the idea of the liturgists expresses an essential but partial view of the parish. Regarded as a community of worship, you said, the parish fulfils the first commandment of the law, but neglects the second, which is like it: it risks making the Christian just a good parishioner, rather passive, who takes his part in the worship and obeys his priest. This concept, right in its own order, needs to be completed by that of the parish as a community of real life: that was, in fact, the object of your conference.

I willingly admit that the parish gains by being considered under several different aspects, photographed, so to speak, from several different angles. That is no more than is necessary in order to penetrate all its riches and potentialities. And in the setting of that congress, devoted to the social structures of the parish, it was right that a theological development, established on that basis, should bring to light the principles which bear on the various technical or practical proposals. But the definition of your subject seemed to me to go beyond the bounds of a choice of method. Your thesis, like the 'I', is stated in terms of opposition, and the concept of the liturgists deserves, in my opinion, to be defended by an advocate from their number.

By limiting liturgical worship to the expression of our relations with God, you risk, I think, giving too narrow an idea of it.

In the first place, public prayer is itself, as such, an act of fraternal charity. Instead of each one praying at home, we join together as a family, 'to pray together': united in the same thought, the same feelings, we sing the same chants, *loquentes vobismetipsis in psalmis et hymnis*. That is even more evident when we assemble for the sacrifice. In the first place, anyone who has sinned against his neighbour ought not to take part in it, as Christ himself tells us in the Sermon on the Mount. And St Paul says: 'Have you not houses to eat and drink in?', and regards those who eat and drink the Lord's Body and Blood unworthily as primarily Christians without fraternal charity. Communion, in uniting us to Christ, unites us thereby to all those who together eat the same bread. And the sacrament of penance, reintegration into Communion, reconciles us to our brethren in reconciling us to God. It is this double representation that the priest guarantees to it.

The liturgy therefore unites us to our brethren as it unites us to God: it takes hold of us also in all that we are, body and soul, person and society, bodies and goods. Through Christ, with him and in him, the whole world, our whole life, all our efforts of the week, rise to heaven, symbolised by the bread and wine we have laid on the altar. And when we come to take our part in the sacrifice, the Father's blessing extends to the whole field of our activity; *per quem haec omnia, Domine, semper bona creas*. . . . The liturgy does not detain the faithful in the enclosure of the sanctuary: when the Mass is over the deacon asks them to depart: but they have realised more fully the collective character of their existence; the week now beginning is the Mass continued, and they are its priests. As Dagallier said, they don't want their Mass to be a lie. Priests and people, by their work and their missionary activity, will enlarge the field of their meditation to the dimensions of the world (Lebret).

For this purpose we must remember the active rôle of the faithful at Mass: *nos servi tui et plebs tua sancta*: it is above all at the Holy Sacrifice that they form a kingdom of priests, and that will be more clearly seen when the Christian people, led by its natural leaders, will itself provide, each man according to his talents, for the upkeep of the house of God, the service of the altar (like the worker 'militants' of Mantes, who on great feast days turn the altar-boys out of the sacristy, don the albs and serve the Mass), the chants and the instruction of the children and catechumens in the liturgical action.

Two facts, one primitive, the other contemporary, may serve to illustrate these considerations. To the Corinthians, who had asked him about precise, practical points, Paul replied with a letter to be read in the course of the assembly—the assembly for prayer has always been an assembly for speech, and the priest has not always been the only one to speak.

When, within the bounds of our parishes, smaller groups become conscious of themselves, they give themselves a liturgy which expresses their union and makes it real in a tangible fashion, by enabling themselves to resolve the problems of their life in common, in the light of the gospel; and the presence of the priest provides them with a beautiful ending to their intercourse by the celebration of the Eucharist, on the table where they have had their meal.

The liturgy therefore opens out a perspective on the whole of Christian life, which it expresses, crowns and transfigures, without mutilating it. In the cloister, after all, the monks are given their work for the day, with the grace to do it well, at the chapter at Prime. The parochial prayer is continued in the same way. It is the highest expression of the Church's life on earth: it is also the most profoundly real. For if man is flesh and blood, he is also, on this earth, son of God and citizen of heaven, and it is the liturgy, 'prime and indispensable source of the Christian spirit', that brings us nearest to heaven: *hic domus Dei est et porta coeli*. It is there that the divinisation of earthly things must culminate: never forgetting those other men who are at the door and must be helped to enter: *Compelle intrare*.

I do not say that all liturgists and all pastors of souls exploit this wealth to the full, but there is nothing to prevent them doing so. In this respect the Roman liturgy lends itself better than others: the offertory suggests that we mingle our offering with the sacrifice of Christ in a concrete manner (without going so far as to drown the consecration under the offertory rites, as is too often done); whereas at the Great Entry in the Byzantine rite the Cherubikon invites the faithful (representing the cherubim) to forget all earthly cares.

Once again, in defending the liturgical presentation of the parochial community and considering it superior to all others, there is no need to exclude a sociological presentation. Our need is definitely to renounce a certain way of presenting things, to revise our discipline of thought. It is a good thing to distinguish, to define certain elements of a whole by their specific differences, so as to avoid confusing everything and ending in chaos. But without forfeiting the benefits of our Aristotelian and Cartesian training, it would be well to subordinate it to a more biblical view of things. To a Jew, concepts are not opposed to one another, they are points of view, each of which reveals the whole reality under a particular aspect. We know well that God does not (really) hate Esau, and that we can love Christ with all our strength without hating our parents. The word of God is at once commandment, prophetic exhortation and teaching of wisdom, even if the priest, the prophet and the sage seem to be at variance. Justice is mercy, and the fear of God is a way of loving him.

Let us learn, as Semitic logic does so well, to surmount the dialectical oppositions, by seeing them as partial and provisional. We cannot parcel out reality into clearly delimited zones, especially when we are speaking of the ineffable unity of the divine mystery in which all the rest finds its substance.

But it is not so easy. The Hebrews could allow themselves violent antitheses, for to them they existed only in language, whereas it is our logic itself which separates, opposes and divides, by making the divisions appear from the outset as definitions: every variation of perspective is considered a change of opinion: —think of our difficulty in understanding biblical expressions and the apparent contradictions we find in them.

Wide horizons and subtle shades of meaning must guard us

from the impoverishment of life and thought caused by the abuse of over-sharpened rational tools.

From Fr Congar—I am very glad to be given an opportunity to deny an interpretation of my thought which really belies it. Fr Roguet of the CPL had already told me, after my conference, that he was on the point of taking up the defence of the liturgy, but he had understood that fundamentally I had not attacked it at all. I had absolutely no wish to criticise the liturgy, which I love, any more than the parish as a liturgical reality, living and being itself through the liturgy. I used no mere flower of speech when I said that everything so well said on this subject was admitted, and I need not return to it. It was, in fact, because the subject has been fully elaborated, especially in the publications of the Belgian liturgical movement. I was only complaining of a certain narrowness in the concept of the parish, as certain liturgists have given it. *Certain* liturgists, I said, whose names and works I quote. So I adhere to all that those liturgists have said on the liturgical reality of the parish, and to all that they and others (including Abbé Pécréaux) have said on the wonderful resources of the liturgy for putting life into our parish communities. But I persist in thinking that a definition of the parish *solely as a community of worship* has something narrow and insufficient about it.

ADDENDA IN 1962

1. If I were to rewrite this study today, I should develop more positively the liturgical point of view, so closely related to the strictly ecclesiological. I should lay more emphasis on the parish as the local representative of the *ecclesia*, of the mystery of Christ; a point of view not only of the studies in note 2, but of more recent works such as those of F. X. Arnold,[51] of Karl Rahner,[52] etc. This is because we now understand better the true nature of priesthood,[53] of Christian worship, of the sacraments, and the place held in these mysteries by the word and faith. These are themes I have expounded, especially since 1952, in numerous conferences and retreats. To explain them as they deserve would require a considerable effort of research in the sources, both of the Bible and of tradition, a criticism of certain ways of distin-

guishing between 'sacred' and 'profane', etc. God willing, I shall return to it later.

2. Since 1948 many studies have appeared on the parish, often written from a pastoral and practical point of view, which I could not deal with here.[54]

NOTES

1. Conference given at the Congrès National de l'Union des Oeuvres, at Lille, 1st April 1948; text published in *Structures Sociales et Pastorale Paroissale* (*Congrès Nat. de Lille, 1948*), Paris, 1948, pp. 48–68. The text is unchanged but for some additions to the bibliography.

2. I refer, for example, to L. Beauduin, 'L'esprit paroissial dans la tradition', in *Les Questions liturgiques*, II (1911–12), pp. 16–26, 80–90, 305–11 (reprinted in *Cours et Confér. des Semaines liturgiques*, vol. IV, Louvain, 1926, pp. 11–42); Herwegen, *Bericht der liturgischen Priestertagung, Wien*, Vienna-Mödling, 1925, pp. 10–11; A. Crogaert, 'La liturgie, principe de vie paroissiale', in *Cours et Confér. des Semaines liturgiques*, vol. III, Louvain, 1925, pp. 117–28; E. Moureau, 'L'esprit paroissial', *ibid.*, pp. 189–96; A. Wintersig, 'Pfarrei und Mysterium' in *Jahrbuch für Liturgiewissenschaft*, V, (1925), pp. 136–43 (French trans., 'Le réalisme mystique de la paroisse', in *La Maison-Dieu*, no. 8 (1946), pp. 15–26), and see also *Jahrbuch*, IV (1924), p. 162; J. Pinsk, 'Die religiöse Wirklichkeit von Kirche, Diözese und Pfarrei', in *Der Katholische Gedanke* (1933), pp. 337–44 (reproduced in *Hoffnung und Herrlichkeit*, n.d., pp. 149–63; French trans., 'La liturgie et la realité spirituelle de l'Église, du diocèse et de la paroisse' in *QLP*, Aug.–Sept. 1933, pp. 192–205; see also by J. Pinsk, 'Die Liturgie als Grundlage für die religiöse Wirklichkeit von Kirche, Diözese und Pfarrei', in *Liturgische Zeitsch.*, 4 (1931), pp. 426–37; M. Schurr, 'Die übernatürliche Wirklichkeit der Pfarrei' in *Benediktinische Monatscrift*, 1937, pp. 81–106; K. Lechner, *Pfarre und Laie. Ein Beitrag zum Problem der Grosstadt-Seelsorge*, Vienna, 1949.
Among the liturgists, Pius Parsch adopts a more pastoral, less particular point of view: see 'Die Pfarre als Mysterium' in *Die lebendige Pfarrgemeinde* (*Seelsorger-Tagung*, 1933), Vienna, 1934, pp. 13–33.

3. *Jahrbuch f. Liturgiewiss.*, IV (1924), p. 162.

4. 'The Church is above all a society of liturgy, a society formed to procure that great common good: worship', Festugière, in *Revue de Philosophie*, 1913, p. 739. Guéranger called a little book, aimed at forming an association of Christians living by the Spirit of the Church, *L'Église ou la société de la louange divine*.

5. It is well known that the Greek word *paroichia* at first meant the local, episcopal Church. In fifth century Gaul, what we call a parish was sometimes called a diocese, and *vice versa*. It was from the sixth century that *parochia* or *paroecia* began to mean the parish as we know it. In St Bernard, in the twelfth century, *parochia* still has the meaning of diocese (see *Epist.*, 178, 1: *PL*, 340); H. Imbart de la Tour, *Les paroisses rurales du IVe au XIe siècle*, Paris, 1900; J. Lesêtre, *La Paroisse*, Paris, 1906; P. de Labriolle, 'Paroecia', in *Rech. S.R.*, XVIII (1928), pp. 60–72. More recently, F. X. Arnold, 'Zur Theologie der Pfarrei', in *Theolog. Quartalsch.*, 133 (1953), pp. 129–59 (French trans. in *Proclamation de la Foi et Communauté de Foi*, Brussels, 1957, pp. 51–74).
One should note here that in spite of appearances the word *parochus*, parish priest, is not derived from *parochia*, but from a Greek word meaning 'provider', 'host' (see de Labriolle, p. 65, n. 23; Canon Fromentin, in *Ecclesia*, Bloud, 1948, p. 1280). The title 'curate' (= parish priest) is found, for example, in a *libellus*

of 1251, text in P. Fournier, *Les officialités, du moyen âge*, Paris, 1880, p. 318. On this title and many others, see H. Schäfer, *Pfarrkirche u. Stift im deutschen Mittelalter. Ein kirchenrechtsgeschichtliche Untersuchung*, Stuttgart, 1903.

6. See for example the article 'Chorévêque' in *Dict. de Droit canonique*, vol. III, col. 686–95 (Leclef, 1939).

7. Thus P. Loew, *En mission prolétarienne*, p. 68. (*Mission to the Poorest*, London, 1950.)

8. St Thomas, *Com. in IV Sent.*, d. 20, art. 4, sol. 1 (ed. Moos, no. 121) et ad primam, and, implicitly, d. 25, qu. 1, art. 1, sol. Pius XI, in his Speech of 19th October 1923 to the youth of Rome (in *L'Action catholique*, Paris, 1932, p. 88), said: 'It (the parish) is like a family, not like a city or a village: it is the earliest home of religious life in the great social family.' Cardinal Ottaviani declared, though in a somewhat different sense (namely, to assert its irreplaceable necessity): 'the parish is to the Church what the family is to the State' (*Osservatore Romano*, 13th Feb. 1954: see *NRT*, 1954, p. 526.

9. See Aquinas, *Com. in Polit.*, lib. 1, lect. 1. And see S. Schwalm, O.P., *Lecons de Philosophie sociale*, Paris, 2 vol., 1910.

10. This point is important, not only in sociology, but in pastoral matters, and conclusions can be drawn from it about various institutions in the Church. I can illustrate it by some examples. It has often happened that schools have vegetated or declined through lack of an environment rich enough in men, possibilities or exchanges. It was so with the schools of Tournai and Laon in the twelfth century; the schools of Paris, on the other hand, lasted and prospered. (See Paré, Brunet, Tremblay, *La Renaissance du XIIe siècle. Les écoles et l'enseignement*, Paris and Ottawa, 1933, pp. 22f). At the beginning of the nineteenth century the transfer of Ellwangen University to Tübingen was of decisive importance in this way. Möhler wrote in 1826: 'Small, isolated institutions seldom give excellent results. They lack everything: links with an intellectual environment, external stimuli, personal energy; a constant mediocrity prevails, gradually killing them. On the other hand, nowhere is the human mind more active than in the heart of a vast community dedicated to the pursuit of great aims. The individual is enlarged by the whole' (Quoted in E. Vermeil, *Jean-Adam Möhler et l'école cath. de Tubingue*, Paris, 1913, p. 25). Finally, this sentiment played a great part in the life of Goethe: his admiration for Napoleon was inspired by it: he was stifled in the narrow provincialism of Weimar (see P. Hamann, *Goethe*, Paris, n.d. (1932), *passim*, especially pp. 86–9).

11. *Com. in Epist. ad Ephesios*, c. 2, lect. 6.

12. See on the one hand Mt 16:19; 18:18; on the other, Mt 24:45; Lk 12:42. To the pope we apply Ps 104:21, which says, speaking of Joseph: *Constituit eum dominum domus suae et principem omnis possessionis suae*.

13. Speech of 20th Feb. 1946, at the bestowing of hats on the new cardinals, *Doc. cath.*, 17th March 1946, col. 172.

14. I mean writings like Crogaert's, *loc. cit.*, or those of Lefebvre, *La Messe du Souverain Pontife*, Lophem, 1929.

15. *Com. in IV Sent.*, d. 25, qu. 1, art. 1, ad 3; see also a series of articles on 'Ordre et juridiction dans l'Église', in *Irénikon*, 1933.

16. Gal 3:28.

17. Cardinal Hlond explained this point well in his great pastoral letter of 1933, *La vie religieuse de nos paroisses*, French text (abridged) in *QLP*, Oct. 1933, pp. 210–21: see p. 214.

18. See Aquinas, *Com. in IV Sent.*, d. 13, qu. 1, art. 1, sol. 2, and d. 23, qu. 2, art. 1, sol. 3.

19. Can. 738; *Sum. Theol.*, IIIa, qu. 67, art. 2, ad 2.
20. Can. 1330f; 1342, sect. 1. St Thomas, *Com. in IV Sent.*, d. 5, qu. 2, art. 1, qa 2, ad 2 and d. 6, qu. 2, art. 2, qa 2, sol et 3; *Sum. Theol.*, IIIa, qu. 71, art. 4, ad 3.
21. *Com. in II Sent.*, d. 11, qu. 1, art. 1, ad 3; *Sum. Theol.*, III, qu. 82, art. 6, c and art. 7, ad 3.
22. *Com. in IV Sent.*, d. 13, qu. 1, art. 1, sol. 2 and d. 23, qu. 2, art. 1, sol. 3.
23. *Com in IV Sent.*, d. 17, qu. 3, art. 1, qa 2, ad 2; d. 13, qu. 1, art. 1, qa 2, sol. et 2m; *Sum. Theol.*, III, qu. 82, art. 3, ad 3. Compare the distinction between the *clavis ordinis* possessed by the ordinary priest, who has power *in his quae directe sunt ad Deum*, with the *clavis jurisdictionis in foro causarum*: *Com. in IV Sent.*, d. 19, qu. 1, art. 1, sol. 3; see also d. 18, qu. 2, art. 2, qa 1, ad 2.
24. See *QLP*, IV (1913–14), p. 243.
25. *Com. in IV Sent.*, d. 18, qu. 2, art. 2, qa 1, ad 2; *Quodl.*, III, art. 17, ad 5.
26. See *Com. in IV Sent.*, d. 25, qu. 1, art. 1, sol.
27. Besides several of the texts cited above, in which the diocese is compared to a city or a kingdom, the bishop is constantly represented by Aquinas as a 'prince' in the spiritual hierarchy: it is his office to carry out the consecrations which create an *excellentiam status*, a social function or dignity. See *De perfectione vitae spirit.*, c. 23 and 24 (ed. Parme, vol. XV, pp. 99–100); *Quodl. III*, art. 17, ad 5m; *Quodl. I*, art. 14, *C. Gent.*, IV, 73; *Com. in IV Sent.*, d. 13, qu. 1, art. 3, qa 2, ad 2m; *Sum. Theol.*, qu. 83, art. 3, ad 2; etc.

In the same line of thought may be found an explanation of this fact, that the higher an authority is and the larger the area under its rule, the more danger there is of its becoming remote and administrative. The family, like the parish, *educates* rather than *governs*. Historically, we see the central power in the Church gradually giving a more official and administrative form to its interventions, the more it tried to govern all the Churches, see, for example, the articles 'Chancellerie apostolique' and 'Décrétales' in *DACL*. Taparelli d'Azeglio rightly notes that government, in its outward aspect, requires less assiduous cares: it is therefore more the work of 'political' power, more remote and superior. In its interior aspect, on the other hand, it must be exercised in closer contact with the governed (*Essai théorique de Droit naturel*, no. 1465, French trans., vol. III, p. 186). The parish priest or the religious superior, who represent a 'domestic' authority in the Church, carried out in daily life, have a more inward ministry than the higher members of the hierarchy.
28. I would refer the reader to my article 'Sacerdoce et Laïcat' in *Masses Ouvrières*, or in *Vie Int.*, (Dec. 1946) or in a brochure.
29. See, for example, the article 'Patria potestas' in the *Dict, des Antiquités grecques et lat.*, by Darembert-Saglio, vol. IV, 1st part, p. 342.
30. Wintersig (German text, *Jahrbuch* . . ., 1925, p. 136) refers, for such a concept, to W. Schwer, 'Die alte Pfarrei in der neueren Stadt', in *Bonner Zeitschrift f. Theol. u. Seelsorge*, I (1924), pp. 60–77. On the question of parishes based on personal or ethnical categories, etc., see P. Thomas in *Parole et Mission*, n. 4 (1959–1), pp. 16f; *Mission sans frontières*, Paris, 1960, p. 40f, 53f, 211f, 221f; *La Maison-Dieu*, no. 36 (1953–4), pp. 75f.
31. Wintersig, *loc. cit.*; *Jeunesse de l'Église*, no. 3, pp. 10f; Mgr Terrier, *La paroisse* (Pastoral letter for 1943); etc.
32. Articles entitled 'Quelques réflexions sur la paroisse', published in *l'Aquitaine*, May and June 1946, and reproduced in *La Maison-Dieu*, no. 9, 1947, pp. 104f.
33. Articles cited in n. 2, above.

34. Think of the opportunities we have for such a task in preparing people for examination of conscience and confession.

35. Rom 4:25.

36. Eph 2:14.

37. Jn 1:17.

38. See J. T. Delos, *La société internationale et les principes du Droit public*, Paris, 1929, pp. 156–84 and 204–7. On society made up of families, see J. Lacroix, 'Simples notes sur les rapports de la Famille et de la Patrie', in *Cahiers internationaux de Sociologie*, 1947, pp. 162–8.

39. *Politische Reden*, vol. XII, p. 376 (quoted by F. Siegmund-Schultze, *Die Einigung der christlichen Kirchen*, Basle, 1942, p. 54).

40. *Ep.* 79.

41. These complaints occurred frequently in the replies to the enquiry on sanctity in *Vie Sp.*, (see fasc. of Feb. 1946). *QLP*, Louvain, which summed them up, promise an enquiry on this special point. Read also Michonneau, *La Paroisse Missionnaire*, e.g. p. 258 (English trans., *Missionary Spirit in Parish Life*, see chap. 8, n. 8).

42. See several reports at the Besançon conference.

43. In Catholicism one does not belong to the Church *because* one is a member of a parochial community: one belongs to the Church, and then, living in a certain place, one belongs to a certain parish. See A. Hagen, 'Pfarrei und Pfarrer', in *Theol. Quartalsch.*, CXIV (1933), 116–28 and 406–24 (published as a book, Rottenburg a. N., 1935): see p. 121. In Protestantism, the Church is built up from below, starting from believers and local communities: see L. Frendt, 'Der katholische und der evangelische Gemeindebegriff', in *Theologische Blatter*, Feb. 1932, col. 42–50: see col. 47.

44. *Paroisse . . . (Congrès nat. de Besancon)*, pp. 28f.

45. Articles quoted, n. 32.

46. I have given some references in the article 'Pour une théologie du laïcat' in *Études*, Feb. 1948, p. 202.

47. See e.g. P. Motte's report to the *Congrès de l'Union* at Bordeaux in 1947: *Evangélisation. . . .* pp. 104–16. Wintersig speaks of the parish as 'a single liturgical person' (*Jahrbuch f. Litw.*, 1924, p. 162). Since the present report I have discussed the question in *Lay People . . .*, pp. 318f: 358. We have also had such declarations as that of the Dutch episcopate, 1st May 1954 (see *Doc. cath.*, 51 (1954), col. 1250). Finally, from the historical angle, on Christian antiquity, K. Delahaye, *Erneuerung der Seelssorgsformen aus der Sicht der frühen Patristik*, Freiburg, 1958.

48. See *Missionary Spirit in Parish Life*, *passim*, and in *Ecclesia*, Paris, 1948, p. 1308.

49. This is one of the conclusions of M. G. Le Bras, in *Rev. hist. de l'Église de France*, 1933, p. 515.

50. Christmas allocution, 1944 (*AAS*, 1945, pp. 13–14); on the Church, Speech of 20th Feb. 1946; see *Doc. cath.*, 17th March 1946, col. 173.

51. See n. 5.

52. In *La Paroisse*, quoted below, pp. 33–48.

53. See above, chapters 5 and 6.

54. See the bibliographies, first those of *QLP*, 1949, pp. 106–11, 135–40; 1950, pp. 81–4; 1951, pp. 180–4; 1953, pp. 131–9; 1954, pp. 294–300; 1957, pp. 165–74; 1959, pp. 152–4; 1961, pp. 80–6; the schemes of work inserted in *Masses Ouvrières*, no. 83 (Feb. 1953); *La Scuola Cattolica*, July–Aug. 1954, p. 292.

I would mention also the following studies: L. Siemer, 'Pfarrfamilie und Ecclesiola', in *Die Neue Ordnung*, 3 (1949), pp. 37–51 (a little too favourable to a certain self-sufficiency of the parish); fasc. 36 of *La Maison-Dieu* on the parish (1953–4); *Pfarrgemeinde und Pfarrgottesdienst, Beitragen zu Fragen der ordentlichen Seelsorge*, ed. by A. Kirchgässner, Freiburg, 1949 (contains, in particular, a very pertinent critique by Fr Karl Rahner of the 'Pfarrprinzip', according to which the Christian ought to seek, and can find, all his spiritual needs exclusively in the parish. On this 'Pfarrrinzip' see *QLP*, 1949, pp. 138f); *Die Pfarre, Gessalt und Sendung*, Session de l'Institut de Pastorale at Vienna, in 1953, Vienna, 1953 (see A. Nyckmans, 'Pour une théologie de la paroisse', in *NRT*, 76 (1954), pp. 524–7; *Die Pfarre*, ed. by Hugo Rahner, Freiburg, 1956 (French trans., *La Paroisse. De la théologie à la pratique*, Paris, 1960).

CHAPTER TEN

Two Aspects of apostolic Work

The Priest as Head of his People and as Apostle[1]

TO TREAT OF THINGS IN THE ABSTRACT IS legitimate, and in its own order is not misleading. But when we are speaking of concrete things, at the level of existential judgement we have to take account of the circumstances and to envisage a complex. This assertion is one of the aspects of truth in existentialism. No person exists 'in himself'; man is always 'in situation'. Another truth, already ancient when Aristotle perceived it, but set in a fresh light since Hegel and the discovery by moderns of 'becoming', is that man's 'situation' is explained largely by his history: that every situation is defined by its co-ordinates, is the fruit of a birth, and is better understood when it is seen as a stage or a moment in development.

Historical antecedents

If, then, we are to judge the problem I want to discuss with you, a problem which is of present-day pastoral concern, we must recall the historical antecedents of the conditions in which we have to carry out our pastoral work. The chief of these antecedents can be summed up in a word: Christendom; the state of Christendom.

The state of Christendom, as it developed, existed and survived, from the end of the Roman empire down to modern times, can be characterised by the following marks: the world, and society as such with its institutions, mean to be Christian, and are Christian or thought to be so. Society itself is constructed in the Church, on the Church's terms, and receives from the Church a positive, express, direct regulation. The Church exists as the people of God in a quasi-political manner, rather in the manner that Israel was the people of God. From this flow three consequences, which give pastoral work a very special form:

1. Men are Christians through the mere action of the institutions and the framework of life. Everything, in fact, is done in the Church, and in the forms fashioned and regulated by the Church. It is the institutions which make people Christians.

2. The Church, or rather the clergy, the priesthood, thus regulate life by using their authority in a juridical way, because their authority is recognised and they exercise a real jurisdiction over society. It makes little difference here whether this is in virtue of the essential rights of the 'spiritual', of the Church, or in the capacity of tutor of Christendom, of the supreme authority generally recognised in the 'Christian republic'. What matters is that the Church rules and influences the life of men by way of jurisdiction.

3. Finally, as everyone means to be Christian, is Christian or is believed to be so, and as the authority of the Church is generally recognised and honoured, practice corresponds in a high degree to the ideal; the facts commonly conform to the law, to the objective, ideal rule formulated by theology and canon law. Things are commonly done in the realm of the 'thesis', not of the 'hypothesis'. Perhaps it would be truer to say that the régime of Christendom is erected into a 'thesis' and finally identified with the normal, regular order of things.

The priest as head of his people

In these conditions the régime of pastoral action makes the priest primarily a head of the Christian people, the supreme head of the people, a people which means to be wholly Christian. And in fact, in that state of hierocratic Christendom, there was in the main a clergy which, in accordance with the three marks we have pointed out, applied itself, firstly, to ensure the working of the institutions: from the priestly point of view, chiefly the administration of the sacraments; much less urgently the preaching of the

G

Word of God; secondly to maintain its authority, to vindicate the general rights of the Church, of the priesthood and the special rights of its dignity or office, against all who threatened them: the lords, the corporations, later the states, even the religious orders; thirdly to ensure the observance of the rule by the faithful, the flock.

Among the clergy of the hierocratic Christendom there were many good priests, and even saints. The pastoral work of the Church was extensively carried out. Yet a sort of internal logic inclined the priest to be above all a man of authority, of dignity, to exert his influence not so much through the worth and substance of his inner life as by the mere action of the institutions and the authority he possessed. This state of things separated the priest sharply from the religious life. The obligation of perfection was imposed not so much on the priesthood as such, as on the religious life, which does not in theory imply the priesthood, and did not then imply it in fact. The missions themselves, that is, the apostolic work before the conversion of the princes and society, before the establishment of the régime of Christendom, was mainly the work of the monks and religious.

We all know how, from the late thirteenth and early fourteenth centuries, a process of laicisation of Christian society began, and went on developing until in the modern states it took the form of a violent rupture and a reaction. In this new state of affairs, in this spiritually divided society, a new type of pastor arose: a type of priest living for his people, devoting himself to them. But for a long time the idea of Christendom persisted as an ideal, that is, a state of things in which Christian institutions, Christian organisations, would by themselves make men Christians. In the 'Days' at Saint-Jacques, to which I have alluded, I showed how the 'works' in the nineteenth century tried to constitute a sort of 'ersatz', a substitute for Christendom.

In this new régime, by dint of devotion and hard work for the sake of the Christian institutions and organisations, which took the place of those of the former Christian society, the priest retained or recovered the authority he had hitherto enjoyed as it were by inheritance, without effort. Devoted to his people, working himself to death for them, he yet continued, on the whole, in the line of a pastoral method belonging to Christendom. He maintained, for what they were worth, both the institutions and his authority, and the 'thesis', at least for those who still submitted to his jurisdiction: the faithful, the 'good' Catholics. He stuck to the pastoral position of a priest-as-head in Christendom, a Christendom reduced in numbers, the really faithful: priest-head of his people, devoted to his people, killing himself with organising and maintaining 'works' organisations, in which people could continue to become and remain Christian, by the influence of these works and these organisations.

The priest as apostle

Especially in the last fifteen years, since the revival of sacred study and since Catholic action and various other circumstances have begun to bear fruit, we can see new features appearing in pastoral activity. We can describe these features in the following terms, corresponding to those in which we defined pastoral work under the régime of hierocratic Christendom:

1. In the laicised and spiritually divided world (to say the least) in which we now live, it is no longer institutions which make men Christians, but men who make institutions Christian. Catholic Action, while pursuing the same aim and looking for similar results, follows a logic which on the whole is the inverse of that of ancient Christendom. Instead of the organisations forming consciences, it is from personal and 'interiorised' convictions, from Christian consciences, that a line of action is followed, affecting the organisations and institutions. Hence the priest, instead of making the influence of the institutions and the permanence of the organisations his only, or even primary, aim, makes it his chief task to form Christian consciences, convictions and personalities. The priest of ancient Christendom preached very little, and until the erection of the seminaries in the seventeenth century, he was often incapable of it. The priest of the Catholic Action age must be an educator of consciences.

2. The pastor of souls in old-time Christendom imposed the Catholic régime on himself and his people by his authority, by the way of jurisdiction. Spiritual authority, of course, remains what it is, and the Church continues to exercise the authority she possesses over her members. But this jurisdiction is far less entangled in the temporal applications and implications it had under

the régime of hierocratic and jurisdictional Christendom. It is applied, not so much in the framework of Christendom, of the 'Christian republic', as in a strictly ecclesiastical framework, in the competence and domain proper to the Church, the society of the faithful. Towards the world, the society of men for whom the Church has apostolic responsibility, the priest no longer exerts his influence by way of jurisdiction, but by way of 'testimony', the 'prophetic' way. What he now brings into play is not so much his authority as pastor, or even priest, that is, the authority based on his title and function: it is his spiritual authority as man of God, his 'pneumatic' or 'charismatic' power, his dynamism as a religious man, a spiritual man.

3. Finally, a state of affairs where only the intrinsic nature is known, has been succeeded by, or at least mixed with, a state where the intrinsic nature is seriously modified by the fact, and the truth of the object is held more or less in check by what may be called the truth of the subject. The pastor of souls in the old jurisdictional and hierocratic Christendom had not much difficulty in obtaining the universal observance of the objective, the intrinsic rule of things. He needed strength, and he brought to the task energy and firmness, but he could do it, and he thus assured the reality of his pastoral activity. On the other hand, more and more priests, excellent priests too, feel that if they always applied objective rules and always tried to make the fact agree with the law, they would be betraying the truth of their pastoral work. For some time now we have realised that in the sphere of the Church's relations with temporal society, since the break-up and dissolution of the old Christendom, we have entered on a world of the hypothesis. To be quite frank, I am not sure if we are all yet sufficiently aware of this fact. But already an analogous fact is becoming clear in the strictly ecclesiastical sphere, that of our pastoral action. Just as we count less than formerly on the institutions and organisations to make men Christians, as the priest appeals less than before to the authority of his function and more to his quality as a spiritual man, so in the administration of the sacraments we lay more weight on the conscience and the subjective disposition; I had almost said, the subjective truth. We take more account of the person's state, the interior personal truth of his deeds and attitudes, and in certain cases we come to

prefer a religious act which is honest and authentic, though objectively imperfect, to an administration of the sacraments which in itself at least is externally satisfactory, but corresponds to nothing personal and true in the subject. I allude to many cases I could easily detail, concerning anointing of the sick or penance or marriage, and even, if not baptism, the communion of children.

In my opinion we have here something very considerable, but it can only be adequately expounded by relating it, on the one hand, to the ecclesiological synthesis and, on the other, to the incidence on Christianity of the characteristic fact of the modern world, that is, the discovery of the point of view of the subject. But that would take us too far afield.

Substitution or synthesis?

Does what I have just put forward mean that for a pastoral régime of institutions moulding Christians, of organisations and works, we must at once *substitute* a régime of apostolate, purely spiritual, personal, 'prophetic'? I certainly think not. I am convinced that the works and institutions are necessary, and good, and do much real good. I think that though, one day, in the truth and fullness of the eschatological order, the Church will be a purely spiritual 'pneumatic' reality, here on earth it is still under a régime of pedagogy and, to tell the truth, a certain régime of law. At bottom, there is always the debate between the law and grace, the law and the Gospel, the form and the spirit. In the earthly reality of the Church, the form guards and serves the spirit, the law helps and supports the grace. Sunday of its nature is a purely spiritual reality and the sabbath has been abolished. But it is in the Christian countries, where the Sunday is observed with the precepts attached to it when Christendom was a reality so as to give it something of the old look of the sabbath, that the 'Lord's Day' is still really and spiritually kept.

But it is extremely important to realise—and here we reach the heart of our subject—that for the priest of today there are two lines of pastoral work, corresponding, in the pastor of souls, to two different attitudes, which it may sometimes be very difficult to reconcile; but it is important to grasp their originality and to respect their specific demands. I shall explain them, if I may, from the standpoint of my own experience, and also, if you will allow me, I shall speak with complete candour. I have such a love for the priesthood, I so greatly enjoy talking with priests about our common priestly responsibility, that I need have no real fear of being suspected of any criticism or low opinion in what I want to put before you.

Outline of two possible attitudes for the pastor of souls[2]

Let me tell you what I have often felt when visiting priests, or more precisely parish priests, when working with them or talking together, whether on occasion of preaching sermons, in the parochial ministry, or as prisoner during the war. Even in the days when, as chaplain of a prison camp, I was myself, in a way, a parish priest, expressly in charge of souls, it seemed that I, a Friar Preacher, was led to seek a direct, individual contact with souls, taking no account of categories and labels. My idea was to go to all, as from soul to soul, and often, at first or at the same time, as from man to man, from believing or religious man to man who was what he was, and on whom I was careful not to pronounce judgement. My tendency—my fault, perhaps, or at least my temptation—in the domain of the ideas I encountered, whether expressed and conscious or unexpressed and implicit, was to see them effectively as pure ideas, trying with joy, sympathy and trust, to lay bare whatever elements of truth they had in them.

Among my fellow-priests of the parochial ministry, except perhaps among the younger men, I seemed to meet a rather different attitude. They considered and applied a whole set of social relations and practical considerations. Their first concern was not to be taken in, not only on the plane of ideas but also on that of persons, and especially of *the rôle played by persons in society, in a given human group*. For them, it was not a matter of socialism or Protestantism, or of what can be thought or said about them, but of a particular socialist, a particular Protestant, and of the concrete *influences*, in the groups where they ministered, of the activity of that socialist or that Protestant, or of what could be said about socialism or Protestantism. In short, we were on a plane which was concrete and social, where we looked, not at ideas in themselves nor at men in themselves, but at ideas and men in their effect, their function, their social influence.

For the parish priest—that is, for the priest with the care of souls, and residing, in order to provide that care, in the midst of a given human group—there can be no question of ideas, convictions, loyalty, witness, apart from consideration of the concrete consequences or interventions of these things in a given milieu and situation. It is always a question of these things as representing concrete crystallisations in this or that milieu: it is a question of a certain attitude having a certain effect or a certain influence; of a particular attendance, of a certain practice or the absence of it; it is a question of marriage in the church or somewhere else, which will give a certain example, good or bad; a certain play or a certain dance at a certain place, which will have certain very concrete consequences; of attendance at a certain youth organisation, managed in fact by so-and-so; and so on. In short, for the parish priest, as I have defined him above, there can be no question of a purely 'spiritual apostolate', but always of positions to be occupied, maintained or conquered, and a certain system of influences and relations.

We find, then, that there are two different lines of apostolic or pastoral work: two lines corresponding to two very dissimilar attitudes and almost two clergies. These two clergies are not so much the diocesan clergy on the one hand and the religious on the other, as the parochial clergy and especially the parish priests on the one hand, and on the other the priests who have not habitually the concrete charge of a *people*: the religious, but also the diocesan 'staff', the professors, certain chaplains: in short, those whose only connection is with souls, or with ideas.

The parish priests have the concrete charge of a people: they are not purely and simply apostles: they are also heads of a people, heads of Christendom. They have to reckon with a mass of concrete situations, habits, relations and influences. Moreover, they are bound, there in the midst of their people, to *stay*. They are not there just for today, they will be there tomorrow too, and for several years more. The parish priests have been called the infantry of the Church. They hold the line, in the trenches, every day and all the time. The religious, the Friar Preachers, for example, are rather like the special corps, the heavy artillery or the commandoes. They are brought up from the rear in trucks, they mount their attack and are then taken back to the rear, to be congratulated and decorated. The infantryman who holds the lines catches the counter-shelling and picks up the bits. . . . We religious come along, we throw out some bright ideas, and it is the parish clergy who have to put them into concrete practice, and sometimes to clear things up behind us.

Of these two kinds of clergy, which is right? Quite clearly, both. Both right, do I mean, each in their own domain? It would be very easy to distribute their rôles thus, as I have done in my summary. But each would thus be terribly impoverished. The priest or religious who, on the pretext of a purely spiritual apostolate completely neglected concrete effects in the existing human groups, would be a rash man and could become dangerous. The parish priest who would be only the head of his people or of Christendom would be failing in a part of his pastoral function. So if we are to take account of the two realities we have here distinguished, we must pursue our enquiry further.

Possible dangers of a purely head-of-the-people attitude . . .

The 'head-of-his-people' priest considers principally the social point of view, the field of relations and interactions between men. He applies his action as it were on the horizontal plane, that of social responsibilities, of relations and institutions.

On this plane he can know, and he does know, what does harm and what makes for good, what is good and what is bad. All his work, his preaching, his interventions, aim at establishing or preserving good influences, good practices, relations or modes of action which make for good; at combatting, eliminating or at least keeping away from his flock, all others. For many priests this struggle has been waged over very concrete points: Masonic politics, the state school, or it may be the dance, or the propaganda of some group. . . .

So far, this is only normal and regular. No pastor of souls with any real sense of his responsibilities can be excused from knowing and saying *what* is bad and fighting it. But, just in so far as the 'head-of-his-people' attitude predominates in a priest, almost so as to exclude any other, there appears a danger into which I fear we sometimes fall. I mean that the priest, letting his whole pastoral activity be dominated by this point of view, may let a social point of view react on the personal: knowing *what* is good and *what* is bad, he may go on to claim to know *who* is good and *who* is bad. The attitude and points of view of the 'head-of-his-people' may blot out and stifle, in himself, the points of view and attitudes of the apostle, the evangelist, the man of the good news for all. Listening to certain priests, in fact, especially those of the generation whose religious struggle was waged largely on the political plane, one has the impression that they have firmly rooted in them this triple conviction: (1) there are good men and bad men; (2) one can know and point out who they are; (3) *we* can know, and point them out.

As a result of this triple conviction, some priests accept the idea that with the 'bad', whom they know, nothing can be done, and one sometimes hears expressions like these: 'Ha! Do they think I'll go to see them?' (or, 'be the first to greet them?'). 'If they want religion, let them come! But if they don't . . . leave them! They're just scum, good for nothing. . . . You're wasting your time!' Or again, in a certain parish, the children of the State school are strictly separated, and at Mass and catechism and the First Communion, are seated on benches apart, and placed behind the children of the church school.

When a man says or does things like those I have quoted, he is very near to considering the administration and protection of the 'good', to the exclusion of the bad, as the object of his pastoral work. Head of the people of the 'good', he no longer acts as pastor of all. Our ecclesiastical mania for classifying people into good or bad sterilises our apostolate. And so one sees priests, excellent administrators of their parishes, really losing their apostolic zeal. They bestow great care on the maintenance of their church, their school; they faithfully administer the sacraments and teach doctrine clearly, which is all excellent; but, without any real concern, they neglect all that part of their flock which needs evangelising. Sometimes they don't even pay sick visits, however elementary, among the world of the 'bad'. When one thinks of the pastoral parables in the Gospel, especially of the lost sheep, one shudders to imagine the result. Nowadays the proportion of the faithful sheep and the lost would rather be reversed. It is not one per cent., but rather ninety-nine, who must be sought outside the sheepfold. But whereas the evangelising shepherd leaves the ninety-nine faithful sheep in order to seek for the hundredth which is lost, don't we sometimes stay with the faithful, at the risk of letting the others be lost? At the same time, obviously, we must not neglect the care of the faithful, nor fail to protect them against the danger of wolves, if there are any about. A difficult and complicated task!

. . . and of a purely apostle-priest attitude

The 'apostle-priest' considers not so much the social relations and influences as the personal relationship of each soul to God. It is not the horizontal plane that interests him, the plane of man in relation to other men, but what might be called each man's third dimension. Every man, whoever he is and whatever he has done, appears to him as relevant to his priesthood. For it is precisely by that priesthood that the apostle has been appointed the servant of all men, *in iis quae sunt ad Deum*, for whatever in them represents their third dimension, their capacity for reference to God. As apostle, as evangelist, the priest must proclaim the good news to all: he is not concerned to know whether a man is a socialist, or rich, or influential. For him there are no labels, only souls. It is the attitude of the gospel, one that we see realised, for example, in St Francis of Assisi.

This attitude appeals to us. To be purely and simply a priest and an apostle, man of God and man of men, giving them to each other, is our very ideal. But we must not hide the fact that it, too, has its dangers: a danger the opposite of that which confronts the 'head-of-his-people' priest. The danger is that, looking only at consciences and their honesty, we may give with an excessive trust in life and in men: as if there were no more wicked men in the world, no more enemies and, ultimately, no more evil.

Examples of the two attitudes: the reunion of Christians

The two attitudes I have contrasted have also their parallels in a domain very dear to me, the reunion of Christians. There is a manner of considering and approaching non-Catholics which corresponds to the attitude of the apostle or evangelist. There is another which, in a domain where loyalty and religious passion may take very acute forms, reproduces the attitude of the 'head-of-his-people' priest, guardian of the good against the bad, conscious of knowing exactly who are good and who are bad.[3] The danger of a purely evangelistic attitude is that, seeing only persons and personal religious lives, we may almost forget that heresy exists, and exists in heretics who, in the concrete, constitute a danger to the whole flock. The danger of a too purely denominational and denominationally militant attitude is that, seeing only heresy, we may forget that there are living souls, to whom, as such, nothing should make us enemies. In the extreme case, the 'head-of-his-people' priest, in whom the denominational militant has completely absorbed the apostle, would accept the idea of a 'crusade', that is, an effort of strength to reduce a 'dissident', considered as an enemy. There is nothing less 'apostolic' than a crusade. Its attitude to men is in no way that of an apostle. To be an apostle is always 'to be with' men. But to go on a crusade is essentially 'to be against'. Even with those whom the priest has to oppose in a certain respect, he must find a way to be *with* them even while being against them. To be sure, the missionary must be against the sorcerer, the parish priest must be against the pimp, or the bad influence which is taking his children from him. But the problem is how to be against these evil agents without being against the man himself, and that is what a 'crusade' prevents being even attempted.

Fundamentally, the 'head-of-his-people' priest and the militant confessional missionary tend to forget the transcendence of God's work. They readily identify the institution they administer with the Kingdom of God, and people's situation in relation to that institution with the religious mystery of souls. They do not see clearly enough that the Church has a reality much deeper than what we can see of it. It extends mysteriously as far as the extent of the mystery of Christ and the Holy Spirit themselves.

Institutions

G. Thibon proposed a very right distinction between *manners* (*moeurs*) and *morality*.[4] 'I call manners', he wrote, 'everything in human conduct which springs from unconscious necessity; in other words, all that is done by instinct, by tradition by spontaneous adaptation to the social milieu, etc. I call morality whatever is related to the *specifically conscious* affectivity. To have manners it is not necessary to share consciously in an ideal: to have a morality, it is. Our ancestors had less morality than we, and more of manners. They were sometimes cruel to their children, *but they had them.* . . .' In general, manners correspond to that part of our life which is regulated by institutions; public spirit, social behaviour: morality is the domain of personal conscience. We come back to our two points of view. On the one hand, one relies on organisations, habits, social pressure, to form and keep Christians: on the other, one appeals to conscience, to its actions, its convictions and its resources. In the emphasis on 'manners' there is a kind of 'politics first' attitude, the feeling that everything is a matter of institutions.

This does not imply, of course, that priests with this tendency are adherents of the views of Charles Maurras, but it inclines them to sympathise with measures which, in the human community of which they have religious charge, would establish a body of relationships, a social pressure in the 'good' direction. Whence the tendency of the clergy to agree that there is such a thing as a good direction, that a good or a bad thing in the political order corresponds to a spiritual good or bad. In the political order: we mean, on the plane of the actual régimes, not merely of the concrete exercise of the powers of police and administration: an order in which, obviously, the spiritual work can either be helped or hindered to the point of being made practically impossible by the direction given from above. But how easy it is to slip from that purely pastoral attitude into one which becomes political and is bound up with the question of the régime itself!

This is specially noticeable in the generation which knew the struggles of the years between 1880 and the Great War. The parish priests have had so much experience of their work being welcomed or frustrated or sometimes suppressed, according to the way in which state policy was directed! In France, unfortunately, we have scarcely known any régime but one of persecution and interference, following on one of favour and 'protection': only rarely a real régime of state neutrality and freedom! What with political institutions doing the Church's 'job' and others preventing the Church from doing her 'job', we have only recently, for too short a time, known the simple but true freedom of a pure apostolic action.

The world of 'manners', of institutions, which is the world of the 'head-of-his-people' priest, is also a world of tradition. It is a matter of returning to the 'cadres', accepting the ready-made. The world of morality, of personal conscience, which is far more the world of the apostle, is nearer to the modern world, which is marked by the discovery of the point of view of the 'subject'. There one appeals to freedom, to commitment, to the powers of personal conscience, to the education of free convictions, to sincerity. We can guess how easily these two attitudes could be related to political sympathies or choices; but that is not our concern here, and there are more interesting connections to note. For here are some consequences or connections of an inclination towards the *cadres* and the ready-made, or towards initiatives and the continual re-thinking of a spiritual apostolate.

Through the tendency of everything to deteriorate, the propensity for institutional or even political formulas easily becomes, in the clergy, a propensity to look for 'dodges'; that is, for recipes, processes, which function by themselves, without appeal to any inner energy or to the persons themselves, without bringing into play a spiritual ideal and a freedom. Our pastoral theory, our conception of the ministry, easily leads us to look for a 'dodge' to make people merely practising Christians, without having to communicate a flame, a movement from conscience to conscience. We should like to have a 'dodge' to get people to Mass, or to their Easter duties. And sometimes we may ask ourselves whether our attachment to the Church school—a very justifiable attachment, which I share with the most positive conviction—does not cover a secret desire to have an institution which by itself will produce good practising Catholics and regularly provide vocations.

The training of priests

Even in the recruiting and training of priests, don't we sometimes feel the propensity for the ready-made? Haven't we sometimes been careful to keep at the seminary and to train, primarily, 'heads-of-the-people'? Men, that is, whose chief concern, once they are established in authority over a community of men, is to ensure or preserve a certain sort of behaviour as the result of certain influences, and to see that these influences are favourable. Haven't we sometimes acted in such a way as to have, not so much creative personalities as men who are guardians of the Catholic citadel and system? Haven't we sometimes positively eliminated, or kept in obscure positions, men of personality, rich in the values of the 'subject', capable of realising themselves in the field of religious values? Hasn't the clergy sometimes been educated mainly to hold on to organised positions which were suited to ensure a certain collective behaviour? And so the clergy has been chiefly anxious to preserve and influence, to hold on to positions which sometimes became political positions: to get Mr So-and-so to act, get him to vote a certain way, to have good Catholics in office, who may be got to intervene for one thing or another.

In short, the fag-end of jurisdictional Christendom.

Preaching

We have seen that in that sort of Christendom the preaching of the word of God held a very small place. Fortunately we are no longer at that stage. But in a viewpoint dominated by institutions, organisations, the ready-made, and where the priest acts primarily as head of the people, preaching will be mainly on the Catholic system and its concrete implications, more than on the gospel, that is, the call to conversion, to faith, to personal religion. The system of preaching is in many cases only feebly evangelistic and apostolic: it corresponds to a ready-made world where objective decisions are accepted by tradition and authority. And of course dogma is not something to be invented: in that sense, we have to preach what is ready-made. But there is a manner of preaching dogma which represents also a testimony, a sharing of conviction, and aims above all at awakening consciences to a personal grasp of the truth, a real answer to real questions. Now this contact with the needs of actual persons is seldom sought and effected in our preaching except in some kinds of apologetics, which themselves are often factitious, and in any case only serve to justify the total submission of the subject to a ready-made object. Our preaching is too seldom the communication of the fruit of a God-possessed conscience to other consciences. It is too often content to deal out ready-made formulas borrowed from authors in whom, to start with, there were more alleged answers than real problems, and for whom the truth was already presented as wholly 'prefabricated'.[5] This state of things sometimes produces in us a sort of spirit, not of humility in presence of the true, but of triumph, a triumphant crushing of the difficulties; not one of personal commitment or communication of a truth which has been made one's own, but the self-sufficient proclamation of information, massive and ready-made; springing from no true problem and answering no real question. In short, what our preaching often lacks is the gift of bringing the objects, which are what they are, into connection with the person: and that is something which we have first to do in our personal life, in our own consciences.

An attempted explanation

This raises a more general problem, which I propose to deal with elsewhere: that of the meaning to be given to our priestly quality as men of God. We are, in fact, both priests and men of God in two ways: *ex officio* and *ex spiritu*. Our priesthood is always an office, a function; it can and must be also a spirit. We can live for the faithful and act pastorally, either as simply men of a certain office and function, or as spiritual men, having really something interior to communicate.

The spiritual-man aspect must be expressed chiefly in preaching and direction. The aspect of office, function and power seems predominant in the celebration of the sacraments. But even there we can and should act as spiritual men. What a difference there is between the priest who is merely the agent of the valid consecration of the hosts, and the one who is really the priest of the community, the leader of the prayer and offering for living souls. . . . The former is man of God apart from himself, so to speak, as a mere instrument. The second is man of God with his soul, with his whole life, by his personal commitment. He does not only transmit ready-made objects, or a life which does not come from him. In him, objects have taken root, they are nourished from his life in proportion as he has himself nourished that life from them: his ministry and his life are one and the same thing, completely alive.

Pastoral theory is only an appurtenance, an extension or an application of ecclesiology. All that we have said about our pastoral attitudes is based on the way we consider the Church and theologically construe its mystery. The idea of the priest as the functionary of the Catholic system, an authority communicating to a subject people the ready-made substance of Christian grace and truth, corresponds to, and is perhaps rooted in, an ecclesiology. I have briefly shown elsewhere how ecclesiology was made into a special and separate department of theology, in circumstances which made it more of a 'hierarchology' than a really integral ecclesiology.[6] The ecclesiology which was laid down and widely taught after Gallicanism on the one hand and Protestantism on the other was devoted almost entirely to regarding the Church as an institution; to developing her aspects of hierarchical mediation of truth and grace, of hierarchical structure. The aspect of the Church as a wholly active and living community was practically forgotten and sometimes even opposed, compromised as it was by certain Gallican, Protestant and Jansenist excesses. The Church was considered primarily as a ready-made framework, in which all we had to do was to enter it and receive; hardly at all as a community in which all have something to do, something to share with one another, in which the Holy Spirit is supremely active and where, quite apart from our hierarchical positions, we are all transmitters for one another of the *agape* of God: that *agape* which has been poured into our hearts by the Holy Spirit who has been given to us.

Conclusion

Integral truth is synthesis and integration. It has never been my purpose to make a radical contrast between two activities of the priest, any more than between two notions of the Church, as if they were irreconcilably opposed and we had to make an exclusive choice between them. The Church is at one and the same time a hierarchical society *and* a living body, institution *and* community, made from above *and* constantly being made from below. Our function as pastors of souls embraces, with varying emphasis according to circumstances and vocations, an activity as head of the people *and* one of pure spiritual apostolate. What I precisely refuse to do is to let either of these activities be sacrificed to the other, and specially the second to the first.

Yes, above all the second to the first. For that is the commoner temptation and the easier decline. For though the law is necessary and the form is beneficial, it must never be forgotten that the law is for grace, the form is for the spirit, institutions and powers are for persons. The Church is built of sacraments and of men, but the sacraments are for men; the sabbath is made for man. The organisations are at the service of consciences.

What we need, then, is to do better and better, more and more purely, what good priests of Jesus Christ have always done in the Church: to steep the form in the spirit, to make the 'works' and organisations, so necessary to the Christian people, become educative of consciences and the inner life,—without which, they are not worth the trouble. We are not priests just in order to enrol people, even in the Church, but to lead men to God: *Sacerdos constituitur in iis quae sunt ad Deum.* That we lead men to God in the Church and that only in the Church can we lead them fully to God, is my conviction, a conviction I should like to proclaim, one day, in a complete treatise on the Church. Let us be priests, then, in the Church, and by the exercise of the sublime ministry we have received in her, of the faith and the sacraments of the faith. As for the acts of our office, of our priestly power, we shall have to strive more and more to exercise them as men of God, as men personally possessed and indwelt by the Holy Spirit. We must never neglect that direct, purely spiritual apostolate, from soul to soul, for which Abbé Michonneau has pleaded so persuasively and with such pastoral realism:[7] an apostolate in which the priest does not act solely as an organiser of works, a minister of the sacraments, head of the Christian people, but as a religious man.

Only thus can our pastoral ministry, and the Church, in that part of it we are called on to build, assume their full dimensions.

NOTES

1. Text of a conference given at Vanves, 31st Dec. 1947, to the directors of the Apostolic Union. Published by *Prêtres diocésains*, Feb. 1949, pp. 81–97. The publishers prefaced the text with these lines: 'The article we present to our readers needs no recommendation, but it should be remembered that it was composed for a restricted audience and refers to the situation in France.'
2. At that time I did not know the book by Max Scheler, *Vorbilder und Führer*, since translated into French (by E. Marmy, Lyons, 1958) under the title *Le Saint, le génie, le héros*. It might be a help in working out more clearly a sort of 'phenomenology' of the two attitudes I summarise here.
3. An example of this second attitude could be found in what we are told of a missionary and his struggles: E. Housse, *Des Andes à l'Archipel de Chiloé. Le R.P. Xavier Munier, rédemptoriste, apôtre du Chili* (1869–1932), Saint-Étienne, 1932; Bk II, ch. 1. In Cronin's *Keys of the Kingdom*, Francis Chisolm acts purely as an apostle. Fathers Kezer and Fitzgerald have, in different degrees, a 'head-of-the-people' attitude.
4. *Diagnostics*, pp. 141 and 144.
5. On the contrary, in *The Keys of the Kingdom*, Francis Chisholm's bishop says to him: 'You're not one of our ecclesiastical milliners who must have everything stitched up in neat little packets—convenient for handing out. And quite the nicest thing about you, dear boy, is this—you haven't got that bumptious security which springs from dogma rather than from faith.' (See my chap. 3).
6. Bulletin d'Ecclésiologie, in *RSPT*, Jan. 1947, p. 77.
7. In *Missionary Spirit in the Parish*.

CHAPTER ELEVEN

The Mission of the Priest
in the Modern World[1]

WE SEEM TO BE FACED WITH A TWOFOLD RE-
quirement: that the Church should be truly the Church and the
priest be the man of God; that contact should be kept with men
and events.

I. FIRST REQUIREMENT:
TO BE TRULY THE MAN OF GOD

The priest's mission is essentially to carry out the ministry of
the apostolic word, the ministry of the sacraments of faith and the
fostering of that Christian charity which creates a Christian community.

1. *The man of the apostolic word*

The priest is first of all the man of faith. Sometimes, when
preaching in country parishes about the priest's mission, I used
to point out how there are two or three houses in a village which
have a different look from the others: the school, sometimes the
mairie and always, at least, the church. This, from the archi-
tectural point of view, is quite distinct, with its steeple indicating
precisely that it is not made to satisfy any of life's horizontal
needs, but man's need in his third dimension—the vertical—the
need of man who stands erect, who is not made only to plough
furrows, to cultivate the soil, to exploit the world, but to look up,
to have a life belonging to another city. And I also showed how

among the inhabitants of the village there is a man who is unlike the others, by his dress and manner of life. He is in fact the man of faith, the man of the church and its steeple, the man who is there, not to teach the people how to till the soil, to exploit the universe, to organise their activities on the horizontal dimension of human life, but as the specialist of the third dimension, the dimension whose distinctive activity is prayer.

In the same line of thought, I used to show how among the days of the week, too, there is one unlike the others, when in principle we interrupt our ordinary work, wear other clothes, pursue other activities. It is the day of eternal life, the day on which we perform the distinctive act of eternal life, which is prayer. So then, the priest is first of all the man of faith, the man of the word of God.

During these days together we have discussed many ideas of sociology and political economy and analysed the social facts of the rural scene. This is strictly necessary, and I shall return to it. But note: we are not economists, we are not even agents for Christian civilisation, we are not meant to tell people how to feed their babies or cultivate their fields: we may occasionally do that sort of thing, but it is not our mission.

There was a time in the Church's history—the second half of the eighteenth century—when this was thought to be the priest's mission: it was the age of 'philosophism', of the philosophy of the Enlightenment or, in the Germanic countries, of Josephism. Men liked to think, and were quite sentimental about it, that the priest was the man who made other men happy, who was there to teach them how to mind their bees, how to avoid illness, etc. You have an example of it as late as Balzac's *Le Curé de campagne*, who is a good fellow in a most attractive way, but Balzac's country priest —quite a different character from Bernanos's—is the man who is really the inspirer of the earthly city in its horizontal dimension, who makes it a happy city in the earthly sense, and teaches men the right way to spend their Sundays, at skittles and country dancing. Today, obviously we have gone beyond the stage of skittles and country dancing, but we can supply its modern equivalent. That is not our job: we are primarily men of another world, witnesses to another world.

2. *The priest is the man of the word of God*

Obviously, this must be a word which reaches souls, and this suggests a criticism of our ecclesiastical preaching and our teaching of the catechism, a thing which is so important because in the greater part of the country practically all the children attend the catechism.

So here we have an absolutely exceptional tool in our hand. I remember, when I was at the seminary of the Institut Catholique, M. Verdier, the Superior, used to say to us: 'Gentlemen, consider that every Sunday we have about 40,000 sermons. What political party has the chance to make 40,000 speeches every Sunday? What have we to show for it?' Well I know that we have miserable congregations: the poor priest who is faced with fifteen children, as many women and two men, if that! It is terrible, I know, the amount of energy needed to fill the void, but all the same, there are still some to hear us, some people who come. Let us be witnesses to them of the other world, witnesses to God, to Jesus Christ: men who affirm the heavenly truths and show people how to reach them. Let our word, then, be direct, coming forth alive from our consciences, a word which can take root in the conscience of other men. We must not be merely a sort of transmitter of catechistic orthodoxy, giving out the material it is agreed that we should give out. That agreed word touches neither ourselves nor others, it does not come from us alive, and so does not take root in human consciences. Don't be afraid, then, to speak even in the first person, to bear our own witness as religious men.

Believe me, I have no quarrel with the fact that we have to teach the catechism, that is, to present objective truth. When I was a boy I was lucky to have a priest who preached in an admirable, very simple manner. Many of his sermons began like this: 'My dear brethren, the catechism says that the Mass' (for example) 'is the unbloody sacrifice of Jesus Christ.' Then he would explain this very simply: he taught. He was a man of faith, a man of doctrine: he taught. And for that reason one was presented with the statement of something solid, Catholic doctrine in all its strength. It was impressive and it certainly left its mark on a generation. But I might have reproached him a little for not giving us his personal witness, with being too much, shall we say, the impersonal reporter of a doctrine which was quite objective, ready-made. I should have preferred him to speak rather in the first person. In our words we are educators, and education is, at bottom, essentially example; it is getting people to do something by doing it with them, in their presence: teaching them to pray, for example, by praying with them, in front of them.

3. *The man of the sacraments of faith*

Here too, what a difference there is between the priest who is simply the minister of an objectively valid sacrament and a religious man who brings about a mystery, and is the first to come under its influence! What a difference in the manner of hearing confessions, between the 'absolution-mill'—I used to know a priest who made records in speed—and a confessor who applies himself, who is truly the father, the man, the man *with* men, the man *with* the sinner's soul, who tries to rekindle it and lead it onwards.

Or take the Last Sacraments: the difference there can be between the wholly objective, dull, dry way of ministering to a sick person, and the way of a religious man who, with powers which the laity do not possess, yet, in the way he ministers, puts himself first of all among the faithful, goes straight in among them. It was one of M. Olier's favourite ideas that the priest, in spite of his powers, must plunge himself in spirit into the body of the faithful, put himself again with the faithful, make himself like one of them, so as to inspire from within both the individual and the little group among which he finds himself as a religious man. There is certainly, too, the way of celebrating Mass, the Eucharist. I know the difficulties, when one knows that behind one's back the children's little legs are shuffling, there is chattering here, scuffling there. I know how hard it is, but there really are priests who succeed in giving the impression of religious men and thus educating their people.

4. *A community inspired by charity*

Finally the priest as inspirer of charity, with the immense influence for good of a group in which charity is present. Have you ever studied the way in which the early Church, the primitive

Church was missionary? For my part, I was astounded to find that the strictly missionary motive has very little mention in the ancient texts. The idea so prominent with us, of going out to attack men apostolically, does not seem to have been of the first importance in the early Church. That Church was apostolic through the radiance of little groups of love, composed of Christians. It was thus that the Church was established, by a radiance from man to man, from small group to small group, far more than by some kind of frontal attack, which in any case would have been practically impossible in the age of the persecutions. I often compare the apostolic missionary work of the early Church to the process by which certain plants, such as strawberries and vines, reproduce themselves: if a shoot is made to touch the ground, it takes root and thus, bit by bit, starting from a single plant, one can plant a whole area of land. I am a great believer in this process of 'layering', as it is called; a transmission of faith, which takes root from one living conscience to another conscience. And this is all the stronger in its effects when it starts from a little community, producing groups of charity.

In all this, what I want to point out is that our priestly function, on its essential side, makes us ministers of the things from above. Remember those terms we repeat so often in the Easter liturgy, which ought to sing in our consciences as a sort of permanent leitmotiv: 'You who have been raised with Christ, seek the things that are above, set your affections on the things that are above: dwell there where your Head is, he who is your motive of life and hope: Jesus Christ, who is in heaven.' And we can never be sufficiently conscious that our life is above, and that, as St Paul says, 'our life is hidden with Christ in God'.

I love that phrase of St Paul's, and I apply it not only to my personal life but to my apostolic life. I am profoundly convinced that our apostolic life too is something which is hidden with Christ in God, which we cannot completely account for, which is a mystery. The Church, you see, is built with men, built up from the earth, but its foundation is in heaven. What we see of it here is comparatively unimportant, it is its *sacramentum*, not its reality of grace. The true reality of the Church is built on the other side of the veil, in heaven. It is built of all that we project beyond the veil of visible things, and shall find again on the other side of the veil, in Christ.

So when we study—as we must: we can never study too much at the present day—the earthly implications of our apostolate, the techniques of insertion and efficiency for our apostolate in the modern world, we must never forget that all this is only an aid: the essential is that invisible part, anchored in the heavens, to which we are the witnesses, the ministers. Briefly, in answer to the question: 'What is the priest's mission in view of the evolution of the rural world?', I believe that the most important thing is for the Church to be truly and purely the Church: that our witness to the things of the other world should be truly and purely borne in every way, perhaps in our failure. It was so with our Lord— his witness was borne on the Cross. And as Paul says, God's plan is the wisdom of the Cross, which prevails over the wisdom of the world.

In your study of the evolution of the rural world you have made some use of the wisdom of the world. That is necessary, but never let it lead us to forget the wisdom of the cross, that is, that the essence of our apostolate is truly the element of mystery, of the invisible, by which we are witnesses to the other world, *mad* witnesses to the other world, and all the madder in that we sometimes feel we are not very sure of what we are telling.

Because, I suppose, you are like me; when I testify to the things of the other world and when I bring them into my life by prayer, I constantly apply to myself those words in the Gospel: 'Lord, I believe, but help my unbelief!' Even while I believe, I know that I waver, that I am not all that sure of what I believe. And here I allude to a difficulty which is always found in the lives of spiritual men, and of believers, but is going to be more and more, I believe, a burning actuality for us. I believe that in a world which terrestrially is being increasingly mastered, in the world of technology in which man is king by his intelligence, it will be increasingly difficult for the man of faith to believe: more and more we shall catch ourselves groping a little, saying to ourselves: 'I tell them this, but what do I myself believe?'

We can only come through this by an act of faith. To that mysterious thing, faith, the key is interior: no exterior key is really effective. There are motives of credibility, motives of apologetics, motives of experience; the things of faith can be felt from time to time. But in the end everything is enclosed in faith.

Often we are alone with that veil, that wall behind which lie hidden the things to which we ought to be witnesses, and it is extremely difficult thus to be witnesses to spiritual things, in the midst of a world which is drawn by a tremendous movement of construction, of life, but without any belief in the spiritual or the supernatural. Yet that is our function: we are called to be the meeting-point of the order of earth and the order of heaven.

Jesus Christ is the sole point by which the world above and the world below have contact. But he is now invisible. He gives himself visible agents, as it were, of his unique mediation; the apostles, the priests. It is through us, poor men, through our wavering faith, that communication has to be effected between the two worlds: the world below with the terrible fascination of its seething turmoil, and the world above, with its immense but hidden riches. We are at the meeting-point, and that is the grandeur of our priesthood. Thus we have to go among men with that awareness of our character as mediators, that awareness that we have to bring about the union of the world below and the world above.

That is our essential mission. If we don't do that, we are not priests. We may be so by our cassocks and in social esteem, by our 'character' and the power received at ordination, but we are not really priests by our souls and our effective activity ('without me,' said our Lord, 'you can do nothing'); we are not in him.

II. SECOND REQUIREMENT:
CONTACT WITH MEN AND EVENTS

To sum up, then:

First: the Church should be truly and purely the Church, by our quality as men of God, witnesses of the faith; from this flows, therefore, our quality as religious men in the ministry of the apostolic word, in the celebration of the sacraments, in the inspiration of communities of Christian charity.

Second: in order to be meeting-points of the world and the world below, mediators between God and men, wielding our function as visible Christs, we must be *men of God and men of men*.

We must in some way be devoted to both parties between whom we are mediators: devoted wholly on high to the things of faith, and devoted wholly below to all the hurly-burly of human activity. We have to be men of God, but also men of men: not just theoretically but concretely, really, with all the implications of that realism.

The modern apostolic crisis—by which I mean the awareness we have gained of the real state of the field of apostolic work—has made us more aware that the Church was also made by men and for men. All kinds of circumstances had led the Church to think of herself rather as something ready-made, a sort of totality of things-in-themselves, a prefabricated dogma, a ready-made worship, which could hold together by itself, even if there were no one to practise it, so long as there were at least one priest to celebrate it.

1. Not 'things-in-themselves' but 'someone's things'

Whether it were dogma in the state of ready-made orthodoxy, or worship in the state of ready-made liturgy, it all seemed to be so to say, things isolated from men, which would hold together by themselves, and even the Church was thought of rather in this way. The Church meant the pope, the hierarchy, the bishops, the whole apparatus which existed as if in itself. It was as if France were the legislation, the law, the constitution, the civil service. We learned our lesson in 1940, that France could not exist if she were no more than that, and were not continually being made by Frenchmen. In the same way we have come to understand that the Church, with her dogma—which does not have to be made, but has been made; her sacraments, which also have been made; her hierarchy, her corps of officials and her machinery—the Church, in spite of all that, would not exist if her faithful were not continually making her. The Church is the society or community of those who have the faith: the faithful.

And so at this moment we are now in process of rediscovering —and I think that is the basic meaning of all the new pastoral movement which is still feeling its way—that the different facts which make up the Church—faith, sacraments, community— ought to be, not things-in-themselves but *someone's things*.

When I think of the state of our dogma, as we find it in our teaching, in the catechism, I find it is a thing-in-itself and is often no longer *anyone's* thing: no one thinks of it concretely as a living thing. We are too prone to be satisfied with a dogma in itself, which has not to be worked out but is all laid down in the catechism or the theological manuals. We retail it, we are purveyors of orthodox theology, and that is all. We are in process of finding out that dogma must be *someone's* dogma or someone's living thought, otherwise it will not bear its fruit.

This is even clearer from the point of view of worship. Bismarck, expounding the difference between Protestantism and Catholicism said something like this: 'If I understand it rightly, in the Catholic Church the Church can exist without the faithful, can exist all alone, since its essential action, the Mass, can be celebrated without the faithful.' That is true: we have a Church which can exist in the clergy alone. Personally, I think it is a very profound truth, bound up with the doctrinal structure of Catholicism. But Bismarck added: 'whereas Protestantism is simply what springs from the community of the faithful. Outside this community it is impossible.'

The whole truth includes the two things: the hierarchical act and the participation of the faithful. Our worship must be *someone's* worship: when we go into a church and put ourselves mentally into the position of one who is not a member, what impression have we? It is my custom, at any Catholic function, to perform a double action: on the one hand, as a believer, as member of the Christian community, to carry out, myself, the action which is going on,—on the other hand, from time to time, to go out of it in thought and to place myself, as Fr Levie has neatly said in a book I recommend you to read, 'under the gaze of the unbeliever'. When I go into a church and say to myself: 'What impression can this give? What does this express? What does this worship, this Mass, convey to one who does not know its doctrine?'—then I conclude something like this: it is something which is done before an audience, but it is not the worship of a community. It is worship performed by a man in front of other men, sometimes in front of no one—but it is not the worship *of* anyone. It is not the worship of a community.

2. *Being with*

We have seen that the Church was made by men and that the priest, for that reason, must be 'the man of the men'. Now mankind is not something abstract, a sort of impersonal mass: it exists in space and time. It is not man-in-himself, but actual men, existing 'in situation'. Men, then, exist in certain conditions of space and time and concrete manner of life. Therefore the priest, mediator of union between the kingdom of God and men, must be *with* men, not just beside them or in front of them, but with them. Gabriel Marcel has made a very interesting analysis of that expression, 'being with'. He shows how being with is something quite different from being in front of, quite different from being beside. For instance, I can meet men every morning in the same railway carriage and travel the same journey with them, without having any contact with them. I am beside them, not with them.

It is impossible for the priest to exercise the function of mediator between God and men unless he belongs really to both worlds, unless he is both *with* Jesus Christ and *with* men. But one can only be with men in the concrete condition in which those men are, apart from which their humanity would be no more than an abstraction.

3. *Prompting the question before giving the answer*

There is more to it than that: in the modern world and especially at this moment, we need not only to answer men's questions and to be with them, know them, be close to them, but also, before answering any religious question, to prompt the asking of it. For the men to whom we are now sent really have no questions, and will let us go about among them in our cassocks, looking at us often sympathetically, sometimes curiously, but very often with complete indifference. To many of them, we and our cassocks and all that we bring them (our sacraments, our message) mean absolutely nothing. So it is necessary, if we are to give them an effective answer, to provoke the question, to arouse in men a desire to nourish their souls in the third dimension, the spiritual. Yet more, we must not only provoke a question but make it possible for them to be attentive to the question, and so, eventually, to our answer. You know how there are certain conditions of life which make it in practice impossible for men to have any spiritual concern for the third dimension, when they are completely hemmed in by the two earthly dimensions and have nothing to spare for the third.

It is a fact which needs to be studied, that a change in the conditions of life, which the Church was unable or unequipped to follow in the nineteenth century, was one of the chief causes of the loss of faith by large sections of the population. It is a fact that when the phenomenon of industrialisation began in the nineteenth century, new centres of human habitation were formed for which there was no pastoral provision, and often not even a church building (because it was very difficult to build them under the régime of the Concordat, which required authorisations not willingly granted by the State). And very often considerable new populated areas grew up, regular little towns or cities, three or four miles from a church, with no properly adapted means of pastoral care.

Now we have other tools: in the first place we have freedom, freedom with poverty—but there is never freedom without poverty—and other intellectual tools, the tools of sociological analysis. Now we find ourselves faced with enormous implications. We must not only say so, we must make that analysis, we must create an organism, and that requires time, premises, men.

Clearly, then, the priest is going to be very largely absorbed in functions which are not strictly priestly, but are absolutely necessary, in apostolic realism, if we are effectively to carry out our function as mediators between God and men, meeting-points between the heavenly, invisible world of faith and the world of men, which is a world of technical transformation, of very ardent and effective exploitation of this planet.

4. *Urgent need for educative action*

In conclusion, I want to draw your attention to a point which always needs emphasising: the need to insist systematically and continually on the educative rôle of the priest. This is necessary on several grounds, but chiefly because of the state of 'non-Christendom' into which the country as a whole has decisively entered.

We can never be too conscious of the fact that we live in a

society totally different from the medieval, which with us was practically continued under the *ancien régime*, and still survives in many regions, for historical situations never begin and end at a fixed hour and day. In many parts of the world there are still medieval situations; the people in them still living in the Middle Ages. The situation of Christendom was marked by one fact: the whole of life, all society, meant to be Christian, even in its organisation, and thus the very institutions were expected to make Christians by themselves, by their own natural action. The family, the school, the trade, all these institutions under the direct regulation of the Church, 'christianised' by their own action. I should say that the situation nowadays is precisely the opposite. Whereas formerly the institutions put people in a Christian atmosphere, now everything depends on individual consciences, and it is from the starting-point of the individual conscience that we can hope, to some extent, to transform the institutions, the collective condition of life. To quote Maritain's expression, we have entered the world of secular Christendom.

The future of religion depends on deep personal convictions. What is therefore necessary is to educate consciences, to educate lay apostles, men of faith and prayer, through and in all our technical activities, all those adaptations to which we are committed by the situations we have analysed.

The faithful have become too accustomed to following ready-made directions, to asking their priests for the solution and simply applying it. I may add that the priests themselves have often been accustomed to the same attitude: to obey and, faced with each situation as it arose, to ask for the solution in order to apply it.

What we need, then, is to carry out an educative work, to educate the religious conscience of our people, and first of all our own, as regards concrete facts, initiatives to be undertaken, responsibilities to be accepted. If we do not, we risk catastrophe; we shall be men who, in the hour of action, have no resource but to appeal to an authority which is absent and too far away, and is itself unable, because of its position, to provide the concrete solution.

I think, then, that we are entering on an age of secular Christendom, which obliges a priest to give educational activity a sort of primacy. Obviously this will always be a personal activity, but we can find the support we need in teams, in the priestly community of those responsible for a given sector, for one man alone is unequal to the task. His conscience, at grips with concrete action, can only develop its powers in the priestly team, which is the real unit of work. It is a fact amply illustrated in the history of the Church in the thirteenth and seventeenth centuries, and in many other ages. Whenever the Church has been fully missionary, fully in contact, fully effective, she has developed her community sense. At the beginning of the thirteenth century this was extraordinarily striking, at a time when the key-point was won in an exceptional manner, and one as difficult as ours, since socially and sociologically speaking it was the emergence of the communes—something quite unlike anything seen before. The key-point was captured by communities.

It was the same in the seventeenth century: the reform of the Church was only possible through communities. After the Council of Trent, the first attempts at priestly training in response to the decree of the Council, failed because they were individual attempts, as for example in the dioceses of Rouen and Rheims. The only enterprises to succeed were those which were based on communities: St Vincent de Paul, M. Olier, etc.

So this apostolic realism, which in the concrete contact of action will engage only the personal consciences of our lay apostles and ourselves, must be fostered in a priestly community: a community which must be based on faith, the sacraments of faith and the community of charity: the three constitutive elements of the Church. Faith: so there must be exchange of spiritual testimonies. The sacraments of faith: therefore sharing worship, prayer together, if possible the eucharist together, according to such ways as are at present allowed by the rubrics. Finally, the community of charity.

These things are now so well known and obvious that there is no need to emphasise them: what is needed is to put them into practice.

NOTES

1. Notes taken at a conference given to the Session of the federal chaplains of Rural Catholic Action at Versailles, July 1950. Published in *Les Cahiers du clergé rural*, no. 122 (Nov. 1950), pp. 385–93.

CHAPTER TWELVE

Christ in France[1]

THIS PAPER IS NOT GOING TO BE A HISTORY OF the biblical revival or the liturgical movement, nor yet of the pastoral and catechetical campaign. I shall not trace the stages of the rise of a Catholic laity nor the chief currents of ideas, the criticism of moralism and the quest for a religion which is adult, true and fitted for men involved in a real and difficult life: nor that rediscovery of the historical dimension of Christianity and its virtue of hope, and of the decisive character of the final goal to which all things tend ('eschatology'). There will be nothing about the worker priests.

Or rather, I shall try to set all these things, and some others too, in their proper perspective by singling out the essential problems with which the Church is faced in our land and by considering their origins and consequences. All this, in fact, has a meaning in relation to an underlying movement which is precisely that of the present life and conscience of French Catholicism. We shall try to grasp what that movement is. Thus we may be able, at the same time, to answer that question often asked by our foreign friends: is it decadence, or alarming crisis, or a revival and vitality full of promise?

For French Catholicism is followed with almost excessive interest and also with concern. France is a land of poor religious practice and of attachment to the great traditional forms of religion: a land of half-empty churches and of worldwide influence; of seminaries too often depleted and of missionary and contemplative vocations. We are bubbling with ideas which are readily carried to extremes, with a sort of generosity or radicalism of mind; thought issues in revolution or a crusade, and discussions take on the semblance of a war of religion. But France is also a traditionally religious and submissive country, whose history shows that it has not the schismatic spirit. With all this, France is disturbing, and there would be a void in the world and in the Church if she ceased to exist and to be disturbing.

All the movement which has begun or is being sought among us has sprung from a realisation of the real dimensions of the apostolic task. In a way it is a reawakening. A reawakening always starts from an experience which shocks, and produces new men. In the sixteenth century, for example, as a result of the reaction against the paganisation of life in Italy and the shock of the Reformation, there took place the great missionary urge which followed the new realisation of the dimensions of mankind and the world. The instrument of this realisation was a new experience of geography and then of ethnography. This provoked, in all that part of the Church which had that experience, an urge and problems unknown by others. Beneath the questions of spirituality, schools and clientèle, the opposition of our Jansenists to the Jesuits was partly the opposition of men wrapped up in their St Augustine and their practices to men who knew the peoples, the spaces and the winds of a wider world.

Our new realisation, the source of our reawakening, is the fruit of two successive and contrasted movements. First, the severe experiences of half a century of history (1876–1914), then an experience of contact, an acceptance of the mingling and then the dialogue and what followed them: our emergence from the ghetto and the rediscovery of a world, that very world to which we were 'sent', the depth and true dimensions of which we had never really grasped.

This world to be won for Christ at first seemed much vaster than we had imagined. Gradually, by the method of investigation practised by Catholic Action, then on the occasion and (if I may say it) with the help of the war, the evacuations, the prison camps, the shared privations, the Resistance, and finally through the systematic surveys of religious sociology, we gained a true view of the real state of the apostolic field of action. The discovery was not only scientific, it was not only lived through by priests and laymen, young men and women truly dedicated to Christ: it was also enlightened by 'prophets', men who recognised God's will in the events of the time: Cardijn, Godin, Suhard, and all who are still carrying on their work among us.

But the greatest discovery was not that of expansion, it was that of density. We saw that we had to deal, not only with men of our own world who were simply reticent or abstentionist or even negative to the demands of religion, but also, around us, surrounding and submerging us, with other spiritual worlds, which had their own consistences, their own values, and were more or less completely ignorant of ours. There were at least two such worlds, not actually unconnected, but more or less distinct, the secular world and the proletarian.

It is an important element in the French situation that France is the land of philosophism, of the Revolution, of 1830 and 1848, of political and intellectual secularism. At one of my baccalauréat examinations I had to write an essay on Michelet's phrase 'the great century, the eighteenth'. France is perhaps the country where the secular world has the greatest consistency as a spiritual world of values *in coexistence with a really live Catholicism*. And its values are not hard to name: respect for man, for his reason, his freedom; a profound, spiritual rejection of clericalism and the arbitrary. The same Michelet saw 'the true light of the modern world' in the phrase he had taken from Vico: 'mankind is its own work'. Along with him, a man like Proudhon would no doubt be fairly characteristic of that France.

He is also the contemporary, and to some extent the prophet, of the appearance of a new people, born not so much from the intellectual, moral and political revolution of the eighteenth century as from the industrial revolution, which here produced its consequences in the first half of the nineteenth century. The word 'proletarian' first appeared in 1817. It is derived from a Latin word which in ancient Rome denoted those who counted in the census only for their *proles*, for the number of their children, but did not belong to any of the orders of the City, and, to quote Toynbee's definition, were in society without belonging to it. Industrial concentration cut the workers off from their roots in the local frameworks and traditions, including the religious, and reduced them to the state of a 'mass' giving them, from the point of view of work, dwelling, transport, culture and defence-organisation, a mass conditioning. Thus was born a new people, outside the motherly care of the Church, which at first did not know it as such: a frustrated people which was soon animated by a reaction and a will for battle, that revolt of the producers against the conditions of production which was spoken of in the *Communist Manifesto* of 1847.

At that date, Pius IX had lately succeeded to the throne of Peter. His first concern was to defend the Church against the violent challenge of the modern revolution, and to achieve Catholic concentration with a view to fruitful reconquests in Europe and overseas. The *Syllabus* of 1864 ended with an 80th (condemned) proposition stating 'that the Roman pontiff can and should be reconciled and come to terms with progress, liberalism and the recently established civil order'. It is also from the middle of the century, or even as early as 1830–1 (*L'Avenir*) that we can date the profound division among French Catholics, who have scarcely been united except on the question of Christian schools (a unity which we may think today is on the way to becoming exhausted). On one side were those who were willing to accept their age, allowing for necessary purifications; on the other, those who absolutely rejected it. The division still exists, although the proportions of the two camps have profoundly changed. It is undoubtedly accompanied by a certain ill-feeling among many, due to the fact that those who are 'against' make much use of secret denunciation to Rome. It is a real disease, in the extent to which the practice has spread, and one specifically French. This too forms part of our situation and our problems.

But our problems are important in another way, and here we reach the centre, the heart, of our situation. That is determined by the call of a world to be regained: in extent, those two-thirds of our brothers who live, indifferent or vaguely sympathetic, as if Jesus Christ were not, for them too, the Saviour and the Truth: in depth, those men who are spiritually alien to what we represent and who constitute another world of life, even more than a certain percentage of non-practising Christians. The chief concern of the Church of France is to be effectively and dynamically present to that world and those men, for the sake of Jesus Christ.

It is impossible to speak of the situation thus created otherwise than in terms of *mission*. This is one of the master words of our generation. Perhaps it is sometimes misused, especially when people speak of a 'missionary country', without sufficient note of the fact that the expression has a precise canonical connotation, which does not perhaps apply to us. But the words 'mission', 'missionary situation', 'missionary sector', even 'missionary parish', are in my opinion undoubtedly accurate. There will be an increasing realisation of the fundamental unity of the missionary problem in the world and the solidarity of all parts of the Church in a *missionary situation* which affects her in all that she is.

This missionary situation can be defined as 'being with', as the Church, for the sake of Jesus Christ. The element of geographical distance is here secondary and accidental. That the Chinese, in order to know the Gospel, need to have men sent to them *from a distance*, is part of the canonical notion of mission: it is neither necessary nor sufficient in order to define a missionary situation of the Church. To be sent to someone does not necessarily involve moving towards him in space: on the other hand, one can be beside him without being sent to him. There is a state of mission when, instead of being apart from someone, or merely beside him or in sight of him, one is truly *with* him: and not for good companionship, for the pleasure of being together, but in the name of something else; as the Church, and for the sake of Jesus Christ. It is no accident that Pius XI was both the pope of the native missionary Churches and the pope of Catholic Action, with his formula (out of fashion today, perhaps, but not really outdated): 'the apostolate of the milieu by the milieu'.

In these conditions, it is understandable that the strongest missionary call was felt to be towards this new proletarian people, born outside the Church's motherly care and never really known by her as a people. The efforts to be *with* that people, at last, for the sake of Christ, shape the aims of the homeland mission, with all the difficult problems which the enterprise has revealed ever more vividly, and which consist above all in this: how, and *how far*, to be with them? The condition of the proletariat here is inseparable from its struggle for liberation. Is it possible, from now on, to be *with* the people, even as the Church, without taking its side in a struggle in respect of the demands of the Gospel, and the liberation (transcendent and total indeed, but real and concrete) which Jesus Christ brings us? We cannot help asking the question of the Christian meaning of history, and lifting the question from the purely personal and spiritual level of salvation to the collective level of earthly history. We can no longer evade the encounter with Marxism, not only as a theory, but as the concrete leaven of the workers' struggle, daily present and active.

To give a dogmatic 'no' to Marxism is simple, and obviously necessary, and the Church has not failed to give it. It does not leave intact the questions raised by Marxism or the answers it offers to the questions raised by the industrial revolution; real questions, however, remain, and valid elements in the answers. Still, everything is not nullified from above by the simple application of the dogmatic truths of an immovably constituted deposit. It is the same with the other great questions raised by the modern world. It was necessary to join this world, too, and to be with it, as the Church, for the sake of Jesus Christ, in its questions, its answers and its hopes, false or half false. If this was a missionary situation, there was ground for seeking it out, not only in the pastoral sphere but in that of thought. Here as there, there were frontiers to be crossed if Christ were not to be deprived of human realms where he wills also to extend his salvation. Here as there, the Church could be either at rest on her traditionally occupied centres, or in process of expansion from those centres, with a view to encountering men's real questions. As Cardinal Suhard said in the sermon at his jubilee on 5th December 1948: 'To save Paris means first of all to save the souls of its inhabitants. But it means also to save the city, to take it in charge as it is, with its past, its future, and the complex problems of its present. If I pass these by, if I have no concern for them, I am neglecting half my mission, for from the moment that they present themselves in my territory, its problems become themselves my diocesan subjects.'

Thus appeared the possibility, and therefore the obligation, of a missionary dimension of thought, even of theological thought. There had always been a pastoral struggle against sin: now there had to be an effort to recover and salvage vast areas of values, as well as an effort to win and heal men. At the bottom it was the same struggle. Only, those Christians who were engaged in it showed themselves to be more vulnerable and they were, in a way, more particularly marked men. If France caused anxiety in 1946 and the following years, it was chiefly because she was, more

than others, the field of these necessary struggles, having a vocation for battles of ideas. Even the most missionary-minded men
in the strictly pastoral field were sometimes alarmed at experiments which were really dangerous.

That it was the same struggle is clear again from that feature
which is certainly the most fundamental, the most characteristic,
of the contemporary French religious movement: the awareness,
realised rather than explicitly avowed, that it is no use bringing
from above an answer wholly possessed, which a darkened world,
has only to receive as it is. For the answer to be valid, it must have
acquired the dimensions and rhythm of the question, and while
coming from above, from the one source of never-ageing truth,
it must enter and develop from below. The authenticity of the
human must be respected and assumed. The root of the new
demands in a country like ours consists, perhaps, in an irrepress-
ible elimination of paternalism, even to the extent of refusing the
good itself if it tries to impose itself from above. We may note in
passing, moreover, that the authority of God, as it is asserted in
the whole economy of salvation, in Israel, in the Incarnation and
in the Church, is far from paternalism, though always sovereign.

It would be quite false to say that French Catholicism has
adopted the modern point of view of an autonomous and closed
humanism, one for which, quite simply, 'mankind is its own
work'; if it had, it would no longer be Catholic. But it is no doubt
marked by a desire to respect the truth of things, by an open mind
to whatever is human, by an attentive and respectful interest in
the depth of man's problems, and finally by the desire for that
authenticity which is found in answers when they arise from
listening to man's real questions. This desire for authenticity as
regards man is expressed in a word which has only recently
acquired the extent and full meaning it has today: we want
something which is not only *true* but *valid*. It is at the root
of the use, in the pastoral field, of a method springing from the
facts, in the manner of Abbé Godin. In the religious science this
corresponds to the readiness to use non-Catholic works, not out
of any rather contemptible fondness for heterodoxy, but with the
desire to welcome everything acceptable and to inspect the questions before offering the answers. When we try to find a common
denominator of the different pastoral experiments of the moment

—renewal of catechetical methods, administration of the sacraments, religious sociology, or liturgy in youth movements—we arrive at some such formula as this: to substitute for what is a mere rite something which meets man's need for truth. When young T., having heard a sermon in a style he does not understand, asks his friend what the preacher said and gets the answer: 'He said everything which had to be said', we may be sure that all the rites of orthodoxy were observed, but that nothing happened. Nothing did happen. The truth in itself was perfectly observed, but there was no truth for the hearers, because their human problems, the authenticity of their real lives, were not taken into consideration first of all.

The problem exists not only on the scale of individuals and little homogeneous groups, it exists as a general problem with infinite ramifications, on the scale of the world. There is the modern world, and already from its womb a new world is coming to birth, with its marks plain to see: the conditions of life will be largely socialised, technicalised. It will certainly be incumbent on Christians to make the needs of the person valued in that world, the needs of the creature made in the image of God, capable of vocation and love. But they will have to accept that world if they are to be able to generate the response and the salvation of Christ in it, on the level and in the dimensions of its requests. The supposedly classical answers, the forms of yesterday, are inadequate or unassimilable for a world born after their time. As Jean Daniélou said at Geneva, God's word to man does not change, but man's answers to God change. One cannot force the man of today to repeat, in historically relative and dated forms, the answers made by the man of yesterday: one could dictate them to him from outside, he could repeat them with his lips, but they would not be *his* answers. In these circumstances, the missionary purpose of the Church herself obliges Christians not to be too hasty in their apostolate, but to respect a first stage of humble presence, which should be a stage of listening and simply understanding. This stage need not necessarily be chronologically previous and distinct, but should be a spiritual stage of attention, devoted to realising all the truth of the 'being with'. In the proletarian mission, where this stage is particularly necessary, they speak of entering 'from below'. Most certainly the deepest aspect of the question of the worker priests is found at this point. But the question goes far beyond those cases, important and decisive as they are. To quote only one other example, which is familiar to me, it is equally at this level, of respectful attention to what is acceptable in the basic requests, that ecumenical work is situated. Here too, our duty is first to listen and to understand, to enter into the depth of a question, to realise all the seriousness of a drama of historical dimensions. Here too, those who think only of immediate apostolic results ask: 'How many conversions?' and point out mistakes, real or imagined, without seeing that it is not just a matter of a mere increase in Catholic numbers, such as they are, but of entering into different or new worlds, so as to live with them, in them, as the Church, for the sake of Jesus Christ.

With the same elements of the missionary situation we could also connect the present practice of 'witness'. According to a meaning now very widespread, which we have no wish to dispute here, witness is that quality of a life integrally led *with*, partaking all the drama of some person, in such a way that it attracts, and produces in the heart of that milieu the beginning of a Christian response, which can be both very purely according to the mind of Christ and integrally authentic from the point of view of man. At bottom, the two things correspond: the purity of Christ and the authenticity of the human. All the researches now going on among us are polarised on those two points, between which there is a tension, the truth of which can only be maintained by being very generously lived.

It is again in these perspectives, I think, that one can understand other rather characteristic manifestations of the present movement of French Catholicism: the multiplication of small communities and the part they play in the discovery of forms of Christian life responding to the double polarity: evangelical purity and human authenticity: the quest for personal attitudes of *faith* going beyond the more or less traditional forms of religion. With this, the quest for an adult Christianity, that of a Church which shall not be merely a body of men 'practising' a 'religion', but a sign upholding faith, a milieu both educative and productive of an adult faith. Then, the corresponding quest for a type of priest whose priesthood, like the Church, should be not only ritualist but prophetic, really adult.

If I were to enumerate and, still more, explain and illustrate all these points, I should never have done. I should have to turn these pages into a chronicle, which is just what I do not want them to be, devoted as they are to discovering the *meaning* of the present religious movement.

If the case is as I have described, we must clearly realise that it raises a certain number of questions, and it is very important to become and remain aware of them. They are *our* dangers, they are what causes anxiety to our responsible pastors and above all to the common Father on our account.

Cardinal Baudrillart said to us in May 1938: 'What I chiefly fear is movements of conquest. One goes off to conquer others, and one is the first to be conquered by them!' In present-day French Catholicism, at least in some of its specialised movements, there is a sort of yearning to meet real men and their problems, to present them with a 'valid' Christianity. This involves them in offering something more than a Catholicism-in-itself, which in any case has never existed and does not exist in its pure state, but is necessarily expressed in certain historical forms, more or less bound up with a given world. In forms which correspond to the demands of our historical world, we look for a Catholicism which shall be true, not only in itself, but existentially, for the men of today. The danger is obviously that we may be so anxious to find a translation for men, an effectiveness in man, that we do not sufficiently assert the necessary primacy of what is given from above, the priority of the *true* over the *valid*.

To guard against this danger does not seem to me so difficult. It simply obliges us, who are engaged in the movement, to keep our eyes always on the already acquired structures, and to respect their imperative demands. The Church has a mission in this world, but she *is* not a mere mission. She has, in the first place, a structure, and she exists in herself, according to her truth in itself, before being something for man or in man. She is an order of holiness apart, which comes from God and the apostolic tradition, and claims to be held and respected, whatever the world's clamour may be. Some can see only this order of holiness, and are little troubled by the fact that men are asking for bread, and that the bread our fathers once baked is no longer digestible. But to others the world's appeals are so loud that they go out to it with too little thought of the Church's essential nature, of the priest-hood, of the dogmatic affirmations. It is in this conviction, and trying to be loyal both to the structures and to the movement that I have always tried—whether it were ecumenism or reforms, laity or mission—to attach the movement to the structure and to erect a structure open to the appeals of the movement.

Another danger, connected with the last: we are going further and further away from a monolithic Catholicism. Monolithic, to be accurate, it has never been, but it was more so, formerly than today because many were content with obedience to the essential nature, and above all it had rather the reassuring appearance of a block without a crack because the Catholics nearly all belonged to a homogeneous Catholic world, with habits which did not disturb clerical traditionalism. But the love of sincerity, the quest for human authenticity, the 'valid', (with all which that implies in practice, of depreciation of the essential nature, the missionary opening and the 'going to the barbarians', that is, the acceptance of a new world), all these have given French Catholicism a new face, and that, in proportion as it shares the general condition of the country. Now with us, while economic democracy is far from real, and political democracy is illusory enough, ideological de-mocracy is flourishing. France is a profoundly divided land. The National Assembly at Versailles made that plain to the world. It must be added that the deep disgust with all totalitarian rule is shared by the great body of Catholics.

The result is that we find ourselves faced with a pluralism which is not without its dangers. Not only is the rather superficial monolithic character of the 'Catholic world' of other days on its death-bed, since that world is being increasingly abandoned, but Catholics, out of loyalty to the problems as they feel them, take divergent ideological choices, sometimes with too little care for the claims of obedience or of the communion to be observed with all their brethren; sometimes with a radicalism which is deaf to dialogue and far from healthy. There is therefore a risk that on the fringes of the legal Church, towards which a sincere but sentimental loyalty is an insufficient attitude, there may spring up ideological côteries, which are a sort of spiritual fatherland and play the part of a real church, but are morally half in schism from the great, the only Church. So we have a latent problem of unity on the level of the Church herself. To raise the problem and look for its solution only in terms of obedience would be quite insufficient, though it ought to be raised on those terms, and it is urgently necessary to stress the duty of obedience among us. We must speak chiefly of the claims of communion, and look for effective support in the profound sense of the mystery of the Church, which has been restored and fostered for more than thirty years by so many things: the mystique of Catholic Action and youth movements, the liturgical revival, theological studies and even those little communities which, with some risk of becoming côteries, have so often been the place of rediscovery of the mystery of God, of Christ and the Church.

We sometimes hear talk of the danger of 'neo-protestantism'. Certainly there have been many things to create a situation which could be called 'pre-reformation', somewhat in the sense that we speak of a pre-revolutionary situation, and by allusion to the period (1494–1517) lately studied by M. A. Renaudet. It was with that situation in mind that I wrote *Vraie et fausse réforme dans l'Église*. It is my conviction that the Catholic Church cannot avoid certain challenges, not perhaps directly from Protestantism (though it is pretty enterprising in this mid-twentieth century), but from certain ferments which have been active since the sixteenth century, and were welcomed by Protestantism when it abandoned Catholic traditions: the bible, an existential and dramatic conception of religious relationship through the Word of God, a new feeling for the person, lay values, in both senses of the word 'lay'. To these must be added later ferments: socialism, Marxism, technical civilisation. Faced with such challenges, there are two things which can be done, before which, once again, men are divided between those who can only do one or the other: either to save the deposit, or to accept the challenge and, putting into practice the double loyalty to the purity of what is given from above and to the authenticity of what emerges from below, to try to bring Catholicism to a new birth as response, in the heart of the world where it receives an unprecedented task, from the hand of him who is the Lord of history. To remain the Church of all time, while becoming the Church of our time.

Within the larger whole of a collection devoted to France's opportunities, it was my duty to present the religious movement of contemporary French Catholicism, and thus leave to be worked out the opportunities of the Church, that is, the opportunities of Christ in our land. I had also to reply to the sympathetic and anxious inquiry of the foreigner: decadence or revival, dangerous crisis or vitality full of promise? Revival is certain: the vitality is great. Revival and vitality are at work on the lines of juncture of the present and the future. So the best opportunities consist chiefly in hope, and they are affected by that element of risk inherent in everything which is a quest. We do not conceal the dangers, but I am convinced that once again France is working for the future and for the whole world—and the world, at the bottom of its heart, knows it.

NOTES

1. Published in *La Vie intellectuelle*, Feb. 1954, pp. 113–30 (special number; 'Chances de la France'). The date is important because of the particular situation of the Church in France at that time.

CHAPTER THIRTEEN

Reflections on the spiritual Aspect of church Buildings[1]

WE MIGHT FIRST CONSIDER THE PROCESS OF building and its preliminaries—raising funds and so on. I live in a parish recently established in a district where a whole new town is due to be built, and a young priest has been appointed to build a church. He has called his parish bulletin *Building Together.* These two words seem exactly to express the essence of the spiritual aspect of the work of building.

But this is more easily said than done. The ideal would be for building work to be undertaken by a living community, or at least a team, who would make it their business, and by their brotherly mode of life would arouse the desire to take part in it.

The temptation, obviously, is to entrust it to a professional. This is nearly always inevitable and has real advantages. But it is still desirable to interest the whole community in the construction of its church, and not only practising Catholics, but the *really outstanding personalities* who live in the parish and are capable of making genuinely creative contributions.

I prefer to consider chiefly the spiritual aspect of the building itself, an aspect that many priests are called to realise or transform. I shall deal with this under three headings which are actually questions.

How are our Churches Places of the Presence of God?

They are, because they form part of the economy of the temple or the presence of God. They are connected with what is the

temple of God in the present stage of the plan of salvation. Now
the New Testament teaches us that there is now no temple but
the body of Christ: 'He spoke of the temple of his body' (Jn 2:21),
of his body, sacrificed and accepted in glory. Our churches are the
temples of God because they are the homes of the body of Christ,
by the eucharist, the Mass and the tabernacle. It is essentially by
the celebration of the mystery of the body of Christ that a place
becomes a church. Up to the fourth century there was no other
rite of consecration, and this fact alone is extremely instructive as
to the Christian meaning of 'the sacred' and, beyond that, of
Christian worship. 'The sacred', in the Christian sense, is *first of
all*, 'the temple not made with hands', the body of Christ offered
and raised up. It is *first of all* what God himself has done in the
framework of the history of salvation, and finally in the fact of the
Incarnation and of Easter—*Haec dies quam fecit Dominus!*—and
which men receive in faith and then express to God in thanks,
and then to men in confession of faith and in *diaconia*, or service
of love.

We can at once see that spiritual dispositions can be inspired
by this dominant viewpoint of the biblical revelation. Our
churches are temples of God in the first place by the celebration
of the Eucharist, which is at once thanksgiving, confession of
faith and source of brotherly service: they are temples in virtue
of the altar and of the tabernacle which holds the presence of the
eucharistic Christ.

I know men who, as they walk or drive through the villages, or
travel by train past the church-towers which dot the country-
side of God and man with their spires, love to salute in thought
the presence of the Lord in the mystery of the altar and the
tabernacle.

We may approach the mystery of the presence of God, not this
time from the side of the biblical theme of the temple, but from
that of the Latin and Greek word for church: *ecclesia*. It is a
highly significant fact that the same word (and likewise the word
'church' in English) stands *both* for the mystery of the people of
God, called to become the Body of Christ and to inherit eternal
life, *and* for the building or place where the Christians meet for
worship. Other names have been tried: *conventiculum*, proposed
by Lactantius, did not survive; *basilica* or *dominicum* (Greek:

kyriakon, whence Kirche, kirk, church) were in use till the fourth century. In the end, *ecclesia* prevailed. In the apostolic age they called it 'the house of the *ecclesia*', that is, of the assembly. As yet there were no special, public places, exclusively and publicly dedicated to the Christians' meetings for worship. Our churches are the places of the presence of God, not only because of the eucharistic Body of Christ, but because they are the places where the faithful come together.

There is a special presence of God wherever two or three come together in his name.[2] If we had to define it technically, we should call it a covenanted Presence: that to which God has attached the fulfilment of the promises of the covenant, not only in their individual and personal aspect ('If a man loves me, he will keep my word, and my Father will love him, and we will come to him and make our home with him' (John 14:23), but in their truly 'ecclesial' aspect.

These two ways in which our churches are the temples of God —housing the eucharistic body of Christ and being the meeting-places of the Christian body—are clearly in close connection. The people of God, too, are the Body of Christ, and are so called in the New Testament. They are the Body of Christ spiritually, which is why we call it the 'mystical body', but 'mystical' does not mean unreal. They are his 'community-body', and it is such a body that we form one single being of praise, one single son full of love for the Father, one single heir of the patrimony of God. This unity is consummated in the eucharist, so that in the last resort it is on its account that our churches are temples of God, on the double ground of his dwelling in his Son and in the assembly of the faithful, members of his Son's mystical body.

Importance of the Fact that our Churches
are Special Places, Particular Buildings

For this is a fact, and one which is an integral feature of our very landscape. Is there anything lovelier and more intimate, more suggestive of a common meeting-place, than those villages clustered round their steeples, in the folds of the valleys or on the gentle slope of a hillside? I enter the village, and at once I am struck by a fact of architecture: among the ordinary houses, rich or poor, but all clearly belonging to little human groups centred on themselves, there are three houses common to all, at once distinct in themselves and open to all: the town hall, the school and the church. The last is generally more striking, and has the peculiarity that it indicates, by its very structure, that it has a vertical dimension, the third dimension of men, who are not made only for the earth, on the two plane dimensions of existence, but for heaven, on a third dimension, which the priests have been specifically charged to arouse and build up in souls.

But since God is everywhere in his presence of creation and immensity, and since the faithful can meet and celebrate the Eucharist anywhere, in a room, in a wood, in the open air—it has happened and happens often: in a camp, in war, in times of persecution—why are there churches? Are churches necessary?

They are not absolutely necessary, and the mystery of the Church would remain what it is if there were no churches, but they are supremely fitting and full of significance. We know how George Fox, the founder of the Quakers, caring only for the inner religious impulse of the immediate, personal and active presence of the Holy Spirit in men's hearts, condemned the churches, which he liked to call 'steeple-houses'. He was not wrong in believing in the Holy Spirit and the inner presence of God, but he was wrong in making that the whole of religion.

For we are no longer, or we are not yet, in that blessed condition of the presence and familiarity of God in everything and in all. The biblical story of Genesis shows us, in the beginning, a time when God was quite close and familiar, both to men and to things; it bears witness to a presence both cosmic and interior or familiar. And similarly we have been promised that at the end 'God shall be all in all',[3] one of the profoundest and most illuminating sayings in Holy Scripture. Once again there will be a Presence both total or cosmic and supremely interior and familiar. But our present dispensation lies between Paradise lost and Paradise restored, in a world deprived by itself of the familiar nearness of God. It is that of an 'already' and a 'not yet' which are inwardly associated: already temple and presence, and not yet perfect temple and presence.

It is because God is not yet 'all in all' that the Church and the world are not yet co-extensive, and that the Church is a particular and sometimes very small group in a vast world, although it represents the firstfruits of a Kingdom of God on the dimensions of his creation. It is because God is not yet 'all in all', because his whole creation is not yet the temple of his glory, that in the midst of the world of men and things there exist *special* buildings, though open to all: our churches.

Their rôle is precisely to be, at the same time, the sign, borne by a particular group, of a call to the whole world to become the temple of God, and a means by which the particular group, which bears the sign, is built up into the people of God and the community-body of Christ. With this double rôle is connected the *sacred* character of our churches.

The Sacred in Christianity

Few notions are more ambiguous than this notion of the 'sacred'. Yet it is something both very real and very important.

Its ambiguity is due to the fact that independently of Christianity and antecedent to it, there is a whole world of the ceremonially sacred in things: its different manifestations have been analysed in, for example, the works of Mircéa Eliade. Now it is very remarkable that of all this 'religious' material practically nothing is found in the New Testament, except what is related to the expression or the structures of the religious reality which is internal to man himself, as, for example, the theme of the new birth, or the very simple and ordinary 'matter' of the sacraments.

Obviously in a few lines I cannot explain and justify a position of which I can here only offer the conclusions, and that in the barest outline. In the present state of my study and reflection I am convinced that in Christianity, in the first place, the only substantial 'sacred thing' is the Body of Christ, and, secondly, all the rest of 'the sacred' has only an educational value, good, profound and necessary withal. That educational value is itself aimed in two directions: outwards, it becomes a sign to those who are outside; inwards, it becomes a means for building up the community-body of Christ, in each of its members and in its capacity as the union of them all.

Our churches are signs: expressions of our faith and our hope, first of all. Witness. Promise and firstfruits of that *Consecratio mundi* spoken of in the Christian Martyrology: it was in its coming that Pius XII saw a particular task of the faithful laity. The men of the Middle Ages loved to represent, in the sculpture of their churches, the seasons, the months and the days, and their labours. More than that, in the plan of the building, in the very use they made of the materials, in many forms of symbolism, there has always been an intention to express, in the construction of the churches, the cosmic aspect of the Christian mystery and the Christian hope. Christ will restore all things: he is even now their King, and he accepts certain firstfruits of creation, in the construction of the churches, in the whole liturgy, and supremely in the bread and wine, the vestments, the lights, the altar and the celebration of the eucharist.

Witnesses to our faith and our hope, our churches are signs set up before all the world to attest the mystery of salvation. They are made from the materials of this world, but wrought by men and so disposed as to express *something else* besides earthly use. There are certain churches which are famous for the way they fulfil this function of being signs of the existence of that truth and something else. Many conversions have taken place or begun at Chartres and at Ronchamps too, simply through the sign of stone and glass. In both cases, incidentally, but especially the latter, we find the proof of that general law that the sign must be explained or made explicit in words. At Ronchamps, if I am not mistaken, the chaplain conceives his presence and function to be chiefly those of a voice, sensitive to the occasion and the encounter, offering itself fraternally to let the sign speak for those who are disposed to hear it. And who has not admired in M. Houvet, the sacristan at Chartres, the wonderfully discreet yet firm way in which he is able to fulfil that rôle? But what human speech completes, the sign, incorporating the *logos* of its maker, itself begins to do. We can never too strongly emphasise that rôle of sign for the use of the countless men who pass through our churches and could fill them. Not only by architecture, but by the decoration and position of the altar, the dignity of the accessories, the arrangement of the notices, the posters, etc. All that is part of the visibility and publicity of the Church and her missionary rôle as sign of the approach of the Kingdom of God.

As regards the people who come to pray there, or end by feeling drawn to pray there, the 'sacred' rôle of art and of our places of worship is essentially *to help the soul to compose itself*, and to foster the dispositions which must be used by the religious relation of faith with prayer. This may be true for each individual person or for the community as such.

There are some things which compose a man, collect his thoughts, calm him, inspire him with reverence and at the same time invite him to go out beyond himself spiritually, by opening to him the door of a world wider and higher than that of his ordinary life. There are certain landscapes which do this, certain musical works, certain buildings. *That* is their sacred character. This does not consist, as some people seem to have thought at times, in external and added details. A building does not have a sacred character by being strewn with crosses, lilies and doves, or by having many sham gables or cruciform rose-windows, but only if it composes one to the religious attitude of reverence, prayer and communion with God.

Where a church is concerned, this ought also to apply to its purpose of bringing together the Christian people for the eucharistic action. This will have to be expressed in many concrete requirements which obviously cannot be detailed here. The effect of intimacy must be allied with that of a glorious place, worthy of a festive celebration. The place must lend itself by its arrangement to the *gathering together* of the people with reference to the two traditionally essential things in a Christian church, the altar and the pulpit (which, of course, may be an ambo). By its arrangement, by the way it blends with its surroundings, the church must appear home-like and yet give one the feeling that one is crossing a threshold; it should give the impression of welcome and yet invite one to pass on to something other than the earthly and the profane.

This sacred character has a sort of inner law, which is its necessary, if not sufficient, condition. All recent works on the subject, like those of Couturier, Régamey and others, agree with the experience which everyone can make his own if he opens his eyes and reflects: that the secret of this sacred character is the spirit of the Beatitudes. For it is not produced by extravagance but by simplicity, not by pretentious grandiloquence but by the transparency, interior discipline and assertion of the glory of God in the poverty of man.

Is this a truism? Art demands artists. Christian art also demands a Christian spiritual climate.

NOTES

1. Published in *Pêcheurs d'hommes* (Oeuvre des Vocations du diocèse de Montpellier), No. 46 (Oct. 1960), pp. 10–17
2. Mt 18:9–20.
3. 1 Cor 15:28.

BIBLIOGRAPHY ON CONVERSION

(See Chapter 2)

---

1. *Biblical studies*

J. Behm and E. Würthwein, art. μεκνόεω, μετανόια, in *TWB z. N.T.* vol. IV (1942), pp. 972–1004 (bibliogr.).

A. Bertrangs, 'Metanoia als grondbeginsel van het christelijk leven volgens het N.T.', in *Tijdschr. v. Liturgie*, 44 (1960), pp. 250–69.

J. Delorme, 'Conversion et pardon d'après le prophète Ezéchiel', in *Mémorial Chaine*, Lyons, 1950, pp. 115–44.

E. K. Dietrich, *Die Umkehr im A.T. und im Judentum*, Stuttgart, 1936.

A. H. Dirksen, *The New Testament Concept of Metanoia*, Washington, 1932.

W. Holladay, *The root sûbh in the Old Testament, with particular reference to its usages in Covenantal contexts*, 1958.

'La Conversion' in *Lumière et Vie*, no. 47, 1960.

J. Pierron, 'La conversion, retour à Dieu', in *Grands Thèmes Bibliques*, Paris, 1958, pp. 119–31.

H. Pohlmann, *Die Metanoia als Zentralbegriff der christlicher Frömmigkeit. Eine systematische Untersuchung zum ordo salutis auf biblisch-theologischer Grundlage*, Leipzig, 1938.

R. Schnackenburg, 'Typen der Metanoia-Predigt im N.T.', in *Münchener Theol. Zeitsch.*, 1 (1950, no. 4), pp. 1–13.

H. W. Wolff, 'Das Thema "Umkehr" in der alttestl. Prophetie', in *Zeitsch. f. Theol, u. Kirche*, 1951, pp. 131 f.

2. *Early Christianity*

G. Bardy, *La conversion au christianisme durant les premiers siècles*, Paris, 1947.

H. Braun, ' "Umkehr" in spätjüdisch-häretischer und in frühchristlicher Sicht', in *ZKT*, 1953, pp. 243–58.

K. F. Freudenthal, *Gloria, temptatio, conversio. Studien zur ältesten deutschen Kirchensprache* (Göteborg Univ. Arsskr., 65), Stockholm, 1959.

A. HARNACK, *Die Terminologie der Wiedergeburt u. verwandter Erleb-nisse in der alteren Kirche* (*T.U.*, 42–2), 1917.
See also A. D. NOCK, *The Old and the New in Religion, from Alexander the Great to Augustine of Hippo*, Oxford, 1933.

3. *Theological studies*

Strange to say, there is no article under 'Conversion' in the great French Catholic dictionaries (*DTC, Dict. Bibl., Catholicisme*); on the other hand, see H. PINARD DE LA BOULLAYE, in *Dict. Sp.*, vol. II, col. 2224–65, and W. KEILBACH, art. 'Bekehrung' in *L.Th.K.*, 2nd ed., 1958, vol. II, col. 136–8.

H. BOUILLARD, *Conversion et grâce chez saint Thomas d'Aquin. Étude historique* (*Théologie*, 1), Paris, 1944.
Principal criticisms expressed, from the Thomist point of view:

A. DAL CEVOLO, *La Psicologia dell' incredulo alla luce del IV Evangelo*, Milan, 1945.

T. DEMAN, in *Bulletin thomiste*, VII (1943–6), pp. 46–58.

L. B. GILLON, in *Rev. thomiste*, 46 (1946), pp. 603–12; 47 (1947), pp. 178–89.

L. B. GUÉRARD DES LAURIERS, in *Année théologique*, 6 (1945), pp. 276–325; 7 (1946), pp. 262–4.

P. HITZ, *L'annonce missionnaire de l'Évangile*, Paris, 1954, pp. 88, 107 f.

La Conversion. Compte rendu des XXXVIIIe Journées universitaires, Caen-Coutances, 25–28 mars 1961: Cahiers universit. cathol., special number, June–July 1961.

Ed. HUGON (above, n. 40); M. T. L. PENIDO (above, nn. 21, 22).

A. ODDONE, 'I fattore della conversione religiosa e le Vie di Dio nelle conversioni', in *La Civilta Cattolica*, 1940, IV, pp. 32–41 and 184–96.

P. PARENTE, art. 'Conversione' in *EC*, vol. IV (1950), col. 491–3.

C. F. PAUWELLS, 'Theological Problems of Conversion' in *The Thomist*, 11 (1948), pp. 409–23.

'Theologie en Psychologie der Bakering', in *Jaarboek*, 1952, pp. 59–76.

F. PETIT, 'La conversion' in *Parole et Mission*, no. 1, 1958, pp. 201–13.

FULTON J. SHEEN, *Peace of Soul*, New York and Toronto, 1949, pp. 230–69.

4. *Psychology of Conversion*

(a) Catholic authors
G. BARRA, *Psicologia dei convertiti*, Rome, 1959.
J. HUBY, *La conversion*, Paris, 1919.

T. Mainage, *Introduction à la psychologie des convertis*, Paris, 1913. *La psycholgie de la conversion*, Paris, 1915.

M. Nédoncelle, 'Les faits de conversion devant la conscience chrétienne', in *J'ai rencontré le Dieu vivant*, Paris, 1952, pp. 9-40.

A. D. Nock, 'Conversion and Adolescence', in *Pisciculi. Festg. F. J. Dölger*, pp. 165 f.

A. Retté, *Notes sur la psychologie de la conversion*, Paris, 1914.

(b) Non-Catholic authors

K. Aland, *Ueber den Glaubenswechsel in der Geschichte des Christentums*, Berlin, 1961 (Prot.).

R. Allier, *La psychologie de la conversion chez les peuples non civilisés*, 2 vols., Paris, 1925.

Gordon W. Allport, *The Individual and His Religion. A Psychological Interpretation*, London and New York, 1951, pp. 36f.

P. Althaus, 'Die Bokehrung in reformatorischer u. pietistischer Sicht,' in *Neue Zeitsch. f. system. Theol.*, 1 (1959), pp. 3-25.

G. Bastide, *La conversion spirituelle*, Paris, PUF.

G. Berguer, *Traité de Psychologie de la Religion*, Lausanne, 1946.

E. T. Clark, *The Psychology of Religious Awakening*, New York, 1929.

S. de Sanctis, quoted above, n. 30.

E. K. Dietrich, *Die Umkehr*, Stuttgart, 1936.

H. Essinger, 'Der Konfessionswechsel in römisch-kathol. und evangelischer Sicht,' in *Deutsch. Pfarr. Blatt.*, 61 (1961), pp. 85-8, 110-11.

R. Ferm, *The Psychology of Christian Conversion*, Westwood, New York, 1959.

L. W. Grensted, *The Psychology of Religion*, Oxford, 1952, pp. 72f.

H. Harms, quoted above, n. 30.

Jackson, *The fact of Conversion*, London, 1908.

A. Jalaguier, *La conversion des adolescents*, Montauban, 1911.

William James, *The Varieties of Religious Experience*, London and New York, 1902.

L. W. Lang, *A Study of Conversion*, London, 1931.

A. Marc, *Raison et conversion chrétienne*, Brussels-Paris, 1961.

Marshall, *Conversion or the New Birth*, London, 1909.

H. Pohlmann, *Die Metanoia* . . . (see above under *Biblical Studies*), Leipzig, 1938.

J. Segond, 'Le problème psychologique de la grace et de la conversion', in *Journal de Psychologie*, 1920, pp. 418-56.

E. D. Starbuck, *The Psychology of Religion*, London-New York, 1899.

R. H. Thouless, *An Introduction to the Psychology of Religion*, Cambridge, 1923.

5. *Stories of Conversion to Catholicism:*

These are numberless. A selected bibliography will be found at the end of Mainage, *Psychologie de la conversion,* and of Huby. Here we give only some symposia or collections, then some characteristic recent accounts:

Bekenntnis zur katholischen Kirche, contributions by M. Gierner, N. Goethe, G. Klünder, H. Schlier, ed. by K. Hardt, Würzburg, 1955.

C. VON ADRIAN-WERBURG, *Ihre Wege nach Rom,* Paderborn, 1929 (about 300 stories).

Sie hörten seine Stimme. Zeugnisse von Gottsuchern unserer Zeit, Gesamm. *mit einem Schlusswort,* ed. by Br. Schafer, 3 vols., Lucerne, 1950–2.

Convertis du XXe siècle, coll. by F. Lelotte, Paris-Tournai, 4 vols.

J'ai rencontré le Dieu vivant, Paris, 1952.

Walls are Crumbling, New York, 1952 (seven Jewish philosophers).

Unser Weg zur Kirche. Religiöse Selbstzeugnisse berühmter Konvertiten, ed. by J. Eberle, Lucerne, 1948.

L. BOUYER, *Du Protestantisme à l'Église,* Paris, 1954.

G. K. CHESTERTON, *The Catholic Church and Conversion,* London, 1934.

CHOLLET, *Quelques retours à la foi,* Paris, 1931.

Conversions, ed. by M. Leahy, New York, 1933.

C. DE VOGEL, *Ecclesia catholica. Redelijke verantwoording van een persoonlike Keuze,* Utrecht, 1948.

W. GORDON GOREMAN, *Converts to Rome,* London, 1910 (names).

H. C. GRAEF, *The Scholar and the Cross* (on Edith Stein), London, 1955.

VERNON JOHNSON, *One Lord, One Faith,* London, 1929.

R. A. KNOX, *A Spiritual Aeneid.*

DOM PIERRE CÉLESTIN LOU, *Ways of Confucius and of Christ,* London, 1947.

IGNACE LEPP, *Itinéraire de Karl Marx à Jésus-Christ,* Paris, 1955.

T. MAINAGE, *Les témoins du renouveau catholique,* Paris, 1917.

THOMAS MERTON, *The Seven Storey Mountain,* New York, 1948.

MIGNE, *Dictionnaire des Conversions* (by C. F. Chevé), Paris, 1866.

J. H. NEWMAN, *Apologia pro Vita Sua.*

MARY LECOMTE DU NOÜY, *Pierre Lecomte du Noüy. De l'agnosticisme à la Foi,* Paris.

A. RÄSS, *Die Convertiten seit der Reformation,* 13 vols., Freiburg, 1872–80.

D. ROSENTHAL, *Convertitenbilder aus dem XIX. Jahrhundert*, 3rd ed., 8 vols., Ratisbon, 1899–1902.

Roads to Rome, being Personal Records of some of the more recent Converts to the Catholic Faith, introd. by Card. Vaughan, London, 1901 (65 stories).

D. J. SCANNELL-O'NEILL, *Distinguished Converts to Rome in America*, Freiburg, 1907.

B. SCHAFER, *Die Wahrheit machte sie frei. Konvertiten schildern ihren Weg zur Kirche*, Trier, Paulinus Verlag, 1958 (15 autobiographies from all over the world).

Wir suchten und fanden. 23 Dänen berichten über ihren Weg zur Kirche. Ges. u. mit e. Nachschrift vers. v. Gunnar Martin Nielsen, Lucerne, 1959.

M. R. SIMON, *The Glory of thy People*, New York, 1948.

Warum wir katholisch wurden. Berichte schwedischer Katholiken, ed. by Sven Stolpe, Heidelberg, 1958.

K. STERN, *The Pillar of Fire*, London and New York, 1951.

A. H. WINSES, *Vie de Sigrid Undset*, Paris.

INDEX OF NAMES

INDEX OF SUBJECTS